SIZING UP A
START-UP

SIZING UP A
START-UP

DECODING THE
NEW FRONTIER
OF CAREER
OPPORTUNITIES

DANIEL S. RIPPY

PERSEUS PUBLISHING

Cambridge, Massachusetts

Copyright © 2000 Daniel S. Rippy

A CIP record for this book is available from the Library of Congress
ISBN 0-7382-0353-X

Perseus Publishing is a member of the Perseus Books Group.

Find us on the World Wide Web at http://www.perseuspublishing.com

Perseus Publishing books are available at special discounts for bulk purchases in the U.S. by corporations, institutions, and other organizations. For more information, please contact the Special Markets Department at HarperCollins Publishers, 10 East 53rd Street, New York, NY 10022, or call 1-212-207-7528.

Text design by Cynthia Young
Set in 12.75-point Garamond 3 by Perseus Publishing Services

First printing, June 2000
1 2 3 4 5 6 7 8 9 10—03 02 01 00

To David

CONTENTS

TABLES

ACKNOWLEDGMENTS

In late 1997, I was working at a start-up company in Seattle. After hitting the $25 million mark, I determined that it was time for me to leave. Yep, after the company had burned through roughly $25 million of investor cash and had little to show for it, I came to the realization that this start-up ship was not headed for IPO glory. On the one hand, it's disappointing when you come to the realization that it's time to leave a venture where you contributed time and intellectual effort. On the other hand, knowing that you've been living on the cutting edge of technology is an incredibly empowering feeling. Moving forward in search of my next opportunity, I was amazed at how interested people were in my start-up experience. They were intensely curious about the process one goes through to identify a start-up company with growth prospects. They were also keenly inquisitive about what I would do differently if I had it to do over again. In talking with friends and colleagues, I realized there was a need for this book. To all of those with whom I spoke and consulted along the way, thank you.

To the extent that this book contains the guidance and answers you are looking for, the people listed below deserve enormous credit; to the extent that it is lacking, I am responsible.

For their input and advice, I want to thank Andrew Blake, Walter Bordewieck, Heidi and Mark Craemer, Bill Demas, Randy Eisenman, Prabhavathi Fernandes, Prentiss Gregorie, John Harrington, James Hardie, Erin Hill, James Hulbert, Paul and Cindy Keung, David Kitching, Alan Kitty, Matt Kursh, Charlene Li, Dan Lieberman, John Lindsay, Shana McBride, Allan and Jennifer Miller, Karen Pape, Adrianna Paradiso, Bruce Pomfret, Geoffrey Raynor,

Andrew Rippy, Judy Schneider, Andrea Venezia, Denise Ward, Ian Wilcox, and Donna Williams.

For their interest and support, I want to thank Jay Abraham, Todd Aiken, Bill Furlong, Kurt Losert, Steven Lurie, Steve Noetzel, Karen Pape, John and Loren Pollard, Kate Rimer, Anne Rippy, Elisabeth Rippy, Ned Strong, Alex Tilles, John Turtle, Ann Watson, and Scott Watson. I'd also like to give a special thanks to the team at Handango for their entrepreneurial spirit and embodiment of all that is great in tech start-up ventures.

I am privileged to be a part of a great business development team at Johnson & Johnson whose members help to influence and shape my thinking every day. At J&J, I'd like to thank Rich Caligaris, Abbey Chung, Jan Egberts, Stan Hall, Wil Harvey, and Mark Zenz.

My agent, Nicholas Smith of Altair Literary Agency, provided invaluable guidance and insight. His knowledge of the publishing process was a tremendous asset. I would also like to thank Andrea Pedolsky at Altair for her efforts on behalf of the book.

I extend deep gratitude to my editor, Jacqueline Murphy at Perseus Books. Jacque was incredibly helpful throughout the process, and her knowledge, insight, and energy were inspirational. Thanks also to the team members at Perseus who helped make this book a reality.

Finally, I extend deepest gratitude to my wife and best friend, Laura Rippy. Her patience, support, insight, and criticism were invaluable. I owe her much for giving me the time to complete this book. She was a huge believer in the project from the outset, and she even used the advice from this book to find and join a tech start-up company!

FOREWORD

Someone that I hardly know is asking me to help him make a critical decision: *Should I join a start-up?*

I've had this discussion on many occasions and it's never the same conversation twice. It's difficult for someone who's never worked at a start-up to imagine what it's like. Often, they underestimate the challenges, risks, and unusual dynamics of the start-up workplace. Just as often they romanticize it, thinking that they have an opportunity to join when the company is pristine—in the early days when corporate legends are born.

Why am I a go-to guy for this type of advice? I co-founded and ran a Macintosh software company that was bought by Apple Computer in 1989. And I co-founded and was CEO of eShop, a developer of Web-based shopping software, which was acquired by Microsoft in 1996. Our products became Microsoft's Internet commerce platform. Later, at Microsoft, I ran several start-up businesses, including Sidewalk, HomeAdvisor, and MSN.com. In short, I have lived and breathed the start-up experience.

I've found that working in a start-up is rewarding in many ways. Dan describes them aptly in this book. The pace is fast, so you'll learn more than you could have ever imagined, and you'll take on broader responsibilities than in a larger, more established firm. Start-ups often feel like large extended families where communications are direct, emotions are on the line, and employees act as if they own the place (because they do, of course). I believe achieving success at a start-up brings a greater sense of accomplishment than it would in a larger company, where you sometimes never know how much your contribution matters.

Arnold Blinn and Greg Stein were two fellow eShop co-founders. Both possess talents and personalities that are ideal for the start-up life. The pair, amazing software engineers, always drive forward at warp speed. They keep deliberations to a minimum. After brief consideration, or no consideration, they made product decisions and started programming. They have great instincts and rock-solid confidence that they'll always be able to make things work. They are blunt communicators with no agenda other than to succeed, and they energize those around them. But good luck keeping up if you don't have a similar hard-driving style.

This fast-paced environment is not for everyone. Startups typically have immature management practices, for example. So, if you're looking to learn the "right" way to organize teams, manage business processes, and build products, you probably don't want to go with a start-up. Start-up situations tend to magnify management problems, so difficult personalities can have negative effects across large groups or the entire company. For better or worse, jobs at these gritty and exciting companies are typically wild.

Our VP of engineering at eShop had impeccable project and personnel management skills. He was very talented. But after several years of gritting his teeth on the job he surprised us and resigned. Over the years, it seems, he came to the conclusion that the start-up world was not his "natural habitat." He thrived in environments that were less chaotic and more deliberate. Over time he realized that he would probably never be able to get the satisfaction he wanted out of the hectic work life at eShop.

Before you decide between start-up opportunities, you need to determine if the entrepreneurial culture truly suits you. If you can afford to take financial risks, want to work long, hard hours, are eager to teach yourself new skills, and flourish in unstructured environments, then a start-up might be what you are looking for. If on the other hand you prefer a reliable source of income, perform best in environments with clear goals, and are not willing to sacrifice personal time in order to manage the latest crisis, this might not be a good time for you to leave your career to join the new economy's latest IPO candidate.

How can you choose which—if any—start-up you should join? My experience tells me this: Join a start-up only if you are wildly passionate about its business and its team. If you join for some reason other than an all-consuming passion, you won't have the energy to succeed.

Note that I am suggesting that you consider the team as well as the business. This is vital because I know something about start-ups that you might not know yet: Their business plans are flawed. (Yes, they all are.) So, as the business grows and changes, you need to be confident that the team driving the business—the CEO/president, vice presidents, key product people—have the smarts to reshape the business for success. If the company's investors or board members are actively involved, you should assess them, too. Do these people have vision? Are they people you can work with? Can they make the tough decisions?

The composition of a start-up's founder and management team has profound implications beyond setting and improving the company's strategic plan. They determine what I call the "corporate character."

There are startups, for example, founded by passionate product people who want more than anything to make their vision a reality for a large group of customers. eBay and Yahoo are great examples of companies founded by product visionaries. These types of start-ups can hire talented, energetic teams and build an interesting product, but without world-class leadership, they might have difficulty figuring out if real customers want the product and how to make money from it.

Some start-ups are established by straight-ahead business types who see a customer need and a corresponding business opportunity. Business-focused leaders often do a good job hiring a strong team, raising money, and building customer relationships. But these organizations sometimes fail to come up with the "big idea" that creates wildly loyal customers. Often they're focused on all facets of a successful business instead of being maniacally tuned-in to the company's product or service.

The type of start-up that is hardest to evaluate is the "all star team." It begins with very experienced name brand managers, sometimes people who have successfully worked together in the past, who then move forward to find business opportunities. These teams have the advantage of experience. They usually have good chemistry from day one, but can suffer from a lack of product or business-focus.

In the early 1990s, I joined a start-up founded by former senior executives from Microsoft, Lotus, and Symantec, as well as the two people who invented the spreadsheet. Although the team was amazing, it never developed the focused vision or all-consuming passion it needed to succeed. Eventually it was sold for a small sum before it really had a chance to flourish.

As described in the pages that follow, there are many other factors to consider beyond the business plan and management team. Look for a start-up with the means and contacts to attract key employees, investors, and customers. Consider location: Does the company's hometown have the talent pool needed to grow the company? And, of course, one cannot forget one last issue: compensation.

Yes, you should most certainly join a start-up that has financial upside, and you should negotiate the appropriate stock option agreement so that you'll share in the success if the company goes public or is acquired. But don't sign on simply because you think it's an opportunity to get rich. After all, there's a real chance that those options will never be worth a penny. They're a gamble; perhaps that's part of their allure.

As with any job, the real key to determining if a start-up is right for you is research. Luckily, you have the perfect resource in hand. *Sizing-Up a Start-Up* is exactly the book you need to determine if the dot.com that's courting you will ever make it to NAS-DAQ. It will also provide the knowledge and practical checklists to help you decide if a new economy company is a match with your professional metabolism. If you're thinking of making a move to an early stage company, this book is the right place for you to begin.

I have loved my time in new businesses, and I hope that you'll get to enjoy—someday, if not now—the unique excitement of building something new.

—Matt Kursh, former CEO of eShop and
General Manager of Microsoft's MSN.com

INTRODUCTION

You may not consider yourself a technical genius. That's fine. Chances are that you did not grow up programming in C++. Nor did you win the high school science prize. Your idea of a good time is not sitting around on a Friday night until 4:30 A.M. banging out computer code, staring into a Petri dish under a microscope, or pursuing some other technical endeavor that does not involve sleep. Maybe you have a liberal arts background; maybe you're an engineer. Maybe you've gone back to business school for an M.B.A. or some other graduate degree. Unlike Bill Gates or Michael Dell, you did not drop out of college to found a company, and you are not worth an outrageous amount of money at your age.

However, you do like to surf the Internet. You've begun to appreciate the benefits of software, e-commerce, and the easy access to news and information the Web has to offer. You have admired the breakthroughs that have come in fields like materials science and biotechnology research. The idea that it may be possible for cars to get better mileage from an environmentally friendly source of fuel is worth pursuing. The knowledge that with modern medicine we can all live to be 120 years old is also pretty intriguing. Moreover, the potential for you to get rich on stock options sounds very inviting.

You've even gone so far as to consider joining the 3 million-plus Americans today who are working in new economy start-up companies. Your reasoning is good. You've noticed that there are scores of jobs in the new economy. Many of those jobs require experience, skills, or knowledge gained from another industry in which you may already have expertise: advertising, architecture, art, banking, computer science, consulting, electronics, financial services, engineering, health care, hospitality, insurance, law, life sciences, medicine, planning and design, public relations, real estate, teaching, travel, and so forth. "New economy" implies that these new companies think and act differently from the older, more traditional corporate icons with which we're all familiar.

You bought this book because you're thinking about joining a start-up company. Perhaps you've interviewed with some start-ups. If so, hopefully you have heard a consistent theme in their message: Their people tell you that their product or service offering is going to solve a tough problem for its customers. It will offer revolutionary benefits by improving a process, enhancing productivity, raising the quality of life or, most likely, some combination of these. You're intrigued and enthused. One start-up seems particularly exciting to you. It has only thirty-five people, but they're thirty-five very excited people. The company offers you a job. For your part, you are very excited about contributing to the knowledge revolution of the twenty-first century.

Of course, right now the talk is just that—talk. There's a lot of hype about the company's revolutionary product, but the market actually seems to be just on the precipice of realizing its potential and harnessing the power it promises. The market is a sleeping giant, slowly awakening. The company that has offered you the position intends to be there to serve breakfast when the giant wakes up.

Maybe you've seen a demo or sample of the company's product, but it was incomplete. The pace of the start-up company, of course, is dizzying. There's so much to do. The employees are convinced they will succeed. It occurs to you, however, that in spite of the hype about the product, there's also a very large, very real risk: Perhaps the product in question will fail to deliver on its promise, or perhaps somebody else's product will get to the market first and lock yours out. Perhaps the company will fail, but perhaps it will win bigger than anybody thought it could. The company can't pay you a salary befitting royalty, but you will also get stock options. What does all this mean?

Before you decide whether to join the company in question, read this book and be sure you can answer the questions it raises. It may mean that before accepting a job offer you have to go back and get clarification from company management or do some additional homework on your own. Be diligent and unapologetic in seeking this information.

*   *   *

This book is designed to provide you with the tools that you need to be optimally prepared to assess and make a decision about joining a start-up company in the fast-moving new economy. It is loaded with rich insights from interviews with veterans of the start-up experience, who offer you their assessment criteria. Moreover, drawing from their experience, the book gives you numerous strategies for how to work effectively in a start-up situation once you're there.

Chapter 1 presents a case example of a tech start-up and how it comes into being. It describes the new economy and the factors that are driving the creation of so many technology start-up companies today. It then discusses start-ups in general, the entrepreneurs who found them, and the common conditions found in all start-ups. Finally, it differentiates the tech start-up from other types of start-ups.

Chapter 2 introduces the New Economy Tech Start-Up (NETS) Stage Factors and how they serve to help you identify tech start-ups and determine their organizational stage of development. It then discusses the three key NETS Stages of development of a tech start-up: Birth, Organizational Infancy, and Organizational Adolescence.

Chapter 3 describes the Birth stage of a tech start-up and discusses the pros and cons of joining a start-up at this stage. It also shows you how to use the NETS Stage Factors to determine if a tech start-up is at the Birth stage. It then explains how a Birth stage start-up takes the next step up, to Organizational Infancy.

Chapter 4 discusses how the dynamics of the company change from Birth to Organizational Infancy and what their impact can be. It describes the basic conditions of Organizational Infancy and the signs of success at this stage. It shows you how to use the NETS Stage Factors to determine if a company is at the Organizational Infancy stage. It then discusses how a tech start-up takes the next step up, to Organizational Adolescence.

Chapter 5 discusses how the dynamics of the company change from Organizational Infancy to Organizational Adolescence and describes the basic conditions of this stage. It shows you how to use the NETS Stage Factors to determine whether a start-up is at the Adolescence stage or not.

Chapter 6 provides a summary of the organizational stages and also describes the pathway to mature Adulthood and what it means for you.

Chapter 7 explores the topic of your personal tolerance for tech start-up career risk. It takes you through an exercise to determine your personal tolerance profile. It suggests a comparative framework for you to weigh various factors that you need to consider in joining a start-up company and then helps you evaluate what you have learned about yourself. Having done so, the chapter suggests how to identify the best start-up options for you based on your scoring from your risk profile results. Chapter 7 also suggests different career paths you can consider, based on how the tech start-up fits into your career goals.

Chapter 8 explores the topic of tech start-up financing in detail so that you understand the process. It walks through the different stages of tech start-up funding: seed round, first venture round, later venture rounds, mezzanine, and ultimately, initial public offering (IPO). The chapter discusses the different investors in a tech start-up and their interests, motivations, and expectations. It shows how funding rounds correspond to NETS Stages of organizational development and defines the terminology you need to know. Ultimately, Chapter 8 illustrates how tech start-up ownership changes over time with additional funding rounds.

Chapter 9 discusses the crucial evaluation points you need to consider in making the decision about whether to join a technology start-up.

Chapter 10 highlights the crucial information you can glean in an interview. It offers insights for learning about and assessing a firm's business plan, the management team and board, the company's market strategy, compensation, and your career plan.

Chapter 11 discusses the key considerations you should make once the start-up offers you the job. You will explore all key factors and strategies in detail, including salary, stock option grants and valuation, benefits, and role and responsibilities. Chapter 11 also points out a few key considerations for prospective tech start-up executives.

Chapter 12 explores how to succeed when setting sail in uncharted territory. It underscores the need for you to look out for your own interests. It also suggests that you need to monitor continually the fit of the tech start-up's people, culture, and strategy with your career goals and interests.

Chapter 13 suggests how you can make the most of the start-up experience. Given the incredibly hot job market in today's economy, a new job is close by if you want it. Working within a technology start-up gives you a bird's-eye view of growth industries, trends, and competition, which provides you with knowledge and learning you can trade on in the future.

Chapter 14 is about the long and winding road ahead in your working life. It suggests that you may have multiple jobs and multiple careers over the course of your working life and explores some of the key advantages of the start-up experience: having fun, expanding your network, and leveraging the organizational learning from the tech start-up. It encourages you to consider your career game plan, both in the short and long term.

The Resources section contains information on career guide and career search Web sites from an array of organizations. It also lists sites for specific knowledge industries in which technology start-ups are exploding: biotechnology, computing, e-commerce, hardware and software, semiconductors, and telecommunications. These sites contain a wealth of information that may help you learn more about an industry and its dynamics, or about the start-up opportunities within it. The Resources section also lists sites that offer information on stock options, a key component of tech start-up currency.

I myself have worked for a new economy tech start-up company. Moreover, in my work in business development I have dealt with technology start-ups often. Although I may have preconceived notions about start-ups, I have sought the perspectives of people at a variety of companies to provide a thoroughly balanced point of view about new economy opportunities.

The interviewees quoted in this book are people who have gone into start-ups before you. They offer perspectives from their experiences and share their successes, failures, and lessons learned. Collectively, they have worked in both start-ups and Fortune 500 companies. They have worked in a broad range of industries, and their start-up experience covers businesses in biotechnology, cable television, computer hardware and software, Internet content, business to business and business to consumer electronic commerce (e-commerce), medical devices, semiconductors, and video games. Their roles have encompassed finance, marketing, operations, research and development, and sales, and their position levels have covered the range from entry level all the way up to president and CEO. They have worked in tech start-up firms at all stages and have seen their firms fail, get acquired, and go public. Some are practically "start-up junkies," who may never go back to a large company again, while others have left the start-up realm and joined larger, more stable companies.

I hope that their perspective and advice will help you to know what to expect if you choose to join a start-up. It is a world that is both exciting and challenging, but it's not necessarily for everyone. However, having said that, there are probably more positions at new economy start-ups right now than can be filled. This book is designed to help you determine for yourself whether the start-up experience is right for you, and under which circumstances.

1

WHY A TECHNOLOGY START-UP IS DIFFERENT

"People join tech start-ups for the ability to create something new and get out of the corporate hierarchy. You have more freedom. It's a high adrenaline rush type of situation that also offers the potential financial reward. You can write your own ticket."

—ADRIANNA PARADISO, FORMERLY PRODUCT MANAGER, NETGROCER, NOW DIRECTOR OF MARKETING, E-STEEL

Based on what we hear and see in the business media, the technology start-up marketplace seems to represent the "Wild West" frontier of today's economy. In many ways, it *is* today's new economic frontier. Every day we read about new technology companies waging battle in the marketplace. Competition in technology is happening at warp speed, and the pace of change is constant. The spoils of victory are enormous. Winners are reveling in their glory, gaining fame, fortune, customers, and validation. People have become instant millionaires by way of their start-ups going public in an initial public offering (IPO). It seems to happen all the time, to just about every start-up we read about. It's an economic phenomenon unlike any other.

Believe it or not, those successful start-ups are the exceptions. That's why they're news. We don't read about the companies that fail and fade quietly into the night. They're not news. The reality is that *any* technology start-up represents significant risks to its employees and investors. Getting rich fast is far from guaranteed, and there is no assurance of long-term success. The cold, hard reality is that if you join a technology start-up you might be out of a job on very short notice because your company runs out of money. My point: Don't join a company simply for the wealth you hope to accumulate.

It's important to downplay any expectation of getting rich quickly and focus instead on your career goals. Getting rich would certainly be a great bonus, but it shouldn't be your sole reason for joining a start-up.

That disclaimer aside, this book will tell you how and why joining a new economy start-up can be an exciting career move. It will also show you how to make the all-important decision of whether to join a specific company. I'll tell you how to identify the ideal start-up situation and how to position the experience in the broader context of your career. Although I caution you not to join a tech start-up for the sole purpose of getting rich, I will show you how to evaluate stock option grants so you can determine if you're getting good upside potential.

A tech start-up is different from just about any other type of work situation, for many reasons. Understanding these reasons will put you in a much stronger position to evaluate career opportunities. The following case example will give you some sense of how a tech start-up comes to be in the first place and why it takes on the attributes that it does.

THE CASE OF A TECHNOLOGY START-UP: THE TORTILLA CHIP COMPANY

Imagine that Tortilla Chip was founded by a group of engineers who had to bootstrap the company into existence, first by using their own funds, then by seeking funding from an outside investor. These engineers at one time worked for a company that we'll call Casagrande Engineering Corporation. While on the job they conceived of an idea that they believed offered advantages to some customer in the marketplace. Their product was a small computer chip that could be used for faster computing. The engineers presented their new, small-chip idea to the management of Casagrande.

The Casagrande Engineering Corporation was a large and publicly traded company that was in the business of serving customers who bought large computers that, for whatever reason, needed large computer chips. Casagrande management wasn't familiar with anyone using anything other than the large type of computer sold by their major partner, the Oversize Computer Company, to whom they were a key supplier. As far as management was aware, all customers bought a large computer from Oversize or one of its competitors. In other words, they didn't think there was a significant market for this smaller chip.

Publicly traded Casagrande had to show steady revenue and profit growth every year or its shareholders would sell its stock, causing its stock price to decline. When the engineers presented their small chip idea to the Casagrande senior management team, they rejected it. Not coincidentally, Casagrande management stood to lose the most in pursuing the small chip project because they were the ones who owned the most Casagrande stock. From their standpoint, the project represented a high risk: an expensive undertaking that would not yield large sales and profits in the immediate future and therefore would be a drag on earnings. A drag on earnings would cause the price of *their* stock to suffer.

In spite of the rejection by the Casagrande management team, a few of the engineers kept tinkering with the new chip in their spare time, at nights and on weekends. They continued developing the chip for a period of about a year. During that time, they talked to each other and to colleagues about the concept and discovered that there were a few people interested in buying smaller computers that would require their smaller chip. Soon they began to realize that there was at least some type of market for the small-chip product. They talked among themselves about how to get their small chip into the hands of customers who wanted and needed it.

Given that Casagrande had turned the project down, the engineers decided that they would go into business for themselves to design and produce the small chip and sell it to a newly emerging group of computer makers. They resigned from Casagrande and used some of their own funds to set up shop as the Tortilla Chip Company. They soon realized that they might need to find more money to continue funding their company while they completed the product development.

The engineers went to the Low Risk Bank for a loan, but its banker rejected them. The banker there figured that if Casagrande management had rejected the project, then it had to be highly risky. After all, the engineers acknowledged that the market for their product at the time was small at best and not well understood. In addition, the same banker had just received a loan application for Crisp Cleaning, a new dry cleaner moving in on the corner of a high-volume neighborhood. There was sure to be demand for the dry cleaner, given that the nearest competition was five miles away. All in all, the dry cleaner was a much less risky project to the banker. The bank loan to the dry cleaner, as well as the interest, would almost certainly be repaid. The dry cleaner would never be a huge business, but it was predictable to Low Risk Bank, whereas the business of the engineers and Tortilla Chip was not.

The engineers next approached Mr. D'Angelo, a retired engineer they knew who had made money in the technology sector some years before. Mr. D'Angelo was an "angel investor," one who could provide the founders with early stage or "seed" funding that would enable them to build prototypes of their products so that they could solicit additional investment funding. As the engineers made their pitch to him, Mr. D'Angelo immediately understood the potential opportunity for their smaller chip and agreed to fund the venture in exchange for a small piece of the company. Although he recognized that there were substantial risks in the project, he invested $200,000 in Tortilla Chip to help the company complete a working product prototype. Mr. D'Angelo knew he might never see his investment again, but he also knew that he might earn a huge return.

It took the engineers several months to complete a rough, working prototype of the new chip. At that point they had completed enough work on the prototype to be able to demonstrate some of its capabilities to prospective investors. If they were to move forward, they would need to solicit additional funds to bring all of the appropriate people on board to complete design and development of the product. Ultimately they would need to produce, market, and sell the new chip product as well. They approached Big Kahuna Venture Capital Partners, a venture capital firm that invested in new technology companies.

Big Kahuna was staffed by former executives of high-technology companies who managed investments in many tech start-up companies. When Big Kahuna elected to back a start-up firm, they provided their technological expertise, advice, and contacts to the start-up, in addition to their investment capital. Therefore, they usually demanded and got a larger stake of the company than angel investors, who simply provided the initial seed funding. In this case, Big Kahuna invested $4 million for a 40 percent stake in Tortilla Chip. Big Kahuna also took two seats on the Tortilla Chip board of directors to help oversee the direction of the company. For his $200,000 investment, Mr. D'Angelo had received a 1 percent stake in Tortilla Chip, although he did not sit on the board. He did, however, serve as an outside consultant.

At the time Big Kahuna made its investment, a number of corporate documents were written up that weren't that important to anyone but did serve to run up a very large legal bill. One document formally allocated ownership of stock in the company to key company founders, managers, and directors. The directors of Tortilla Chip also appropriated a pool of company stock to be used in granting stock options to other future employees of Tortilla Chip, as incentive to recruit them to the company. The company was unable to pay lavish salaries at the time because it had to conserve cash. Stock options were considered an effective way to recruit people in light of the modest salaries the company offered. If the company ever issued stock publicly, then hopefully the holders of stock options would profit nicely from their equity ownership.

Although it had received a first round of venture capital financing, Tortilla Chip would probably have to obtain more investment through additional venture funding rounds to put in place the necessary staff and resources before it could go public. Once the product concept was sufficiently proven, the goal would be to take Tortilla Chip public so that the company could raise funds for marketing and selling its product in the marketplace. The Big

Kahuna board members urged the engineers to get their new chip product to market fast because they were aware of another company that was attempting to develop a similar product. The engineers, eagerly getting started, rolled up their sleeves and began the race to market. More than once during the ensuing journey they thought: "This tech start-up stuff is a whole different ball game from a dry cleaner. Tortilla Chip really *is* a new economy company."

THE NEW ECONOMY

For purposes of this book, the *new economy* can be characterized by the fact that everything is happening and moving faster. As a result, companies are finding themselves in ever more competitive business environments. Today's new economy is one in which companies, large and small, are thinking about and doing things differently out of necessity. They must react faster and be more creative than ever before in the way they compete for customers and employees.

Companies must be willing to do more to serve their customers and accept less profit for doing so. Increasingly, companies are offering employees, especially valuable employees, more generous employment terms and benefits to retain them. Perhaps you've read about employees who are being allowed to set their own work schedules or bring their pets into the office with them!

The creative efforts that companies pursue to stay competitive are also causing them to redefine how they see their customers and markets. In short, successful companies are proactively changing their business models, the ways in which they do business and generate sales and earnings. They are making such changes with the help of technology.

Advances in technology of all kinds are increasing the speed with which things happen in today's marketplace. Technological development and progress in many fields has accelerated. The Internet is perhaps the most obvious example of a current technology acceleration. Today you can order a book, make a travel reservation, view the interior of a home, shop for a car, and access the

Library of Congress, all from your computer. As recently as five years ago, none of this was possible.

Computer processing power has improved immensely over the past few decades, while the cost of that processing power has plummeted. The result is that functions that were performed on a mainframe computer the size of a neighborhood block a few short decades ago can be performed on a laptop computer today. Wireless telephones are becoming ubiquitous, and we are seeing the emergence of wireless telephones that connect us to the World Wide Web, so that we can do the same things on the Web from our phones that we can do from our personal computers.

Computers have accelerated technological progress in the area of biotechnology. In fact, experts predict that the progress that we can expect to make in the next twenty-five years in biotechnology will surpass all of our prior achievements combined. As an example of how computers are driving this acceleration, DNA sequencing was impossible without computers to document and categorize genetic molecular strands. Now we are within a few years of mapping the entire human genome.

In other areas, years of research are paying off now. We have already developed several approaches to growing human skin equivalents, or skin substitutes, that are on the market today, and efforts are presently underway to grow an array of other human organs. When we add it all up, it makes sense that the groundwork that has been laid by technology in the past will enable us to leapfrog to new developments in the future.

One of the biggest resulting changes of technological acceleration is the way in which more people work today. In our parents' generation, it was common for someone to spend his or her entire career at one company. By comparison, people are moving around more and doing so more often today. They are more mobile, and they have learned through layoffs or by being approached by other companies that one can get ahead economically by moving from one company to another.

Judy Schneider is a consultant who has served as Vice President of Content, Community, and Personalization at Onhealth, an online healthcare content and e-commerce company based in Seattle. Judy describes the situation this way:

There used to be a penalty if you just stayed with a company for four or five years. But that's not the case any more. In the Internet business, everybody knows you're . . . up for grabs to the highest bidder if a good deal comes along.

That people are switching companies more, and doing so more frequently, is no longer seen as a liability. Indeed, to Judy's point, the heightened competition in business today has spurred companies to become more competitive in recruiting talented people. Companies themselves are, in fact, part of the reason why people switch jobs more often today than they did in the past. Because this heightened demand for talent by companies is contributing to people's switching companies more frequently, company recruiters are hardly in a position to criticize those doing it.

How does technology in business raise the competitive bar among companies? One of the key reasons that business competition is becoming more intense is that as technology advances, prices fall. With the possible exceptions of new sport utility vehicles, barrels of oil, boxes of cereal, fine wines, and maybe a few other things, prices for most products are falling. What is more, product prices are declining even as product performance improves.

We see a cycle here that shows no signs of abating. Technology advances, causing prices to fall. Companies respond by refining their business approach or model through technology to be more price competitive. This brings about new technological advances or more innovative uses of existing technology. As a result, prices fall once again, and the cycle continues.

Meanwhile, people are going to work for companies (many of them tech start-up companies) that seek to exploit new technologies and business models. Some succeed, while many do not. When companies fail, or possibly beforehand, their employees jump ship to a new company whose prospects for competing in a more competitive marketplace look good. We can now see why it is more acceptable for people to switch companies more frequently in the new economy environment. The market picks winners and losers faster than ever before. In the past, the game changed more slowly.

The term *new economy,* therefore, reflects a company and career environment in which the market dynamics operate with unprecedented speed. The element that is "new" is the rapid pace of change. Businesses still operate to generate revenues and profits, as they always have, but they must be ever more nimble in figuring out how to do so and in executing the strategies that will get them there. If you've bought this book, then you already realize that the new economy, which involves ever-faster-paced competition and innovation every day, is a very exciting place to be.

Although the new economy is all about speed, it is not solely the domain of tech start-ups. Many large and established companies are moving aggressively as well. General Electric's online order procurement system, TPNPost, is but one example of an established company taking bold, aggressive action in e-commerce. The big U.S. automakers are following suit with their own initiatives to integrate their suppliers into their business processes online. In addition, although most traditional financial services firms have been slow to take up the online banner, companies such as Merrill Lynch and Goldman Sachs have started serving their customers over the Internet. So as you think about going to a new economy start-up, look to see if a larger, cash-rich competitor hasn't trained its sights squarely on your firm's target market.

WHAT A START-UP IS

The Tortilla Chip case should have given you some idea of what a start-up is. The case actually involved two start-ups: Tortilla Chip Company and Crisp Cleaning. Although both are start-ups, only one, Tortilla Chip, is a *tech* start-up. We'll explore the differences between the tech start-up and other types of start-ups later. For now, let's explore the business category of start-ups in general.

A start-up is so called because it is a new business venture. Often, a start-up involves some type of financial bootstrapping to get started. In other words, an up-front investment is required to start the business. In reality, many if not all start-ups are money-losing ventures for some period of time after they begin operating. The key challenge for a start-up, as with any business, is to make money, to actually get to the point at which the company is making a profit from its operations.

The reason start-ups have an aura of swashbuckling and daring is that they are risky endeavors; many will never actually make a profit, and will, in fact, go out of business. Investors of all types understand that a start-up company's failure is a real possibility. Even Crisp Cleaning can go out of business if it is not managed efficiently. There is a higher element of risk, often a significantly higher one, in a start-up than in a larger, more established company.

Part of what you as a prospective start-up career searcher will need to assess is your tolerance for start-up risk. Your personal risk profile is explored in more detail in Chapter 7, but stay attuned to the risks of start-ups as you read through the other chapters. Many of the people quoted throughout this book share their perspectives on different elements of start-up risk, both from a company and a career perspective.

Who "Starts It Up?"

Start-ups are typically founded by entrepreneurs who have an idea about how to solve a problem differently. It could be that their solution solves a problem faster or cheaper, or that it addresses a market need that they believe is not being met adequately. In technology start-ups, these are usually people who have a background in some field of science or technology. Such people might be computer scientists, engineers, doctors of medicine or other sciences, laboratory researchers, or some combination of these. Of course, the founders don't have to be strictly scientists, but it certainly helps if they have experience with, and an affinity for, technology.

Alan Kitty, President and CEO of Link Tank, L.L.C., a consulting firm in Lawrenceville, New Jersey, notes that the founding entrepreneurs of a technology start-up have a tremendous need to stand out and prove something. Alan's company advises technology start-ups in marketing, sales, and business development. Prior to founding his own firm, Alan worked for several start-ups, including Corel Computer, a spin-off of Corel Corporation, and Design FX, an Internet start-up. In fact, Alan says that the need for the founders to prove something is often so great that they can't help but pursue a start-up. To Alan's point, there is tremendous drive among the founders of tech start-ups, something you need to remember as you interview. They take their work seriously.

Often, the entrepreneurs who found start-up companies have experience in a particular industry. Their prior experience has given them a vantage point from which to learn about markets, customers, and competitors. Of course, this isn't always the case, but a start-up developing software for, say, the banking industry is usually better off having someone with banking experience on the management team.

There are instances in which it may be an advantage if the founders have no prior experience in a given industry, especially if the vision is literally to reshape that industry. Many technology start-ups are in the business of doing just that. As an example, Jeff Bezos did not own a bricks and mortar bookstore when he launched his company, Amazon.com. Amazon offers a completely new way for people to buy and sell books as well as other products. Amazon did hire people with an existing base of experience in areas such as logistics and supply chain management, because having competency in those areas is valuable to a company like Amazon.

Another key attribute of successful start-up founders is that they are passionate about wanting to solve a problem. They usually feel very strongly about the market need that they seek to address. Many founding entrepreneurs are not in the business just to get rich. If becoming wealthy were their sole motivation, it is unlikely that most entrepreneurs would be innovative enough to find the creative solutions that they do. Although becoming wealthy and being one's own boss are certainly desirable objectives for many start-up entrepreneurs, more often than not their reason for founding the company runs deeper than that. Your goal as a start-up career searcher is to find those entrepreneurs who truly are passionate about their desire to solve a problem for a lot of people—and to get paid well for doing so.

Basic Conditions Found in All Start-Ups

Start-ups are entrepreneurial endeavors. Having only recently been "started," they are obviously new. As new businesses, they typically don't have that many employees, often because there simply hasn't been enough time to hire more. The following are attributes that are common to both tech and non-tech start-ups.

Working in a Start-Up Is Hard Work.   Whether a start-up is a newly opened restaurant, a software start-up, or a new biotech venture, every single person with whom I've talked agrees that working in a start-up is hard work. Prabhavathi ("Prabha") Fernandes is President and CEO of Small Molecule Therapeutics, Inc. (SMT), a biotechnology start-up in Montvale, New Jersey. Prabha sums up the nature of a start-up in this way: "Enthusiasm is flowing and the energy level is high because you have to roll up your sleeves and do what it takes to make it a success." Although there can be a difference in the incentives between the tech start-up and the non-tech start-up in getting people to do the hard work required, at the end of the day, all start-ups involve hard work.

Roles Are Broad and Widely Defined.   At an early stage of a start-up's life, one employee may fulfill numerous different roles simply because there is no one else around to perform them. An accounting person may do some marketing, absent someone else to perform the marketing role. An engineer may be trying to balance the books. A CEO may be putting cubicles together. In tech start-ups, the opportunity to take the initiative and play a multitude of roles is part of the appeal to many people.

Bill Demas is Vice President of Marketing at Vividence Corporation, a business-to-business e-commerce company located in San Mateo, California. Bill is in hiring mode at Vividence, and he clearly recognizes the need for broad role definition: "At a start-up, people are very naturally doing things completely outside of their box." He notes that this happens out of pure necessity, because in rapidly growing start-ups, one can't hire talent fast enough.

The Founders Are a Unique Group of People with Specific Attributes.   Adrianna Paradiso, who has interviewed with, and worked for, numerous start-ups, describes three key attributes that the founding team members of a start-up should have: a vision or idea, the ability to execute the idea, and the ability to manage the business. Although the abilities of the start-up founders may over-lap among these attributes, it is rare that one person possesses all three. It is even more rare for one person to possess all three and be able to fulfill them successfully, particularly as the company grows. For a person who has strength in execution, such as a pro-gramming engineer, it is not a valuable use of his or her time to balance the books, do fundraising, or secure office space. Other people should manage those functions. The founding team may comprise two people, or five, or ten; there's no rule for the number of founders in a start-up. Irrespective of their number, the found-ing team members need to possess among them the three attrib-utes noted above if the start-up is to be successful.

HOW A TECH START-UP DIFFERS FROM OTHER START-UPS

You may know intuitively some of the key differences between a tech start-up and the traditional start-up, but they are worth defining because they can be subtle. Making the distinction be-tween tech and traditional start-ups will help you clearly under-stand the dynamics at play in start-up companies.

Goal

The goal of a tech start-up is to get as big as possible as quickly as possible. By big, I mean in terms of revenues. You might not think that the business goal of a research stage biotech company is the same as that of a Web-based e-commerce company, but it is. Both seek to get big fast. If you talk to the investors backing that biotech company, you can be sure they didn't invest so that some-body could win a Nobel Prize or that they were trying to help someone run a nonprofit research lab. Any start-up company in technology wants, and needs, to get bigger in a hurry.

The reason the tech start-up needs to drive revenues is to be-come self-sustaining, so that it doesn't have to rely on investor fi-nancing. Generating higher revenues is a sure fire way to improve its financial situation, as well as to bolster the firm's prospects for going public in an IPO. Although many firms go public without having sales, the reason for doing so in such instances is to raise money to enhance the firm's ability to grow sales. In these cases, the firm will use the money it raises from its IPO to hire people to help develop and market its product. This has been a common practice in biotechnology, materials science, and communications. In the late 1990s, even Web-based e-commerce companies have been going public before having substantial revenues. For many of these companies, the amount of capital—and time—required to complete or market a product can be significant, so doing an IPO is an obvious choice for raising the funds, even before a firm has significant sales. However, even for companies that go public before having significant sales, the goal is still to grow revenues as quickly as possible, because doing so improves the perceived value of the company, thereby driving the stock price up.

People and Capital

A tech start-up usually involves more people and capital than traditional start-ups. The reason a technology start-up needs funding in the first place is to hire the people necessary to complete the development of its product or service and then to market and sell that offering. Technology companies typically seek to provide solutions to problems that are hard to solve. Trying to develop a medicine for rheumatoid arthritis, a new superior semiconductor chip, or a Web-based grocery ordering and distribution service is difficult. These goals certainly require more manpower than, for example, opening up a new restaurant, a local information technology help desk service, or a limousine service. Not that operating any of those businesses is easy, but they require less manpower.

Wait a second, you say, just about anyone can throw up a Web site; that's not difficult to do. Although it is true that literally anyone can put up a Web site, building a Web-based business that is successful is tremendously difficult. There is significant competition for many Web-based businesses precisely because the sites themselves are so easy to build. To compete successfully in the consumer e-commerce space requires significant marketing and promotional resources and talent, software development resources to refine and improve one's site, business development people to cut deals with other sites to channel traffic to the site, financial and human resources talent, customer service and support, order fulfillment capabilities, and so forth. Add it all up and what do you have: more manpower. In summary, then, because the human demands of tech start-up companies are typically greater than more traditional start-ups, so are their capital demands.

Going Public or Being Sold to a Larger Company

A tech start-up seeks to go public or get sold off to a larger company. It does not seek to be a private, independent entity for very long, if it can help it. This is so because if, as an incentive to join the firm, it has given employees stock options, the company seeks to provide them—and its investors—with a favorable payoff on their equity in as short a time frame as possible. The way to accomplish that is to issue company stock publicly at higher prices than the price at which the equity was made available to the investors and employees. An alternative would be to sell the company off to another firm at a higher price than the price at which the investors and employees were able to buy in. Either an IPO or the sale of the company should provide a start-up firm's investors and employees with a positive—ideally, a highly positive—return on their equity in the start-up company.

Although more traditional types of start-ups may have the goal of going public or being sold off as well, they do not all have that goal. As an example, the primary goal of the Mom and Pop hardware store is probably to provide a source of income for Mom and Dad, not to attract huge investor interest. Of course, if the opportunity for Mom and Dad were big enough, they'd love to get rich off their store, but Mom and Pop shops, by definition, typically address smaller market opportunities.

The Wheelgrease Financial Services Company is another fictitious example of a non-tech start-up. Wheelgrease began as a two-person accounting operation and grew in eight years to 200 people. Wheelgrease seeks to go public. It has attained the critical mass at which it will be able to attract investors to do so, but it does not have to go public or sell itself off to keep its employees and investors happy. For eight years it kept its employees happy by providing them with good salaries and benefits. The equity that it may or may not have distributed to employees in the firm was not a key factor in attracting and retaining its employees to work there. After eight years of being in business, attaining revenues and profits to pay its bills, it doesn't really qualify as a start-up, as we shall see.

Roles

Roles are typically less defined in tech start-ups than in traditional start-ups. Why is this so? Consider for a moment the risk of a tech start-up versus that of a more traditional start-up business, and their potential sources of financing. More traditional types of start-ups, if they carry less risk, and many of them do, are far more likely to qualify for bank financing. As demonstrated in the Tortilla Chip example, the Low Risk Bank is going to be more willing to lend money to a traditional start-up endeavor than to a new technology start-up venture. Not always, but more often than not. So what is required of a business that seeks to get a loan from the bank? Among other things, the bank will require a business plan. That business plan will articulate roles and responsibilities of key company management so that the bank can understand how the business, and the people within it, will function. Although roles within that business plan may be somewhat vague, chances are that they are more defined than those of a tech start-up at the outset. They have to be more defined to persuade the banker, Mr. Skeptic, to loan money to the company.

In contrast, a tech start-up these days can (and many do) get its first round of venture funding from a *napkin*. Because there is so much money out there looking for good ideas, many start-ups are getting initial rounds of funding from angel or venture capital investors as the result of an idea that has been "drawn on a napkin." Okay, maybe the idea was drawn on a whiteboard, lunch bag, or placemat. The fact of the matter is that the idea itself was enough to get the first round of money needed to get the firm off the ground. Somebody was willing to pony up millions of dollars to the company based on a drawing (Leonardo DaVinci, eat your heart out). The company will have to produce a business plan at some point to attract additional rounds of money from other investors, but at the outset the product or service idea alone will do. This idea, its development, and the degree of its completion are crucial determinants of the stage of a tech start-up company.

If the idea itself is just now in the post napkin stage, it is hard to imagine that the roles of people within the company have been defined with any real scope. The company's founders may know that one person will head the engineering group and another will focus on business development and fundraising, but beyond that, role definitions are undefined. Of course, as the company hires more people and grows, it will define people's roles and responsibilities more clearly. But when starting at ground zero at a tech start-up, much is undefined. Again, this is not to say that roles are completely defined in non-tech start-up companies, but they are likely to be more defined than in a tech start-up in its earliest stages.

High-Technology Product

A tech start-up typically involves a high-technology *product*. Another distinguishing feature of tech start-ups is that they will almost always involve some type of high technology as part of their product or service offering. Maybe someone can point to an exception somewhere, but I can't think of one. For purposes of this book, high technology is defined as the scientific application of advanced equipment, devices, or know-how. It's easy to see how things like wireless communication devices, semiconductor technologies, and anything involving computer science or biotechnology research fall under this description.

This is not to say that our CPA friends at the non-tech Wheelgrease Financial Services lack advanced knowledge of a given field. They have a highly specialized skill, the use of which is a service to their customers. Most, if not all, of what they do is a service. They may render an opinion about the financial status of a company and produce a report of the company audit, but that paper-based product is hardly high-tech. They may use a sophisticated accounting software package to help them in their work, but they are in the business of rendering a service—in this case, financial advice.

Just as tech start-up companies almost always involve some type of technology product, they will very often have a service component to their business. Most tech companies offer some type of customer service and support. If you've ever called a help desk, you know there's a service component to technology. Very often that service involves someone covering for the company twenty-four hours a day, seven days a week (24/7). Try getting that type of customer service from an accountant! What is more, that service component to a tech company's business may, in fact, be the hardest part of what that company does. Building a front-end Web site to take orders for groceries isn't that difficult compared to determining the logistics and distribution of delivering those groceries and optimizing the number of delivery trucks and their routes.

All of these attributes are guidelines rather than hard-and-fast rules. In most cases, they will be reliable for you if you are trying to distinguish a technology start-up from a more traditional start-up company. This is not to say that if you find a more traditional start-up with great prospects you shouldn't join it. It could well be that the traditional start-up faces a lower level of risk and could provide you as an individual with greater upside than any high-tech start-up company you're considering. However, much of the job growth in the new economy these days is happening in tech start-ups and technology-related companies.

WRAP-UP

Once you are familiar with the dynamics of tech start-ups, what they are, and how they differ from traditional start-ups, and have some sense of the types of people who conceive them, you are ready to start thinking critically about their prospects for success and their stage of organizational development. Your ability to do so will become crucial as you interview with tech start-ups and consider the types of opportunities that might be right for you. A framework of the key variables to explore with any tech start-up will help you to make the determination that only you can make. That framework is the topic of the next chapter.

2

INTRODUCING THE NEW ECONOMY TECHNOLOGY START-UP (NETS) STAGE FACTORS

"I knew I wanted to make a change. I wanted to be in a much faster-paced business. Handango offered a great opportunity to grow really quickly."

—ANDREW BLAKE, DIRECTOR OF
DEVELOPER RELATIONS, HANDANGO

Contrary to how the term might sound, NETS Stage Factors are neither growth hormones nor improved hair care ingredients. New Economy Technology Start-Up (NETS) Stage Factors are a series of attributes that, used in combination, will help you to identify two things: whether a given company is a tech start-up and the development stage of the tech start-up. Once you know how and why they work, you can use them to plan your interview strategies with tech start-ups. Doing so will help you make an accurate assessment about a given start-up, its prospects, and whether you are comfortable with its development stage.

You already know why it is important to be able to distinguish a tech start-up from a more traditional start-up business. The NETS Stage Factors will help you make that distinction even more clearly. Over time, as you interview with different companies, it will become second nature for you to conclude quickly whether the start-up you are dealing with is tech or non-tech and its current development stage.

Knowing the stage of the company's organizational development is important because it determines the risk-reward trade-off that the start-up represents to you. You should be concerned with this risk-reward trade-off from both a financial and a career perspective. Financially, you must consider your compensation and potential upside from stock options. More important from a professional standpoint, you must consider the implications for your career and the potential a tech start-up offers you in experience and skills.

The financial opportunity costs are fairly obvious: The difference between getting paid $45,000 per year at a tech start-up and $70,000 per year at a more traditional firm is easy to understand. In this case, if you go with the tech start-up and your stock options are never worth anything, then you will have realized an opportunity cost of $25,000 per year. From a purely financial perspective, then, you'd like to have fairly high confidence that the company's options will be worth at least $25,000 per year to you.

From a career standpoint, the opportunity cost can be more difficult to quantify, but the principle is the same. Although a start-up at a very early stage may offer you a position that could lead quickly to a role with major responsibility, it could also lead nowhere just as fast. As an example, let's say you join a tech start-up as the Vice President of Marketing. We'll call the start-up Titanic.com. You sign on, and the company stays afloat for six months, then tanks. You're out of a job. Now what?

The title and responsibility you had for six months might not mean very much to other potential employers. In this scenario, the opportunity cost to you would be the value to your career of taking a different position at another company where you might have had a greater impact for a potentially longer period of time. Let's say that in your six-month stint as VP of Marketing at Titanic.com you had a staff of three and never launched a meaningful product. In contrast, perhaps another opportunity would have led to your managing a department of twenty-five and launching a multi-million dollar business in the same time frame. From a recruiter's standpoint, it's easy to see which experience would appear more valuable.

The NETS Stage Factors help you consider these implications. Over the course of this book, you will evaluate the NETS Stage Factors (Chapters 3 through 5) against your personal risk profile (Chapter 7). By combining that information with start-up career search diagnostics (Chapters 9 and 10), you will have a potent combination of knowledge and insight that will help you ask the questions to give you the answers you need. Ultimately, by synthesizing the information you learn about a tech start-up and insights about yourself, you will be able to make a highly informed decision about joining a given start-up.

The five NETS Stage Factors are

- Cash position
- Sales status
- Business model status
- Demand status
- Product status

Let's take them in turn.

CASH POSITION

The key thing to remember about a tech start-up is that its investors want to own a stake of equity in the company for the potential upside that the investment may deliver. In contrast, Crisp Cleaning from the Tortilla Chip case would not represent the ideal start-up equity investment. Rather, Crisp Cleaning is an ideal loan candidate for a bank. As opposed to making an equity investment in a tech start-up business, a retail bank typically seeks to loan money to a non-tech start-up venture, with the expectation that the loan will be paid back. The bank in that scenario does not acquire a piece of ownership in the business.

In terms of cash position, a tech start-up company has received equity investment from investors. These investors may be the founders or others who acquire a stake of ownership in the firm.

You may say that lots of start-up companies, not just technology start-up companies, are set up that way, and that's true. But what differentiates a tech start-up from other types of start-ups is its use of technology.

The other important financial consideration is that the tech start-up company's overarching goal is to go public or get bought out by a larger, more established company. As stated previously, this is not always the goal of other types of start-up companies. Because of the risks in tech start-ups, investors seek to take these companies public as quickly as possible to generate a (hopefully high) return on their investment. Although typically the founding entrepreneurs' key driving motivation is to solve a market problem, they recognize that investors have backed them for financial reasons, not out of the kindness of their hearts. Therefore, they understand the need and desire to go public or get sold off.

SALES STATUS

Sales: cash registers ringing, credit cards a-swiping, money flowing over the wires. Actually, because by definition a start-up is a new business venture, it typically has very limited sales at best. Put another way, a tech start-up has no to low sales. Whatever level of sales it may be generating is, in all likelihood, insufficient to cover its operating expenses. Therefore, if the firm does have revenues, it is probably not turning a profit yet. Why is this so?

First, if the company is profitable, then it is probably not a start-up. If it is a profitable start-up, it is unlikely that it is a technology start-up because technology start-ups typically require a large up-front capital investment relative to most other types of start-ups. We know the reason for this is that technology start-ups seek to address potentially big markets. A tech start-up that is profitable almost immediately, addresses a large market, and requires a very low up-front investment is one I'd like to invest in, so if you hear about one, tell me about it!

As an illustration from Tortilla Chip, Crisp Cleaning is more likely to be profitable sooner than our engineering friends making a new computer chip. But if the personal computer market takes off and they get their small chip product to market in time, then Tortilla Chip will earn far greater *total profits* than the local Crisp Cleaning. The market potential of Crisp Cleaning is simply much more limited than that of Tortilla Chip.

BUSINESS-MODEL STATUS

The company's business model, the way in which it will generate sales and earnings, can be described in some way and is used to motivate investors to finance the company. For many tech start-ups, the business model is fairly straightforward. As an example, if the company is a biotechnology research company and it intends to pursue a partnership with a major drug company, the business model is probably pretty easy to understand. The biotech firm will develop a molecule and license it to a large pharmaceutical company that will manufacture, market, and sell the product. The biotech company will earn a royalty on sales of the product.

For other tech start-ups, the business model may not be so simple. Bruce Pomfret is now a software engineer at Perot Systems in Boston, Massachusetts. Bruce describes the situation at his former employer, Nets, Inc., a Boston-based e-commerce start-up that ultimately ran out of cash and was sold off to Perot Systems: "They went off course a bit. . . . They tried to pursue a lot of ideas even if they were only tangentially related to their original idea of getting an e-commerce platform going." Many other interviewees describe similar gyrations at their start-ups while management was trying to find the right business model. Such exercises in searching for the right business model are fairly commonplace in Web-based e-commerce companies.

It doesn't matter if the business model that was first proposed is still the one that the company is pursuing. What matters is that a business model was or has been articulated for the tech start-up to raise investment funding. An interview insight for you, if you are focusing on Web-based e-commerce start-ups, is to ask your interviewers to what extent their business model has changed. Their answers may be revealing.

DEMAND STATUS

Obviously, if a company has no product, it has no demand. That isn't to say that there isn't market demand for the product that it intends to make and sell. It just means that the company can't sell the product without having one. Of course, having people line up at your door waiting to buy a product that isn't finished yet sounds pretty good to me, so if you find yourself interviewing with such a firm, you could be getting in at the right time.

The challenge for many new technology companies is that it can be unclear if there is significant demand for the company's product or not. Suffice it to say that for a tech start-up to come into being there is some level of perceived customer demand for the company's solution. There has to be, otherwise investors would not back the company in question, or any company for that matter. However, as we saw in the Tortilla Chip example, it may be unclear exactly how much demand exists. Mr. D'Angelo, the angel investor, and Big Kahuna, the venture capital firm, were willing to invest in Tortilla Chip because they believed there was market demand for the Tortilla Chip product. However, Mr. Skeptic, the banker, would not loan money to Tortilla Chip because he did not know if sufficient demand existed to justify the company's existence. In essence, for a tech start-up somebody has to perceive some level of demand for the company's product. In the case of tech start-ups, it very likely will be the angels and venture capital firms and not retail bankers who perceive that opportunity, because tech start-ups are too risky for retail banks.

PRODUCT STATUS

A tech start-up will typically involve some type of high technology as part of its product or service offering. Thus, the product itself is a key factor that differentiates tech start-ups from other types of start-ups. As I've said, high technology is defined as the scientific application of advanced equipment, devices, or know-how.

For an early stage start-up, the actual physical product may not exist at all or it may exist in a partial form. The only requirement for the company to be a technology start-up is that the product, which involves high technology in some way, exist at least to some degree on a piece of paper. At the very early stages of a tech start-up's life, a piece of paper may, indeed, be the *only* place where the idea exists. Of course, for a start-up in the biotech field whose goal is to find a cure for cancer, it is likely the molecule or technology being sought has not been discovered yet, but the idea—a cure for cancer—can still exist on a piece of paper.

By existing on a piece of paper, I mean that the idea can be articulated conceptually in some way. For later-stage funding of tech start-ups, the ability to build upon the initial idea becomes important, but for initial stage tech investment, a drawing on a piece of paper has succeeded in obtaining the required financing. If a drawing of the idea was all an investor required of the company founders at that birthing stage, why should you require more? A piece of advice to you as you interview with tech start-up firms is to ask interviewers to articulate the company's vision and where the company is in pursuit of that vision. Their answers can give you significant insight into the company's prospects for success.

THE NETS STAGE FACTORS: CONCLUSION

You now have some sense of how to use the NETS Stage Factors to identify a technology start-up company. Such a beast will be a start-up that

- has received equity investment financing with the ultimate goal of going public or getting acquired
- typically has no to low revenues
- has a business model that can be described
- has some perceived level of market demand for its product
- produces or will produce a product that utilizes high technology in some way

To briefly recap a few points: It doesn't matter where the company's initial equity investment came from. Somebody ponied up some money to get the company off the ground. Most likely the company is unprofitable. The physical product doesn't have to exist yet. In many cases, it won't, or it will be evolving. Finally, somebody will have perceived some demand for the product; otherwise the company would not have received any investment in the first place. However, the actual demand may not be measurable to any accurate degree.

THE NETS DEVELOPMENT STAGES

There are three key NETS Stages, or stages of organizational development, which you need to understand clearly. These are the stages during which you are most likely to join a tech start-up company. The three primary NETS Stages are

- Birth stage
- Organizational Infancy stage
- Organizational Adolescence stage

There is also a Pre-birth stage that happens before Birth, and an Adult stage that happens after Adolescence, if the firm makes it that far. Each NETS Stage has its own unique combination of NETS Stage Factors.

Birth Stage

As you might expect, Birth is the stage during which the tech start-up is born. It is the stage when the founders decide they're going to stop doing whatever else it is they have been doing up until now so they can devote their efforts full-time to the tech start-up. Obviously this is not a decision people make lightly. At the time of Birth, there is really no one else around except the company's founders. The start-up at this point is funded by the founders and or by angel investors. Venture capitalists have not yet arrived on the scene. The company typically has no sales at this stage.

Organizational Infancy

Organizational Infancy is triggered by the firm receiving venture capital investment. It is also the time when the company has employees other than founders in its ranks. The company has raised enough capital that it can afford to pay people other than the founders to come on board. A company's product and business model will typically be more defined at this stage than at Birth. The company generally lacks significant sales in Infancy.

Organizational Adolescence

In Adolescence, the company does have meaningful sales. The combination of funding that the company has raised plus the incoming sales is enough to sustain the company for the next two-year period. Typically, an adolescent start-up can sell more of its product if it hires more sales and marketing people, something that is not true of start-ups prior to this stage.

WRAP-UP

The NETS Stage Factors are the five crucial data points on any start-up that you need to obtain. While they may seem like a lot to remember, if you distill each term into its essence, you can come up with a convenient way to recall them, such as the following model:

**Cash + Sales + Business Model + Demand + Product =
"CaSe BuilD uP"**

Case Build Up? It's another weird acronym, I realize. But it's a convenient way to remember the terms if you have difficulty doing so.

"Case Build Up" is an appropriate reminder for at least two reasons because you will use the NETS Stage Factors to build a case on two levels. First, as you talk to different tech start-up companies, you want to determine their NETS Stage, otherwise known as their development stage, and prove to yourself why they are at a given stage. Second, you will assess whether they can build a compelling case for how and why they will be successful. The NETS Stage Factors provide you with a framework for doing both.

Each NETS Stage has its own unique combination of NETS Stage Factors, and therefore its own case build-up. You are now ready to use the NETS Stage Factors to identify the different NETS Stages of a tech start-up.

3

WHEN A START-UP REALLY STARTS UP— THE BIRTH STAGE

"Birth is right at the point when you're just getting your seed funding. It's only a very tiny cadre of people at this point, but you know what you need . . . people with ideas and specialties to bring the idea to fruition."

—BRUCE POMFRET, FORMERLY WEB PROGRAMMER, NETS, INC., NOW SOFTWARE ENGINEER, PEROT SYSTEMS

The Tortilla Chip case provided some insight into what is happening at the birth of a tech start-up. The engineers who founded Tortilla Chip Company were still working at Casagrande for a year before resigning and forming their own company. When they founded Tortilla Chip, they did so with their own funds initially. Later they solicited more seed funding from Mr. D'Angelo, the angel investor. Up to this point, the only people who were involved in the company were the founding members.

Generally, the Birth stage tech start-up is a small group of people working on a very early-stage concept. People are performing many different roles at this stage, and their roles vary more during the Birth stage than at any other. Much of the tech start-up is not in place yet, namely, the people and resources. The company's executive offices may still be someone's garage or bedroom.

PROS AND CONS OF
JOINING A TECH START-UP
AT THE BIRTH STAGE

Although joining a tech start-up involves career and financial risks, one of the key purposes of this book is to demonstrate to you the career value you stand to gain from the tech start-up experience, no matter what. Therefore, I am inherently biased towards the career benefits you can realize from a tech start-up experience. However, having said that, there is definitely much more career risk in joining a tech start-up at an earlier development stage than at a later one.

That is true unless, of course, you are a founding entrepreneur. If you are a founding entrepreneur, then you perceive virtually no career risk to the tech start-up, and in fact there may be no choice for you but to pursue the venture. Your passion is putting together businesses. Career risk is not relevant to you in any significant way. If this start-up fails, you are very likely to pursue another.

Pros

The career and financial benefits of joining a tech start-up at or shortly after the Birth stage are potentially very high. You stand to gain great career experience. You can learn many new skills. You are following your passion. You will have major opportunities to demonstrate leadership in a field you care deeply about. You are getting in on an opportunity on the ground floor. If the company takes off, you could run your own department. You also have huge potential upside from stock options. Even if the start-up fails, the experience will be worthwhile.

Cons

The opportunity costs, from both a career and a financial perspective, are also potentially very high. The company could go out of business with very little advance notice. You could be out of a job, having to go look for another job, trying to explain what happened in your prior experience.

If you have rationally considered these risks and are still willing to join a tech start-up in its early stages or very close to it, then none of these prospects should cause you much concern. In fact, you're probably way past worrying about it. If nothing about the Birth stage intimidates you, then you are probably a fairly accomplished person professionally who could freelance or consult on your own, and therefore any risks to you are fairly low. You are highly passionate about what the tech start-up is setting out to do, which is in fact why you are willing to sign on at such an early stage.

USING THE NETS STAGE FACTORS TO DETERMINE IF A START-UP IS AT THE BIRTH STAGE

A framework of the NETS Stage Factors will serve as a guide in defining any stage of a tech start-up, starting with the Birth stage (see Table 3.1). This framework contains key NETS Stage Indicator questions that you need to ask yourself as you go through the interview process so you can determine the development stage, or stage of evolution, of a given tech start-up. You will become familiar with the NETS Stage Framework as you refer to it throughout this book and as you go through the interview process at tech start-ups.

If you have already identified the company as a NETS company and you answer "No" to all of the NETS Stage Indicator questions in Table 3.1, then the company is at the Birth stage. You could even have said "Yes" to the Business Model and Product Status questions and you would still have a Birth stage start-up on your hands. Let's explore the reasons for this.

Cash Position

The source of the company's cash provides you with the single greatest clue as to whether the company is a Birth stage start-up. At the Birth stage, the start-up has founder or angel investor financing only. It does not have venture capital investment funding. At this stage, the founders through their efforts are driving the

Table 3.1   NETS Stage Factors: Birth Stage

NETS Stage Factor	NETS Stage Indicator Questions	Birth Stage Answers
Cash Position	1. Has the company raised venture capital money from investors?	No. Financing at this stage is from founders or angels.
	2. Are there any nonfounders who are full-time dedicated employees of this company?	No
Sales Status	Are the company's revenues and finances such that they will enable it to cover its costs within the next two years?	No
Business-Model Status	Is the company's business model documented as part of a business plan or other company document(s) that was used to motivate investors to finance the company?	Maybe
Demand Status	If the company hires more marketing and sales people, will it sell more product?	No
Product Status	Does the company's product exist on more than just a piece of paper? (Note: Even if the product is not fully built or tested, if some part of it exists, answer Yes.)	Maybe

work of the company. The founder or group of founders may also have contributed some personal money as seed funding. Even if the firm does have a founder working on the idea full-time or close to it, until it raises the venture capital investment it needs to hire more people (nonfounders) to help develop the product, it is a Birth stage start-up.

Sales Status

It will seem obvious that if the company has raised minimal investment capital for the purpose of completing a demo or prototype product, then it will not have any revenues. In fact, absent any cash, the idea around the technology may or may not even have been formulated into a company yet. Once a start-up company receives venture capital investment, it enters the very early Organizational Infancy stage, which we explore in greater detail in Chapter 4.

Depending on the type of tech start-up, the company may or may not generate revenues for a long time to come. If the company were some type of e-commerce Web site, we would hope that it would generate revenues sooner than would, say, a new biotechnology drug. As we will see later, generating revenues is not an absolute requirement for a tech start-up to evolve to later stages of development, particularly biotechnology and other research-based companies. Suffice it to say the Birth stage tech start-up is definitely not generating sales from its end product.

Business-Model Status

At the Birth stage, some idea about the firm's business model may or may not actually be documented. However, it has definitely been articulated in some form. Undoubtedly the company's founders will have given some serious thought to how the company's business model will work, but it need not have been fully documented for an angel investor to provide financing. Recall that angel investor Mr. D'Angelo provided the founders of Tortilla Chip with funding so they could complete a prototype. The engineers didn't know if the product would work until they had completed some major part of it, let alone what the exact business model would look like for their new chip product. However, actual documentation of the business model *is* often a requirement for later stage venture capital financing.

The firm's business model essentially follows from the product concept. If the product concept has been developed, then the next challenge company founders must address is how to sell it and make a profit doing so. Is there a viable business model in which to sell the product? In the Birth stage, even though the company's business model may not be defined fully, the firm's founders will have thought about it and should have some specific ideas about how it will work. Would you pony up money to fund a start-up when its founders can't tell you how their firm will make money? I think not. Of course, many of our interviewees who have worked at Web start-ups found their companies trying different business models quite frequently. We've already heard from Bruce Pomfret about the Nets experience in experimenting with different business model ideas. Creating sustainable, defensible business models on the wild frontier of the Web is tough. Keep that in mind as you look at Web start-ups.

Demand Status

Because at the Birth stage the start-up does not have a complete product, having more marketing and sales people will not help sell more of it. As an example, Bill Demas waited to join Vividence until the company was at a point where it had a proven product that could be marketed. In the Birth stage, a company is trying to finish the development of its product, which is why more marketing and sales people join tech start-ups after the Birth stage, during the Organizational Infancy stage, when their services are much more critical to the firm.

At the Birth stage, it's very difficult to know how much demand there will be for your start-up firm's product or service. The good news for you is that you don't really need to know at this point, as long as you think that demand is going to be big. It would be nice to be able to pull out a crystal ball, look into it, and see that your firm will be printing money two years from now, but alas, it is much more difficult than that to foretell your firm's future. To join the Birth stage firm, you want to be confident that there is a big potential market. Of course you will steer clear of start-ups in which you think there will be little or no demand for the product.

Confidence that the opportunity will be big is different from proven physical demand in the form of customers standing outside the company's door in droves waiting to buy. You don't need that just yet. You will want to see that throng of customers a little later. At the Birth stage, the company is probably able to service its existing demand because there is probably very little demand for the firm's product in its current, incomplete form. Demand probably does exist for a proven, completed product, and the Birth stage firm is hoping it will be the first to tap into it. You begin to see the importance of being first to market. The winner of the race to finish the product gets to serve all of that pent-up demand.

Product Status

At the point at which the company receives angel investor funding, the product may or may not exist on more than just a piece of paper. Perhaps half of a prototype product has been completed. Now you may be wondering: How do some companies get their seed round of financing from a simple drawing on a napkin? Good question. The answer is that the idea exists in someone's mind as well as on that piece of paper. Although that drawing may be fairly simple on the napkin, its execution is often far more complex.

WHEN DOES A START-UP TAKE THE STEP UP TO ORGANIZATIONAL INFANCY?

From a strictly definitional standpoint, a start-up is catapulted from Birth into Organizational Infancy (OI) the minute it obtains venture capital investment funding and has nonfounder employees working full time on the effort. What has changed is the firm's ability to hire at least some of the people it will need to drive the completion of the product or concept. The firm is now in a position to develop organizationally. Once it has raised venture capital funding, it will proceed to do just that, barring any major disaster.

WRAP-UP

You should now have a sense of how a tech start-up is born. Using the NETS Stage Factors, you know how to identify a tech start-up company in the Birth stage. Organizational Infancy, the next step, is the topic of the next chapter.

4

LEARNING TO CRAWL— ORGANIZATIONAL INFANCY

"Start-up companies are organic things. . . . The species evolves."

—DONNA WILLIAMS, VICE PRESIDENT OF MARKETING,
BIGSTAR ENTERTAINMENT

Although Organizational Infancy (OI) is a strange term, it does serve a purpose. It refers to an early stage of a start-up firm's existence. At organizational Birth, the firm's earliest stage, there was only an embryo of an organization. Maybe two or three people were present; maybe four or five. At the Birth stage it is unlikely that enough people were present to field a full soccer team. Maybe the firm had a basketball team, but probably no bench. Most likely a Denny's or International House of Pancakes would not have had to shuffle chairs and tables around to accommodate the firm's first "company meeting." Instead of whiteboards, napkins were likely the presentation medium of choice.

At the Birth stage, to call that first embryonic group an "organization" would be overstating the case. The company at that time was mainly an idea. The founders probably had been ruminating on the idea of a new company for some time, possibly many years. They were contemplating leaving stable jobs to pursue a new idea about which they cared passionately and which they discussed enthusiastically among their colleagues. They probably pursued the idea in their spare time away from their regular jobs, and they may have persuaded some of their old work colleagues to join them in forming the new company.

Most of the early founders of the company were probably techies—highly technical people. There may have been a finance or marketing person present as well, but the majority of your firm's founders were real rocket scientist types. They had a deep technical background in the field in which the firm competes. They would have needed such a background to conceive a way to build a better mousetrap. Erin Hill, a marketer who has worked for several online start-ups in Silicon Valley and Seattle, has described a start-up firm at the early OI stage in this way: "You're in a room with five engineers all day, 150 hours a week." It couldn't have been all that bad. Erin is on her way to becoming a product manager at Loudeye.com, a start-up that sells digital media applications for publishing, hosting, and managing audio and video content online. It will be her fourth start-up experience.

HOW DO DYNAMICS AND ATMOSPHERE CHANGE FROM BIRTH TO INFANCY?

As discussed in Chapter 1, a start-up firm's founders have completed a set of important, painstaking tasks to give birth to the company. They've worked on a prototype product, obtained angel investor financing, and maybe even scoped out some space for the new company. Once the company takes on venture capital funding, thereby moving past Birth, the organizational broth really starts to percolate. The firm has entered the OI stage, which requires a whole range of talents and abilities that the founding members lack. Moreover, the workload is such that the founders simply cannot tackle it all themselves in the twenty-four hours of a given day. If the firm has raised any significant money at all, and it probably has, then it will require a controller or chief financial officer to manage its funds appropriately. At the OI stage, the firm may need a head sales person, or *any* sales person. The same goes for marketing. A human resources person, and possibly a public relations person, may be needed at this stage. Enter the non-techie.

Techies and Non-Techies

Non-techies usually start to show up in start-up firms at the OI stage. This stage of the organization's life is so characterized because the "firm" has evolved from a disorganized handful of people who are talking loudly about an idea into a larger group of people who actually have job titles. They may not be able to recite full job descriptions, but they probably have titles that give some insight into their roles or functions within the organization. As you interview with a start-up firm, take note of your interviewers and surroundings. Chances are good that the firm with which you are interviewing is at a stage of Infancy or early Adolescence.

At the OI stage, the firm has discernible arms and legs in the form of an organizational chart. Generally, the firm's people know the appendage to which they belong in the organization—not always, but in most cases. The firm has moved from being a mere embryonic blob to an amoebic-looking form that actually has some shape and substance.

If you're a non-techie, you should know that there are some very good reasons why "non-techies" start to appear in start-ups at the OI stage. In many cases, non-techies from outside the field simply are not present at organizational Birth because without the technical grounding to know the way to build that better mousetrap, a non-techie would not have wasted his or her time on something about which he or she knew nothing. Despite their technical shortcomings, however, non-techies, with some kind of generalist or liberal arts background, tend to be adept at thinking a problem through logically, which is why they show up in start-up organizations. Once they have an understanding of how or why a better mousetrap can be built, they get excited about it and can add value in many ways. They can help obtain financing for a better mousetrap, or they can market or sell the better mousetrap more effectively than some of their more technical, rocket scientist counterparts. They can figure out how the firm should marshal its resources and get the most bang for its development, sales, or marketing buck.

How Does an Organizational Infant Behave?

The primordial soup that is the start-up in Organizational Infancy percolates in all sorts of dynamic ways. There are many smart people, techies and non-techies alike, running around its hallways, doing all sorts of great things. Their personalities range widely, from eclectic, enigmatic engineering types to polished sales stalwarts, from bookish financial folks to savvy marketing mavericks. No two are alike. Such personality differences can produce incredible results, but they can also result in conflicts.

Unless you're a founding member, by the time you join a start-up firm, Birth is an event of the past. Your firm may even have already undergone a management change or two. The original CEO who spearheaded the formation of the company may still be running the show or may have stepped aside. Maybe that person is still with the firm, maybe not. Other founders may have departed. Such events could have occurred over firm strategy, roles and responsibilities, philosophical differences, or sheer egos. Early-stage start-up organizations are not famous for their harmonious interpersonal symphonics.

In the OI stage, the firm attempts to do those things that infants do: get traction and crawl, clutch things, sink its teeth into them for better comprehension, play around with stuff, try to understand the things that affect its environment (marketplace), and generally plod along and make a mess. As you walk through the halls of a start-up firm in the OI stage, you may wonder what in the world the investors had on their minds when they elected to fund the operation.

You should now have the impression that there will be a multitude of dynamics at play when you join an OI stage start-up firm. In contrast to a larger, older company, all of the start-up firm's people are assimilating to their new environment, a process that is prolonged due to a regular influx of new hires. It takes time for people to become acquainted with each other and learn roles, responsibilities, and managerial styles. Throughout this already impressive flurry of organizational activity, the start-up firm's people are collectively learning about its customers, markets, and competition. As someone new to this situation, you may say to yourself, "Wow, there's a lot going on here."

What Does OI Mean for You?

What should you take way from all of this excitement as you contemplate a start-up career? Have an open mind. Know that you will do things you've never done before and recognize that you might not get everything exactly right the first time through. That's okay. Donna Williams makes the point well in describing a couple of super hires at BigStar Entertainment: "They didn't have any preconceived ideas about how things should go." In other words, they were objective thinkers, willing to try unconventional approaches to solving problems.

Recognize that your company is going through a very natural acclimation process that is exciting, and at times uncomfortable, for everyone involved. You may feel insecure, and you will not be the only person feeling that way. As President and CEO of SMT, Prabha Fernandes recognizes that the OI process was critical for associates in "learning strengths and weaknesses. That takes time. They've got to learn about each other . . . live with each other, work with each other."

Remember when you were a kid, playing on the playground? You had to learn how to play with your colleagues. You learned how to "get along" with them. You had to learn how to share toys and take turns. You learned how to avoid bullies and please your friends. Organizational Infancy stage start-up firm dynamics are not all that different from those of kids on a playground.

"BASIC" CONDITIONS FOUND IN ORGANIZATIONAL INFANCY

A number of basic conditions characterize OI in tech start-ups. The following sections discuss them briefly, share real-world examples, and point out their implications. The discussion also offers insights about what you should look for along the way in your interview process with OI stage start-up firms. You may want to refer back to this section of the book periodically throughout the interview process as you observe different situations.

You Will Have Many Roles and Responsibilities

"If you have any inclination towards being a jack of all trades, you're better off at a start-up."

—Donna Williams, Vice President of Marketing,
BigStar Entertainment

Although you may think that the OI stage start-up firm is doing the equivalent of playing around in a sandbox, the good news is that you probably will be presented with some type of job description when you interview with one. Maybe it won't be profound in its level of detail, and maybe it won't be written down anywhere, but there are probably at least a few main priorities you will know you need to tackle. Although much of your job may not be defined, if you're a marketing honcho the odds are good you won't be expected to conduct genetic research. However, having said that, be assured that the start-up will give you an opportunity to do many things you haven't done before.

That much of your job description may not be defined can be a real opportunity for you to take the initiative and carve out areas of responsibility that are meaningful to you. Bruce Pomfret was a Web programmer with start-up Nets, Inc. He later joined Perot Systems when it acquired Nets. Bruce describes the situation this way: "In order for the [start-up] company to work, you get the latitude to do what it takes to be successful. You don't get that in established companies."

However, a caution is in order here about the evolution of job roles and responsibilities in OI stage start-ups. The process is inherently sloppy. As Donna says, "It's very difficult to be process-oriented in a start-up." There's a whole lot of activity at the OI stage, and no one is standing around to direct traffic.

In the OI stage, it is likely that you and your colleagues will cherry-pick those areas of responsibility that are appealing, possibly leaving behind some of the less attractive but still important ones. Such an occurrence is perfectly natural, but as Erin Hill cautions, the less appealing projects and tasks still have to be done:

> A start-up is a place where everybody's going to take turns taking out the trash. Not everybody's prepared for that. . . . You have to do a lot of grunt work yourself. . . . What do you mean I have to do my own Fed Exes?

As you contemplate joining a start-up firm, it is important to make sure you don't end up holding the short end of the stick all the time. Although being part of a small company can have its advantages, Adrianna Paradiso summarizes the OI stage at NetGrocer: "The big company systems weren't there. There was much more squabbling. People were jockeying for positioning." Such jockeying for positioning is an okay thing, because eventually people will have more crisply defined areas of responsibility, and hopefully they will self-select themselves into managerial areas in which they excel or have a keen interest. The "squabbling" factor can be okay as well, although it can also be a hindrance to you and your potential employer.

In virtually all tech start-up firms, employees are shareholders. Therefore, what's good for one employee is good for another. However, differences of opinion can abound. As Erin says: "Everybody has their own view of what's going to be successful." At some point, everyone needs to stop having his or her own point of view and band together to move forward. Often, people take positions out of a desire to have an impact.

If you are a self-starter, making contributions will not be a problem for you in a start-up, and you won't have to play politics to strut your stuff. You will have abundant opportunities to have major impact in a start-up company. However, if there's one thing that nearly everyone who has worked in a start-up will tell you, it is *be flexible.* In fact, your being flexible will be a matter of necessity. John Lindsay, who worked in various roles for USData in Dallas, Texas, for eight years, and who was with the company when it went public, describes it this way: "In a small company like that, you wear a lot of hats." John should know. He worked as a programmer, salesman, and product manager—for multiple products—while at USData.

Prabha Fernandes of SMT echoes the sentiments of the others: "You should be able to drop (one thing) and move on to the next thing." Her company had started out developing a series of drug compounds before focusing on the specific ones that have generated the most interest from large pharmaceutical companies. At the outset, she says, "We didn't know which technologies would pan out."

Flexibility can help you in ways you may not even imagine in a start-up company. For Bruce Pomfret at Nets, his flexibility paid off in spades. Shortly after Bruce joined Nets, the company ran into serious financial trouble. It was losing money "hand over fist," and there was no outside investor willing to step up to infuse more cash into the company. During its last days as an independent company, its people were leaving in droves.

However, Nets management pleaded with Bruce to stay on to help manage its *Lead Story* Web site while trying to stave off bankruptcy and after laying off all but a handful of its employees. The nearly defunct company paid Bruce cash bonuses every week for about two months for his efforts while standing on the deck of a sinking ship. Then, when Perot Systems acquired Nets, the company asked Bruce to join them. Perot Systems gave Bruce stock options, and shortly thereafter the company went public. So, in addition to having stock options that were "in the money," Bruce got a higher salary and greater job responsibility, and he was working for a company whose future was very secure. Bruce could never have dreamed in his final days at Nets that he would find himself in such a fortunate position. Clearly, his willingness to take risks and "take out the trash" in an OI stage start-up paid off for Bruce.

The Company Is Trying to Validate Its Business Model

"People forget that over ninety percent of start-ups don't work out."

—Bill Demas, Vice President of Marketing,
Vividence Corporation

The business model of the OI stage start-up, the means by which the company expects to make money, is not proven yet. In general, the company's business model works on paper and was clearly compelling enough to entice investors into backing the company. However, there is still uncertainty about whether, and to what extent, the business model will work. The OI stage start-up company is literally a living laboratory that will, in all likelihood, try numerous variations and refinements to its business model until it finds exactly what works best.

Although it may not seem that way at the time, what your potential employer does not know can, and very well may, hurt the company. For example, if a firm is selling into the wrong market and fails to understand why sales are not closing, it may be out of business before it figures out the cause of the problem. Such potential pitfalls abound among start-ups. Indeed, ignorance about a market, product, or competitors is probably one of the single greatest contributors to the demise of start-up companies.

Adrianna illustrates a business-model stalling point from her experience at NetGrocer. NetGrocer's business involved selling bulk grocery products online to consumers via mail order. In theory, it was supposed to eliminate the need to go to the grocery store for most products. The problem was that customers still had to go to the grocery store to buy many of the groceries they purchased on a regular basis because NetGrocer didn't offer them. NetGrocer did not substantially eliminate the need to go to a grocery store. Adrianna believes NetGrocer should have focused on being an augmentation to the grocery store, not a replacement for it. It was neither at the time.

None of us has perfect information, and as a career searcher you should not expect yourself to be able to predict exactly the outcome of a given start-up company. However, if you ask the tough questions about a company's business model—the way it makes money—as you go through the interview process, you should be able to identify start-ups that have better chances of succeeding. If you can do that, you're already one step closer to start-up career success.

From his experience at Nets, Bruce Pomfret was able to answer some of the key questions you should consider before joining a start-up, only in his case it was after joining the OI stage start-up company. Nets was paying five editors to write content for *Lead*

Story, the business news site that Nets operated. Bruce was one of the editors. The site essentially had about $12,000 a year in advertising revenue. He had wondered how the company was able to keep all those editors on a site that generated so little revenue. Weeks later he had the answer to his question: The company couldn't keep it up, and he and his team were told that *Lead Story* would be closed within two months. Even though the *Lead Story* site was unprofitable, Bruce says, "It *did* get accolades as a nice place to get business news." As the adage goes, sometimes you just don't know until you try it. OI stage start-ups are all about trying, testing, and refining business models. Bruce says he is much more focused on looking out for such company mistakes these days.

Corporate mistakes can take many forms: an error in market strategy or market segmentation, a lawsuit, a failure to understand completely the price-performance dynamics of a given product or service, and so forth. As a prospective employee in a start-up situation, not only will you need to trust in your management's ability to respond quickly and decisively to such pitfalls; you should know that you will have to be on the lookout for them yourself. It could well be that you discover such a danger point and bring it to the attention of others in the company, ultimately saving a great deal of pain and effort.

Mistakes that are converted into some type of advantage are commonplace in new economy start-ups and elsewhere. Pick your favorite guitar player. Mine is Peter Buck of R.E.M. The legendary stories of famous guitar players like him, making mistakes on their guitars only to integrate them later into hit songs, is completely relevant to the way products, technologies, strategies, and markets can be discovered by happenstance in the world of start-ups.

One observation is worth noting here. Drawing from her start-up experience at Onhealth and elsewhere, Judy Schneider comments that the more focused the founders are at the Birth stage on mission and vision, the more directed the firm will be heading into the OI stage. Therefore, there should be less experimentation around the firm's business model. Bill Demas echoes this sentiment by pointing out that the organizational structure at Vividence is configured to scale up and accommodate the employee growth that he anticipates as the company evolves in size from 27 people to 100 or 150 people. Such planning was very deliberate. Not all start-up management teams understand the importance of advance planning around firm purpose and employee growth.

As you interview with start-up companies, think about those whose people impress you with their innovative and flexible thinking. Which companies have hired the people who, even if the company gets into a tough spot, will be able to adapt to the situation and improve the company's standing? None of us is a super-hero, and you're not looking for superheroes at start-up companies (although if you find some, more power to you!). However, you are looking for people who will put in heroic effort in the face of adverse conditions.

The Company's Product Is Vaporware (or Vapor—Depending on the Industry)

"They could have told me anything. . . . I would have believed them."

—John Lindsay, formerly with USData, now with Microsoft Corporation

One of the telltale signs of Organizational Infancy (OI) is *vaporware*. Vaporware is a software term for a product that doesn't exist. Applied to biotechnology, the term becomes *vapor*. Your prospective firm does not yet have a product, at least not a complete product that the market is buying in hordes. That's why your firm is a start-up. If you sign up for a job with an OI stage start-up, you may know that the product is not yet complete. You may hear all sorts of great talk about what the complete product will look like and accomplish. Hopefully, you will be very excited. Great visions will fill your eyes. Now there's some sobering news for you. No, you haven't bought a car from a used-car salesman—at least in this case—although you may feel like you have. The company's representatives will sell you a great vision to recruit you. When you think about it, they have to. However, once you join the company, you may learn exactly how far the company has to go to attain that vision; often, the answer is *pretty darn far*.

Part of your challenge will be to keep your enthusiasm up every day on the job, in spite of the fact that your product is still largely vaporware. You will need to stay positive regardless of the hurdles that stand in the way of your firm's creating and launching its product, and ultimately, hopefully, making money. It will be challenging at times, no doubt about it, but if you can think of your situation as an adventure, you'll be much better off. Bruce Pomfret sums up the situation this way: "Start-ups involve risk. There's something about putting it on the line." Not to mention, he adds, you have "the potential of really hitting it big."

The Work Environment Is . . . Different

"It's not for the faint of heart. The basement is not just a breeding ground for mould and mildew."

—Alan Kitty, President and CEO,
LinkTank L.L.C.

Where is your prospective start-up based? Chances are good that it's located in a warehouse, basement, or low-rent high-rise. During your start-up interview process there may be an exciting, almost romantic aspect to the fact that the firm's offices resemble a garage, dump, closet, or whatever. In reality, however, after spending eight—or, more likely, ten or fifteen—hours in a gray cube without a window in a building whose face needs a lift, you may start to think that shiny high-rise corporate offices with great views aren't so bad after all.

Donna Williams tells a funny story about BigStar's humble beginnings: "We moved into the mailroom of the company that a friend owned." Eventually, "We forced the company out of the mailroom." The company grew in size, both in people and funding, and now, in their new offices, people joke about it. "Everyone can say they started in the mailroom," Donna quips.

It may help you to go outside during the day, take a walk, get some fresh air, maybe exercise outdoors or at a gym (certainly the firm won't have its own). The proper start-up environment is decidedly unglamorous. Judy Schneider notes that you can always personalize your own space, no matter how small it is, with pictures and other personal effects. She then adds, "And frankly, you know what? You're going to work so damn hard you're not going to notice."

If your firm's atmosphere is glitzy in any way and the firm has yet to realize sales, you should be concerned. What can be most challenging about your lackluster surroundings is not knowing when your situation will change. If you join a start-up firm, you may hear your firm's CEO talk periodically about some potential company move, which may happen six or twelve months down the road. Tell yourself that move will happen if your company starts to progress down the OI track, either by selling products or, potentially, by raising more money. If the move is contingent on your company's raising more money, then you should hope that the space is no more expensive than the one your firm currently occupies, which brings us to our next point.

Keeping Costs Down Is Critical

"You need to ask yourself: Are they spending money wastefully?"

—Erin Hill, Product Manager,
Loudeye.com

One of the great ironies about start-ups is the way in which senior managers can purport to keep costs down, only to prove wasteful in their efforts. Everyone has his or her humorous insights into start-up financial waste. Adrianna describes an instance when one of the co-presidents' wives wanted to decorate the offices at her OI stage company. Given that the company in question didn't have revenues despite having been in business for more than two years, it seemed ridiculous that management would opt to decorate its offices at that seemingly inopportune time. "You can see why they didn't have good financial control," Adrianna notes. There's plenty of fodder here for Dilbert, so prepare yourself for some amusement.

I can recall a situation from my own start-up experience in which the firm spent tens of thousands of dollars jetting most of the senior management team out to visit a prospective customer on multiple occasions. As management explained it, such executive attention was necessary to close the business. Imagine their surprise when they learned, after several trips, that the company in question wasn't even a viable prospect! Shuttling your firm's management team across the country is an expensive way of customer prospecting, and I don't advocate it. Neither would any investor whose money is being spent on such forays. Ironically, had senior management bothered to ask the firm's product managers whether the prospect in question represented a good fit, they would have learned that it wasn't. So much for good communication.

Erin Hill has firsthand experience with start-up waste. Onlive, a Silicon Valley chat Web site, raised $23 million in a third round of financing. The company then hired legions of new people and started literally burning through cash, while not bringing any sales in the door. The company ran into serious financial trouble and ultimately sold out for $14 million, having never made it out of the OI stage.

There is a fundamental principle at work here. Efficiency in a business sense is simply bang for your buck: return on your investment. What has been done with the dollars invested in your prospective firm? Is management using them efficiently? Are they being used to grow the business in demonstrable ways? On the flip side, it is especially important for start-up companies to time their hiring appropriately to gain the greatest efficiency, so that people are brought in at the right time to contribute to the company's (hopefully meteoric) growth.

Prabha illustrates this point wonderfully from her experience at SMT. "Initially, we had planned a lot of people growth," she says, referring back to the company's founding in November 1997. Her management team realized training and learning needs were much greater than previously had been planned, so the company downshifted on its hiring plans, and the "people productivity," according to Prabha, has become "tremendous . . . much greater in terms of discovery." In the biotech business, where discovery is the name of the game, that higher level of "people productivity" Prabha describes is worth its weight in gold. Many OI stage start-ups can learn from this example.

In these days of high-flying stock prices, it's incredibly easy to forget that it really does matter how closely your prospective employer's management is minding the store. Although this concept is fundamental for any business, it is especially the case for start-up companies that haven't turned a profit yet. Keeping costs down will always be one of the key ways that enduring companies keep their capital free to grow their businesses and turn profits faster than the competition.

John Lindsay, reflecting on his days at USData, offers this advice to would-be start-up employees: "You really have to determine if the [management] capacity is there to manage resources." John should know what it takes, because he joined USData when it was at the OI stage and saw it progress through Adolescence, then an IPO, ultimately burgeoning into Adulthood. Resources, particularly within a start-up, can be limited, but, as Prabha's experience with SMT shows, it's amazing just how much a firm can get out of those human resources if management really tries.

As you interview with start-up companies, look for signs that management is spending its money wisely and in the right areas. If an OI stage company has a finished product, or something close to it, then it should be apparent to you by virtue of the presence of sales and marketing people. It is better for your prospective start-up company's surroundings to be unglamorous and staffed by a management team that has a keen focus on executing its vision than for it to be beautifully furnished by a management team that lacks focus.

Effective Communication
Is a Key Challenge

"You see some of these people grouped around a single desk in a . . . vociferous debate. And this butting of heads is actually a positive thing."

—Bruce Pomfret, formerly Web Programmer,
Nets, Inc., now Software Engineer, Perot Systems

If you've read any business news, the odds are good that you're familiar with the difficulty large corporations have in coordinating their operations and aligning the entire organization along major corporate parameters such as R&D, strategy, and marketing. Although they have a small fraction of the infrastructure of large corporations, start-ups, too, can stumble in trying to coordinate their internal functions. Communication is at the heart of this matter, and start-ups are not exempt from the need to communicate effectively. The causes of poor start-up communication are really twofold: lack of adequate human resources, and politics.

Failure of communication is commonplace in start-up situations because people are often doing the jobs of three or more people. However, it is precisely because of that heavier workload that more effective communication becomes so important. Start-ups generally lack the resources to do things over again several times from scratch. They make mistakes, but the effective ones learn from their mistakes and eliminate them.

Add politics to this mix; bake for forty-five minutes under investor scrutiny at 350 degrees. You think you might be escaping company politics by joining a start-up company? Wrong. Politics in start-ups can very often be the cause of the left hand's failure to communicate with the right. Just as start-ups can ill afford to repeat mistakes, so politics really are detrimental to a start-up's culture and internal communication. What's different about politics in start-ups is that they can really kill the firm, whereas in larger corporations, if one division tanks, there may be several others to pull the dead weight for a while.

Adrianna, drawing from her experience at NetGrocer, says that politics can get pretty entangled, and there can be a lot of infighting. Although interpersonal skills can be lacking in a start-up, when dealing with people with whom you might cross wires, Erin notes that if you extend yourself and go out of your way to understand their viewpoints, you'll build better rapport with them. This notion sounds like pure common sense, but it is amazing how often one needs to remind oneself of such truths in a tech start-up situation.

When interviewing with tech start-up firms, emphasize the importance that you place on effective communication and teamwork. Much of the work in tech start-ups revolves around interdependent teams, so you've got to be comfortable with it, notes Judy Schneider. Be prepared to offer recruiters examples of where you may have led a team or directed an effort successfully and in which your ability to communicate was a key factor. Such examples will be of keen interest to OI stage companies. Make notes to yourself about the communication skills of your interviewers and envision yourself interacting with these folks daily to help you develop a sense of how and where you'll fit in best.

The Workload Is a Sea of Constantly Shifting Priorities

"With a start-up, my marketing plan changes every . . . month!"

— Donna Williams, Vice President, Marketing,
BigStar Entertainment

Fighting fires in start-ups is, to a large extent, much of what the work of start-ups is about. Donna says that the importance of triaging is "tenfold" more important at a start-up than in a larger company. It's important for you to consider that your work routine in a start-up setting could change dramatically and suddenly, often on limited or no notice. Your goal as a start-up career searcher is to find the start-up company that demonstrates the greatest control over its own destiny. Even in such a situation, your work routine will vary greatly and you will experience many interruptions. However, you should seek a start-up situation in which you can be as productive as possible, and for most of us, that means having greater predictability over our workload.

Sometimes a change in priorities can mean organizational survival, if firm management correctly identifies the appropriate strategies and tactics. Such changes can also hasten organizational disaster if management miscalculates. For employees in a start-up setting, such changes can be terrifically invigorating or enormously frustrating, depending on the situation.

John Lindsay recalls a tumultuous, frustrating time while he was a product manager at USData. Management completely changed the company's product plans overnight. Many planned products were scrapped in favor of other, much less complete products. This happened to John just after his company had gone public, ironically enough. Even though John did very well from the IPO, he was "just livid" about the changes in product plans. He never did understand the change in direction, but by that time he didn't have to. Thanks to his stock options, he was able to leave the company and take some time off.

Shifting priorities are bound to occur in a start-up setting, but by going in with your eyes open, you won't be surprised by their reality. In fact, let's face it, part of the huge attraction of the start-up is the ever-changing nature of the work it offers. As Donna puts it: "If all you want to do is one thing, then don't join a start-up." Remember that priority shifts can occur for very positive reasons, such as a firm's success in the form of increased sales.

You Will Be Stretched (Thin) in Many Directions

"It's been great for me. I acquired skills I wouldn't have acquired elsewhere."

—Bruce Pomfret, formerly Web Programmer,
Nets, Inc., now Software Engineer, Perot Systems

Part of the reward of working for a start-up firm is the breadth of exposure and experience you will have. On the other hand, you will wish you had two clones of yourself to help you manage your workload. You will very likely struggle for balance in managing all your projects and responsibilities, for extended periods of time. This state will continue for most of the Organizational Infancy phase. It may subside after the firm enters Adolescence or goes public, but more likely it will never go away entirely. Of course, if the firm has gone public and you got yourself a good deal on the way in, if you feel burned out you can leave and enjoy your new-found wealth.

Being stretched thin means you will work long hours to accomplish your workload. This can be intimidating. You will find yourself juggling multiple assignments, all with tight deadlines. The benefit is that you will reap tremendous rewards in the form of accelerating your learning curve, which will be of enormous value to you for the rest of your career.

You Need to Know How
to Hire the Right People

"They have security in the self. . . . They say, 'I feel the energy, the enthusiasm.' They immediately want the job.

—Prabha Fernandes, President and CEO,
Small Molecule Therapeutics

At some point during the OI phase, if the company is doing
things right it will need to hire lots of new people rapidly. Visual-
ize yourself as a new employee in the company. A colleague comes
to you and requests that you interview a job candidate. Ironically,
you were just interviewing on the other side of the table yourself a
few weeks earlier. Although you may be very new on the job, you
may very well be expected to interview people and help evaluate
them as potential hires. You may wonder whether you are re-
motely qualified to do such things.

Chances are good that you really should be interviewing those
new potential candidates. Even if you are a non-techie, you obviously brought a needed skill set and/or experience base to the table
when you joined the start-up. Moreover, you probably have some
previous experience—from school, other jobs, or both—that has
relevance to your firm. Depending on your experience, you may
also have some sense of the squishier side of organizations: culture,
behavior, and so forth. Depending on your experience and how
long you've been with the firm, you may have a keen ability to assess people's skill levels, experience, and ability to work with others within your firm.

Then again, you may not be interviewing any job candidates.
More likely, you may interview some, but not all, job candidates.
After a time you will find it dizzying to see a new face in the hall-
way every time you turn around—the new employee du jour. Of
course, the good news is that the company must be doing something right to be making so many new hires. This is not always
the case, of course, as we've discussed. However, a boatload of new
hires should be a good sign.

Just remember that not all the people you hire will work out.
Donna hired two people at BigStar who left within *one day* of be-

ing at the company. "They were concerned with titles, having an office. . . . Those kinds of perks didn't exist. . . . I was very frank with them about the realities of the organization." You may find yourself interviewing people like these. If you have concerns that an interviewee is overly oriented towards things such as job title and office (or cube) size, it's perfectly okay to address them with the candidate. It's better to get issues out on the table and discuss them before a candidate takes the job, rather than later.

You can't win them all. But hopefully your firm will hire many more people who work out than those who don't, and you'll get along with most—if not all—of them swimmingly. The nice thing about personnel growth in start-ups is that you will seldom be the last person hired, and new hires are always looking to meet people and make friends.

Disorientation Is a Way of Life

"You've got to be flexible in a start-up. You have to understand change."

—**Adrianna Paradiso, formerly Product Manager, NetGrocer, now Director of Marketing, e-STEEL**

Congratulations. You've joined a tech start-up company and, with your first two weeks on the job behind you, so far everything's working out fine. But wait, what's this? Just when you have gotten used to the latest office layout, a "reorg" (short for reorganization) happens and you find yourself back at square one. Maybe it's a space layout reorg, or maybe it's a personnel reorg. Both are disorienting. Hopefully the coffee machine hasn't been moved in the process, and your firm's CEO wasn't replaced with Attila the Hun. Maybe your firm has moved into a new, nicer space, but unless your company has just gone public, don't count on it.

The OI stage for most start-ups is generally turbulent, so fasten your seatbelt and prepare yourself for it. You will go in prepared, recognizing that reorganizations can be disorienting. If you decide to join a start-up firm, make sure you go out of your way to help new hires feel comfortable in their new jobs. You will be grateful to those who do the same for you when you come aboard. Show people the bathrooms, the coffee machine, and where the good lunch places are.

Above all, don't let the confusion get to you. Keep the situation in perspective. You may be joining a start-up firm for many different reasons, but excitement should be one of them. Enjoy the excitement! If you decide life in a start-up is too exciting for you at some point, you can always find a situation somewhere that offers less.

FIVE POINTS YOU CAN USE TO MEASURE WHETHER A COMPANY IS AT THE OI STAGE

The odds are great that any start-up company with which you interview for a position will be at least at the OI stage. How do we know this? Well, if you're interviewing for a position, then it's fair to assume that you weren't on hand for the company's birth. In addition, certain things would already have happened for the company to reach the point of hiring formally, such as the writing of the business plan, pitching it to investors, raising money from those investors, and so forth. Refer once again to the NETS Stage Factors to determine whether a tech start-up is at the Organizational Infancy stage (see Table 4.1).

If you answered "Yes" to all of the NETS Stage Indicator questions regarding cash position, business model status, and product status, and "No" to the questions about sales status and demand status, then the start-up is in the Organizational Infancy stage. Why is this so? Let's explore the reasons.

Cash Position

If the company has raised money from venture capital investors, then you know immediately that it is at least at the OI stage. You may be wondering if you can freely ask company insiders about the company's cash position during your interview process. Absolutely. Tech start-up managers love to brag about the venture money their firm has raised because having venture investors is a validation of the firm and its business model. Such information is

Table 4.1   NETS Stage Factors: Organizational Infancy (OI)

NETS Stage Factor	NETS Stage Indicator Questions	OI Stage Answers
Cash Position	1. Has the company raised venture capital money from investors?	Yes
	2. Are there any nonfounders who are full-time dedicated employees of this company?	Yes
Sales Status	Are the company's revenues and finances such that they will enable it to cover its costs within the next two years?	No
Business-Model Status	Is the company's business model documented as part of a business plan or other company document(s) that was used to motivate investors to finance the company?	Yes
Demand Status	If the company hires more marketing and sales people, will it sell more product?	No
Product Status	Does the company's product exist on more than just a piece of paper? (Note: Even if the product is not fully built or tested, if some part of it exists, answer Yes.)	Yes

typically made available publicly by start-ups and their investors for a whole range of reasons. In fact, if the company does not disclose this information to you, that should raise a red flag.

If, to become self-sustaining, the company needs to raise more capital, either from private investors or from issuing equity or debt securities in the public markets, that is a further indication that the company is at the OI stage, because it is not yet in a position to operate on its own without financial help. The same holds true for companies that may not need to raise more capital in the two-year time frame but are drawing down on that investment-funding bank account. Just as a young child rides a bicycle with training wheels until he or she is stable enough to ride without them, so the infant company needs the assistance of outside capital to give it a boost in life until it generates sufficient sales to make it on its own. If the company will become more self-sufficient in the next two years without reliance upon additional capital, then it is probably at the Adolescent stage.

As you go through interviews, remember that you need to be able to make a fairly accurate prediction about the company's ability to become self-sufficient within the next two years. To do that, you won't need to run any complex mathematical formulas. You just need to know roughly how much money the firm has raised and its burn rate.

The company's burn rate is the rate at which it is spending its money. To calculate a rough estimate of a firm's burn rate, take the number of employees and multiply it by the average annual salary package—say, $80,000—and add to it your estimate of what the firm spends on overhead expenses (rent, phones, etc.), let's say another $480,000 per year. Then divide by twelve. That will give you the amount of money the firm is "burning" per month. Now, take the firm's total capital and figure out how many months of burn the company can sustain. Using the above estimates, a company that has raised $6 million and has sixty employees is burning cash at a rate of $440,000 per month and can sustain itself without any additional cash coming into the coffers for a period of almost fourteen months ($6 million/$440,000 per month = 13.6 months).

If the company has any nonfounder employees working in a full-time capacity on behalf of the company and has venture capital financing, then it is past the Birth stage and is an OI stage start-up. The venture capital investment funding is key because of the strategic intent of new economy start-ups discussed in Chapter 1. The goal for these companies is to go public or to be bought out to provide a return on that venture investment.

Sales Status

The company's revenues and finances are not such that they will be able to cover the company's operating costs within the next two years. In other words, neither sales, cash reserves, nor a combination of the two will cover the company's burn rate. The company will not break even for a profit within two years. A company in this situation will need to raise more money from investors within that two-year time frame. Clearly these companies are Infancy stage material because they will require those financial training wheels for the foreseeable future. If the company expects to move substantially closer to covering its costs for the next two years from now, it is migrating out of Infancy into Adolescence.

The reason you should use two years as a time frame is that for technology start-ups the visibility for anything beyond two years away is nearly impossible to gauge. If you think it is possible for a company to be operationally self-sufficient within, say, three years, then you should still consider it an OI stage company because there is too much uncertainty as to whether it actually *will* become self-sufficient at that point. With biotechs and some hardware businesses, a company can be in the OI stage for three or four years easily. In these cases, the company's fortunes stand to gain from key milestones such as successful clinical trials or the granting of a key patent, either of which can take a year or longer.

Business-Model Status

Although you should not require OI stage companies to have a fully completed or proven product, they must have a partial product. Similarly, although an OI stage company will have a planned business model, you should not require that it be fully tested or proven at the OI stage.

To qualify for OI status, a tech start-up must have a documented business model that was the basis for obtaining funding from investors. This business model should work on paper. You should be able to explain to yourself how the start-up in question will succeed by profitably selling product or service X, with its assumed benefits, to customers at price Y, in a given manner (direct, mail order, over the Web, etc.). Customers will purchase product or service X because it will help them make money, save time and money, or fulfill a personal need.

The business model will be described in the company's business plan and in other company documents and presentations. You definitely should discuss the company's business model in your job interviews. Your questions relating to the business model will be some of the most important ones from an assessment standpoint and will demonstrate your critical thinking ability, a crucial asset for start-up company employees. Of course, you must be sure to posit your questions in a tactful, nonconfrontational manner.

Although determining for yourself whether the business model actually works is not really a tool for determining the company's stage of evolution, it is important for you to have enough confidence in the company's business model to sign up as an employee. Note that just because investors funded the company on the basis of a given business model does not automatically mean it will work. However, it helps you to know that if the company obtained funding on the basis of a given business model, then clearly someone thought the business model would work. That can potentially reduce your risk, but you still should assess the business model independently.

A business model may look good on paper, but as we all know, plans can work out differently. OI stage companies aren't proven successes yet. If you already know a given company's business model will work, then probably so do a lot of other people, like investors, employees, and customers. Chances are that the company in question is at the Adolescent stage or beyond. Therefore, the business-model test for OI stage companies is that it works on paper. Couple with that the need for you to be satisfied personally with the business model to consider joining the company.

Demand Status

If the company in question hires more marketing and sales people, it will not sell more product. The market demand for the company's product or service is currently not so great that the company can't support it. Typically, this will be because the company's product is not yet complete or is not complete enough to satisfy mass market demand.

Let's assume that, based on your answers to the NETS Stage Indicator questions up to this point, the company is shaping up to be an infant, and that you answer "No" to the question on demand status. At its current operational levels, a given company is losing money and rising sales will not enable the company to reach profitability within the next two years. Demand for the company's product has not taken off, so hiring more marketing and sales people will not generate greater sales and, therefore, will not solve the company's problem of losing money, at least, for now. This scenario may change eventually, but at present customer demand for the current product or service (and it may be incomplete) is not running wild. Therefore, the company is at the OI stage.

Product Status

The company's product exists, at least to some degree, on more than just a piece of paper. It is amazing how many concepts in the tech start-up world get funded on the basis of the now-familiar napkin. Sometimes these ideas become tremendous success stories, such as the Compaq personal computer. At other times these ideas are meteors that crash and burn before people are assembled to implement the concept. Although Birth stage companies may have products whose existence is documented only on a piece of paper, to qualify for Infancy stage a company must actually have something tangible, even if it's just a part of the end result. The product doesn't have to be proven yet; it simply has to work conceptually as more than a drawing. The company believes that product X will work based on research it has done in a given field. The angel investment funding allowed the company to develop some type of working prototype, which attracted venture capital investment to the firm.

In fields such as biotech, this concept can be difficult to gauge. It may be helpful to think of it this way: If the company has been funded to discover the cure for Alzheimer's disease, then theoretically it has some specific, documented ideas about how it plans to pursue that discovery. Its founders aren't simply going to throw darts at a board; they probably have ideas based on prior research methods that will help them make the discovery. The same holds true for concepts in communications and materials science: Some part of the product or technology must exist. Very often, as with biotech, it will be based on prior research or technology.

Sometimes an entrepreneur will develop a prototype of a product before obtaining the funding to finance a company. The prototype will be the impetus for investors to fund the concept. In such instances, the company is still at the Birth stage. Until all of the appropriate pieces (e.g., venture capital funding and full-time nonfounder employees in addition to product concept) are in place, the company is not at the OI stage. You begin to see how all

of the five NETS Stage Factors work in combination to help determine organizational status.

SIGNS OF SUCCESS IN
AN OI STAGE START-UP

Now that we've discussed OI dynamics, the "basic" conditions of
OI, and the five NETS Stage Factors for identifying an OI stage
start-up, you probably already have a good sense of some of the
signs of success in an OI stage start-up. The NETS Stage Factors
provide a framework within which we can see what the signs of
success might look like. These are telltale signs that you should
look for when interviewing with start-ups. Take note of a firm's
progress that its people describe to you. Are trends moving in the
right direction? With the NETS Stage Framework, you'll see how
easy it can be to measure success.

Cash Position: Improving

The cash position of the company is improving. Because by definition an OI stage company is losing money, what does this mean? It
can mean the company is losing *less money* than it did, say, last year,
or last quarter. Although ultimately the company will still need to
spend more money than it already has to become self-sufficient, if
it is losing less money it will need to raise less money to get there.
That's a good thing for you and anyone who owns equity in the
company.

Depending on where a company is in the OI stage, a favorable
cash position can also mean the company has an improved ability
to raise money from investors. Although raising more cash can dilute everyone's ownership holdings in the company, an improved
ability to raise cash is a big plus because it means others, namely,
investors, are bullish on the company's prospects and are willing to
put up bigger bucks to help the company realize its potential. If
someone says to you in the course of your interviews that the company raised $5 million in its initial round of financing and then
raised an additional $10 million in a later round, that's a positive.

Understand that the company may lose more money before its financial picture improves, but this should be a short-term trend with which you are comfortable before making an employment commitment.

In your start-up interviews, feel free to ask the appropriate people within a start-up company about its ability to raise capital. In addition to the CEO or CFO, the firm's public relations people, marketers, and even human resources personnel should be able to speak with authority about this topic on behalf of the company. In fact, everybody should. If they can't, that should tell you something.

Ask yourself: Is the cash flow of this company improving? If not, why? Maybe the company is hiring more programmers, engineers, or researchers, bulking up on the brainpower it needs to deliver the product. That's okay. In your interviews, just ask polite, general questions. Don't get into too much financial detail. You already know a rule of thumb for calculating a firm's burn rate, and the company will probably disclose to you how much capital it has raised. You can figure out how long the company can last without raising more capital, and you will need to assess the company's ability to raise more capital if and when it will be needed.

An important distinction is in order here. New economy tech start-ups don't want to take on more outside investment money than they need because doing so leaves less equity for the firm's employees. You should be more interested in a company's ability to raise capital than its actual need to do so. If it is able to raise more money quickly, that means a lot of investors believe in it. You want prospective investors to be lining up to invest in your prospective start-up. You don't necessarily want these same investors to own all your company's equity, however, because there would be less for the employees, including you.

Sales: The Picture Is Getting Brighter

Because not all OI start-ups are actually generating revenues, you want to see signs that the outlook for revenues is improving. In the case of say, software, this trend should be evident over a time period as short as half a year or even three months. In your interviews, you can check for such a trend by asking someone to explain the progress that has been made on the main product or service over such periods of time. Customer interest—in the form of inquiries and requests for sales presentations—should be rising in conjunction with product development. In the biotech field, six months is not much time at all. However, you're still looking for the same trend, so you may want to ask about a given company's clinical trial plans and its results to date, as well as interest in the company's research from the broader medical and investment communities.

Of course, it's much easier to spot improvement in OI stage companies that actually have revenues. The company will have a sales history, and its people should be able to talk with you very specifically about sales growth. The company may even be reaching a point where market demand for its product or service is beginning to outstrip its ability to supply it. At that point the company is on its way to Adolescence.

Validating the Business Model by Gauging Demand: Is the Market Saying "Yes"?

Validation of the business model can be measured by customer demand. Is the company's phone ringing more often than it used to? Maybe it's even ringing off the hook! Higher sales and—absent sales—higher levels of customer interest will be the key validation of a company's business model. If customers say it works, then it does. Just remember that eventually the company needs to be able to serve its customers profitably. You can't serve your customers if you're out of business. At the end of the day, you want to see your company struggling to keep up with customer demand, while making a profit. It's one of those really nice problems to have.

Product Status: More Complete

The status of the product or service and milestones along its path to "market readiness" should be identifiable to you by the people with whom you interview. Is the company making progress? Is it hitting its milestone targets? Ask about development and corporate milestones of people throughout the firm to get a diverse set of viewpoints. Assess their consistency. If a product marketing person tells you a product is two weeks from being complete, but the development program manager tells you it's going to be six months, that should raise a red flag.

WHEN DOES A START-UP TAKE THE "NEXT STEP UP," TO ADOLESCENCE?

By using the five basic factors, you now know how to track improvement in the status of an OI stage start-up. Although there are really just a few key changes that happen to an OI-stage start-up as it transitions to Organizational Adolescence, their overall impact on the organization, as illustrated in Chapter 5, is quite large. Moreover, getting to this transition point is a monumental achievement for any OI stage start-up company. The number of those that successfully make the transition from OI to Adolescence is far exceeded by the number of those that don't.

From a financial standpoint, the company will need less money than it already has raised. Its ability to become self-sufficient will improve substantially within the next two years. It may opt to raise more money than it absolutely needs to prepare for future growth. The management of a company in this situation might well be considering taking the company public in an IPO or possibly selling out to a larger corporation that has taken note of the company and its growing market.

Revenues are coming in at a rate such that the company does not need to rely on the capital of investors to be self-sustaining. The company's sales may not yet be sufficient to fund all of its operations on a stand-alone basis. However, the company will either be profitable or much closer to profitability within the next two years. The company will realize more sales—and eventually, profits—if it hires more marketing and sales people. If this is the case, then the company is clearly at a point where *it* is the only limiting factor to its growth. The marketplace has validated the company's product and business model at this stage.

WRAP-UP

There are many start-up issues to consider in Organizational Infancy. Like infants, start-up organizations at a young stage in their lives are messy, funny, childish, sad, temperamental, and blissful, all in the space of a day! This can make working for them fun at times, but also frustrating. You may see behavior in a start-up that is accepted as normal that would never be tolerated in a larger, more established firm. Those within the start-up would argue that in the hard-charging world of start-ups there isn't time for polite demeanor all the time—battles are being waged, races are being run—and it is critical for your team to get moving. As a start-up career searcher, you have much to gain from learning under these conditions.

From the people we've quoted and the examples we've discussed, you should now have a good sense of what the day-to-day environment and dynamics are like in an OI stage firm. With the Nets Stage Framework, you now have a resource for measuring whether a start-up company is in the OI stage. Additionally, you now know the questions to ask that will help you track a given OI start-up's progress and how to gauge signs of success. You have a good sense of when a start-up is poised to take the next step up, to Organizational Adolescence, the subject of our next chapter.

5

GROWING PAINS— ORGANIZATIONAL ADOLESCENCE

"I would imagine it {SMT} to be like a thirteen or fourteen year-old kid at this point. . . . You've determined what your strengths are, what your weaknesses are, you've decided what your business is going to be . . . how to optimize and what you thought would be your biggest thing . . . how to get the biggest bang for your buck."

—PRABHA FERNANDES, PRESIDENT AND CEO,
SMALL MOLECULE THERAPEUTICS

Think back. Remember what it's like to be in the eighth grade? It was an embarrassing time for a lot of us. Zits were a major concern. Trying your best to look cool consumed an inordinate amount of your time and energy. Such efforts to appear cool were made all the more difficult for those of us who had braces on our teeth. In the school hallways, who was dating whom was easily more important news than key world events of the day.

As an eighth grader, you lived at home, and you probably had responsibilities to your parents, like performing household chores: taking out the garbage, mowing the lawn, and so forth. Maybe you received an allowance. You probably didn't need to use it to put food on the table for your family, it was really more for fun, but it taught you to appreciate money. Maybe you saved that allowance money for something you wanted. Maybe you had a big piggy bank full of coins. Basically, when you were in eighth grade, you were starting to learn how the world worked.

Adolescent tech start-ups are so much like adolescent people it's scary. They do all of the same things you and I did in eighth grade, and often they do them nowhere near as well as we like to think we did them. They definitely try to look and sound cool. They have to: When they're trying to recruit you, not to mention investors, they have to come across as the coolest thing since sliced bread. Perhaps they will try to dazzle you with their talk of technology. Maybe they will show you some of their technology, hyping why it is the latest and greatest.

Like eighth graders, tech start-ups are very up to speed on who's dating whom in their industries. It's a huge issue for them. A partnership between a tech start-up and a larger partner firm can literally cement the success of the start-up. Partnerships in general are very good for tech start-up firms, for the obvious reason that every partnership secured is a further validation of the firm's idea. A start-up that secures a partnership can be expected to trumpet this news in the form of a press release.

However, you may need to be a little careful here as well. Start-up firms are known to hype almost any little accomplishment as a way of building investor and market interest in them. A start-up firm can't issue a press release that says something like "Company CEO has a pulse," but it can come awfully close sometimes. Publicly traded companies with the tech start-up mentality will do the same thing to try to drive up their stock price. You have to know how to sort out the company hype from the significant stuff. It's a little like parents trying to figure out if their eighth-grade child has done his or her homework without having to inspect it. Tech start-up firms will also trumpet their new star hires to drum up the interest of anyone who will listen. As with partnerships, succeeding in bringing a star on board is a validation of the firm's ideas. In fairness to the countless tech start-ups that practice press release hyperbole, you do have to look at it from their side. If you were in their shoes, wouldn't you do the same thing? In fact, some of their press releases are indeed relevant and important.

Although tech start-up companies don't typically fire off press releases for every hire they make, they are probably doing lots of hiring at the adolescent stage. These new hires have a lot to do with the organizational changes that take place between OI and Organizational Adolescence (OA). Depending on when you join a tech start-up, you may or may not be around for all of them. Of course, no matter at what stage you join a tech start-up, you will definitely see change. Very often, the structure of the tech start-up, which may or may not have been very well defined in the past, starts to take on more definition at the OA stage. The company itself takes on a larger constituency: a larger base of employees, a larger group of investors, and hopefully, a larger group of customers.

HOW THE TYPICAL TECH FIRM
MATURES INTO ADOLESCENCE

"It was [an] exciting time. Those products were really blowin' and goin'."

—John Lindsay, formerly of USData,
now with Microsoft Corporation

If you were ever in the Cub Scouts or Brownies and you graduated into the Boy Scouts or Girl Scouts, you may have some sense of what this change is about. You must assume more responsibility. No longer do you have a den mother peering over your shoulder, counting change for you at McDonald's to see if you actually can pay for that milk shake you just ordered. You are now expected to be able to do such things as managing your lunch money on your own. You are in a new league, but you are at the young end of your new group, and there is much you don't know—yet. You will listen to your fellow colleagues who are older and, theoretically, wiser than you, about what to do and how to do it. In time, you may become a leader, but for now, you need to learn the ropes.

The OA stage tech start-up firm is making the same type of transition. A key attribute of tech companies transitioning to this stage is that by now they have taken on several rounds of investment funding and with it have entered into a new realm. No more are these companies novices, swimming in the swift, vast marketplace on their own. They have received guidance from their venture investors, who, in return for their counsel, investment, and connections, have demanded a significant stake of ownership in the tech start-up firm. From the standpoint of the venture capitalists, they are worth it, and frankly, in many cases they are.

When venture capitalists invest in a start-up, it is fairly common for them to place some of their handpicked people in the firm's executive ranks. I've seen it happen many times, and it's usually for a good reason. Very often the founder running the show up to, or possibly even through, Infancy is the idea person, but he or she may not be a seasoned manager who has a track record of managing a full-fledged business. Indeed, many such idea people do not want to be responsible for the day-to-day operations of a business. They typically prefer to focus on refining and evangelizing the vision of the firm.

Recall for a moment the idea that Adrianna Paradiso shared with us in Chapter 1: A successful start-up firm typically has an idea person, someone who can execute that idea, and someone who can manage the business on a day-to-day basis. Many founding teams of start-ups don't have all three attributes among them. Indeed, it would be fairly rare if they did, and, what is more, the start-up may not necessarily need all three until the late Infancy or early Adolescence stages. However, at or even before the Adolescence stage, when serious money is invested in the firm, it becomes imperative for the firm's management to possess all three attributes. The reason is that at the late Infancy and early Adolescence stages the firm begins to hire larger numbers of people, and hopefully, it is much closer to marketing and selling its products in the marketplace. It forms an infrastructure that must be managed on a daily basis. This type of nuts and bolts activity is not something everybody likes to do.

Changes in the Chain of Command

"People have to understand that if they report to the CEO originally, that may not happen going forward, and they have to get used to that."

—Adrianna Paradiso, formerly Product Manager, NetGrocer,
now Director of Marketing, e-STEEL

When a firm hires more people, an inherent need for more organization within the firm emerges. It doesn't necessarily mean there have to be fifteen layers of management between the highest and lowest levels in the company, but it does mean that there are probably a couple of management layers in the organization.

Reporting relationships can change a great deal in a short period of time at a tech start-up. Bruce Pomfret recalls a situation from Nets: "The person who headed up our group . . . was reporting to the CEO, then he wasn't reporting to the CEO, then he was, and just before we went bankrupt, he wasn't again." A CEO will try different reporting structures and, quite possibly, different people in different roles until he or she finds an approach that works. Although such experimentation happens in larger, more stable companies, it can happen more, and more frequently, in tech start-ups.

However, it doesn't necessarily have to be that way. Bill Demas, talking about the aggressive growth plan for Vividence, does not anticipate any changes in key management for the foreseeable future. That Vividence top management will be in place for the long term is a good thing for would-be employees, because it means that they can anticipate a stable management team that is directed toward and focused on driving the business forward, unhindered by managerial vacancies.

Judy Schneider emphasizes that the fewer organizational changes, the more organized and better off the firm is. It makes sense that if a firm has a solid management team in place with a coherent mission and strategy, the potential for success is much greater. If you are looking to join a tech start-up company at a level that is lower than senior management, look for such assurances. Of course, if key management is in place and the business is clearly on stable footing, your risk is also lower, and therefore your upside will probably be lower as well. However, should you join such a firm, you will probably sleep better at night than you will if you join a firm experiencing managerial turmoil.

One last comment about chain of command. The chain of command at a start-up can change at any time for practically any reason. Adrianna Paradiso worked at one start-up in which the CEO died. It was a huge blow to the firm. In a business where people truly make the difference, the passing of this charismatic and capable leader was the undoing of the firm. The caliber of people matters tremendously in tech start-ups.

Potential Pitfalls in Making the Transition from Infancy to Adolescence

The key potential pitfalls in making the transition from Infancy to Adolescence relate to managing the firm's growth, usually in terms of employees, and its culture. Regarding number of employees, Bruce Pomfret cautions that it is possible for companies to hire too quickly and, on the flip side, too slowly. "You're choking your business in either case," he notes. I have seen more than a few companies "over-hire," and the results are not good. If the firm is not able to use an employee's talents at a given time, it puts both the firm and the employee in a tough situation. The firm is paying a salary to the employee at a time when perhaps the cash should be conserved, and the employee is underutilized, making him or her feel awkward. It may even cause the employee to doubt his or her potential worth to the company, and even leave.

Hiring people at the right time truly is a challenge in tech start-ups. It seems to be part art, part science. Bill Demas has a good idea about what the Vividence hiring plan will involve because it will be driven by product development and rollout plans:

> The technology needed to be built and tested. And that took some degree of time. Once that's done, you go ahead and bring on Marketing. So now . . . I'm really growing the marketing team, and the next area that we're going to grow . . . is the sales force. And later on . . . we'll build the operations team.

Once again, a focused, stable management team can manage and coordinate hiring much more effectively than the firm that is still refining or transitioning its strategy or business model. Prabha Fernandes employed a similarly methodical approach to hiring at SMT.

Culturally, all sorts of things can happen at the Adolescence stage. I've seen quite a few changes, and heard about many more. I've seen venture capitalists step in at the Adolescence stage and drive the founders absolutely nuts by proceeding to call all the shots, effectively neutralizing the founders and their business ideas. It really is possible for a company's founders to "sell their souls" to a venture capitalist who may not know what is best for the company.

Other cultural dynamics can come into play if a large number of people within a start-up came from one company. This group of people can become known as the "insiders" because of their presence at the genesis of the firm and their favored status among the key founders. As Infant and Adolescent firms start to hire additional people, cultural conflicts may arise. Such conflicts aren't necessarily negative. Indeed, such clashes can serve to preserve what is good about a firm, staving off potentially detrimental influences. Conversely, a sense of "group think" can develop among a start-up's insiders relating to strategy or business intent, and if such thinking is misdirected, it can mean the death of the firm. Groupthink can cause management to reject or ignore information about the market that is crucial to the firm's success. It can also cause resistance to key managers who are trying to implement change. It is important for a tech start-up's management team to monitor the firm's culture to ensure that it is not ignoring potentially crucial information.

If a firm's management has established a culture that is open minded and willing to change course if necessary, the firm should be on solid footing heading into Adolescence. That a firm has even survived into Adolescence means that it has many of the right things going for it, and many tech start-ups fail to make it that far. Moreover, for those that do make OA, it is still quite possible to stall in that stage and either fail or be sold off at a loss relative to total capital invested. Keeping a successful culture intact throughout the OI stage into Adolescence is of paramount importance. Definitely ask top managers in your interviews with tech start-up firms how they would define a successful culture for the firm and how they expect to maintain it as the company grows.

"BASIC" CONDITIONS FOUND IN ORGANIZATIONAL ADOLESCENCE

The "Oh Yeah, We Do That" Syndrome

"I've really had to take on the role of an educator."

—Erin Hill, Product Manager, Loudeye.com

Start-up companies need great sales people who can sell anything. They'll tell your firm's customers that you can deliver anything they want, on a platter: "Oh yeah, we do that." In software, particularly, this practice of selling futures is standard operating procedure. The thinking here is that by the time customers actually decide they want your firm's product, your firm will be able to deliver the functionality they want. The challenge is to manage what you say you can deliver. You have to recognize that it's a good thing that there are people within the company walking around with starry-eyed visions about the future, because most likely that vision is what opened up the coffers of deep-pocketed venture capitalists to jumpstart your company in the first place.

However, having a healthy dose of skepticism is also required to offset excessive exuberance. The customers who buy your product want it to work, not to hear about how it will work in the future. They need solutions today. They may be willing to wait for the whole product solution enchilada, but it is highly unlikely that they will buy your product without its solving a significant portion of their problems.

An extension of the "Oh yeah, we do that" syndrome is the "Oh yeah, we do that. . . . Don't we?" syndrome. In this case, a sales person commits to delivering functionality or benefits that your firm does not provide—"Oh yeah, we do that"—then rushes back to the product team to find out if, in fact, you do have it: "Don't we?" This excessive enthusiasm can also affect firm strategy, and not necessarily positively. If your firm signs up to deliver functionality for one customer in three months that it hadn't intended to complete until a year later, it may adversely affect your firm's ability to sell to other customers. Sometimes the ability to target entire market segments is jeopardized by this type of overreaching customization. Such over-commitment has killed companies. Geoffrey Moore highlights many of these key tech start-up organizational dynamics in greater detail in *Crossing the Chasm.*

The challenge is to be able to deliver just enough of the functionality or performance that your market seeks so as to gain a few customers, while continuing to deliver the right functions or benefits that the larger market demands. Again, the firm doesn't have to solve all of a customer's problems as long as it solves enough of the important ones. Also, sometimes a partial solution to a customer problem is infinitely better than no solution at all, in which case a customer will gladly wait until your firm gets around to delivering the full solution to that particular problem. This has long been true in the drug industry, and has certainly proven to be so in software as well.

Let's look briefly at an example. HST, my start-up company, intended to serve the managed care information systems marketplace. This market requires a report called the expense-to-budget report. Sounds straightforward enough, right? Actually, to produce such a report requires some fairly serious functionality. Although we didn't produce what the health services industry considered an acceptable expense-to-budget report at a summary category level, we did do it at the bottom-line level, which was definitely better than nothing. Because this was not the most critical need of the industry, many prospects were willing to wait on a full expense-to-budget report because our product delivered so many other important benefits.

Sometimes your sales people actually can say, "Oh yeah, we do that," recognizing that a partial solution they are selling is better than what the customer has currently and that other functionality that the product provides is actually more important to the customer. However, customers don't like to be misled. Therefore, where and when possible, it's best to clarify if the product delivers a partial solution. The odds are good that if a product has enough core functionality that customers need, they will appreciate your honesty and recognize that your firm is moving in the direction of solving that problem.

Turbulence

"Turbulence is the process of creation. A start-up is about turbulence, period."

—Alan Kitty, President and CEO, LinkTank L.L.C.

Your firm is gaining momentum. It's taking off like an airplane. You are making your way through the low-lying cloud cover into the blue skies above. The captain turns on the seatbelt sign. You are hitting positive turbulence.

On the other hand, your firm may not be taking off like an airplane at all, but rather may be sinking like a rock, in which case the turbulence your firm is hitting is negative. Under conditions of really negative turbulence, you will probably see telltale signs, like your CEO getting fired or your engineering team revolting and leaving. Perhaps the firm initiates a reduction in force (RIF), and lots of people lose their jobs. How long you wish to wait before parachuting to safety is up to you.

Positive turbulence means many things to the Adolescent start-up firm: reorganizations, hirings, firings (usually more hirings than firings), and customers who want stuff—now. It's all part of a natural progression. Ironically, in school we are seldom taught that learning and growth are messy, sloppy, haphazard endeavors. Our teachers never told us that we learn the most by failing, or at least stumbling. There's plenty of stumbling in a start-up firm that is growing successfully into an Adolescent. It will be frustrating. There will be a chronic shortage of people. There won't be enough hours in a day to get through your to-do list. This is natural and normal, so don't despair. Your firm wouldn't be in this situation if it weren't doing at least a few things right.

Fumbling Around for Precision

"The long running joke in the office was 'We're approaching clarity.' There were all these e-mails from upper management about how clarity would be established at any moment. And this went on for months."

—Bruce Pomfret, formerly Web Programmer, Nets, Inc., now Software Engineer, Perot Systems

There are all sorts of fun analogies for the start-up firm transitioning from babyhood into Adolescence. Riding whitewater rapids is an appropriate one. Your firm's senior managers are furiously paddling at your side trying to keep the boat steady. It keeps wildly tossing in the currents, but somehow, miraculously, it never overturns. You keep expecting to be thrown headlong into the cold, churning waves, and yet, somehow, the boat stays afloat.

If your experience feels something like that just described, and your firm's boat successfully navigates the treacherous waters, then no doubt it has been fumbling around for precision—successfully. The start-up ride is never a smooth one. Indeed, if everyone expected to have a smooth ride to success, everyone would be joining tech start-ups.

It is amazing how even the most successful of today's companies—including many of those in the Fortune 500—started out on shaky ground. 3M is a classic example. The company was founded initially on the intention of mining corundum and, upon being confronted with extinction, quickly shifted its business into manufacturing sandpaper and grinding wheels. The rest is history. The strategy your firm ultimately employs to achieve success may be a far cry from that which its founders initially envisioned. Indeed, the strategy that the VC firms backed in your firm's business plan—the one that prompted them to open up their coffers to the tune of several million dollars—may change radically over the course of time as your firm fumbles its way to success.

Examples of such switches in strategy abound. In software, particularly with Internet applications, start-up companies practically redefine their business models daily. In the drug and biotech arena, a firm seeking one indication for a drug may find that it actually yields great results in another treatment area. In materials science, product applications for new materials can vary dramatically from the inventors' original intent.

Fumbling around for precision goes hand in hand with turbulence. Positive turbulence is caused by the chaos that your firm experiences as it first gets slammed by the high tides of the competitive marketplace. The firm then jockeys to gain a stable position in the marketplace, and, if successful, gets slammed again by increased demand as droves of customers line up outside the door wanting to buy your firm's product. Conversely, fumbling around for precision also happens furiously at start-ups when it is clear that current strategy will not work and a new one must be found.

Just as hindsight is 20-20, after fumbling around for precision, you will look back and say, "The right strategy was so obvious." But in fact, at the time, the right strategy was far from obvious. You had to fumble your way there. By fumbling around for precision you are learning by doing.

Now You Know

"The market should drive direction and not current customers."

—John Lindsay, formerly with USData,
now with Microsoft Corporation

Having fumbled around for precision and bumped your nose a few times, you begin to develop a much better sense of what works and what doesn't work. The knowledge your firm lacked before, it has now gained. You are in a position to harness that knowledge and apply it in new business situations, either within your start-up firm or elsewhere.

The beauty of reaching the "now you know" point within the firm is that, regardless of firm success or failure, you have new and valuable knowledge. Because the firm has failed through pursuing various avenues that did not lead to success, you can now explain what doesn't work because you saw it firsthand. There is no better way of preventing a mistake than having already made that same mistake before. Fumbling around for precision is not only learning by doing, it is learning by *failing*.

The best companies in the world learn by failing. They do enough things right that even if they make a mistake, they are around to play another day. As you may know, Microsoft was a little late to the Internet party, but with the release of the Bill Gates "Internet Tidal Wave" memo in May 1995, Microsoft turned on a dime and since then has launched an arsenal of Web-based businesses. Admittedly, not all have panned out successfully—yet—but some appear on their way to becoming successes.

Many great companies know that some ideas will fail and, indeed, prepare for it by placing multiple bets. As an example of the way others learn by failing, we can look at Microsoft. To solve a particular problem, Microsoft may have several internal development efforts going on at any given time. It is generally known that not all projects will succeed in delivering the optimal result. However, everyone attacking the problem is aware that the end goal is to deliver the best technological solution to the problem, so that even if certain projects fail to bear fruit, the company will win in the end by developing the right solution for the marketplace need.

When you have reached the "now you know" point, which is the start-up equivalent of realizing you could have had a V-8, you have insightful knowledge that is valuable both to your start-up firm and other firms. Thus, if your firm's learning experience, paid for by VC dollars, ends in the firm's learning too little too late about how it should have done things, your knowledge and experience will be highly valuable to another firm. At the end of the day, the insights that evolve from the fumbling process are the single most valuable asset you can take away from the start-up firm experience—bar none.

Precision Begets Precision

"There has to a sense of discipline, because some things work, some things don't work."

—Prabha Fernandes, President and CEO, Small Molecule Therapeutics

Your organization will work to plug the holes to execute on the strategy that actually works. If everything is firing on all cylinders, you will start to notice an intensified focus on executing, doing things—even the things that before were perceived as smaller issues. The good news about a higher level of precision is that the bigger strategic matters have been resolved, and now people can focus on the smaller issues. The firm will demonstrate an unprecedented level of traction around hitting deliverable targets. The fumbling-around-for-precision phase yielded targets, and targets are much easier to hit when they're defined. A higher level of precision within the firm enables everyone to divide up the workload into defined segments with specific, achievable endpoints.

High Tech, High Touch

"(One company) couldn't operationally meet their demand. . . . They couldn't install equipment correctly to maintain business. They were so backlogged that people left [for a competitor]."

—Adrianna Paradiso, formerly Product Manager,
NetGrocer, now Director of Marketing, e-STEEL

Although your firm may have the ultimate "high-tech" strategy in place at this stage, it will be exceedingly important to manage "high touch" customer issues as well. At the end of the day, business is about people negotiating and communicating with each other. In fact, the execution on the customer front is actually where battles are won and lost. There are numerous examples of companies that had technologies superior to those of their competition but who lost the game in the marketplace because they failed to execute on the "high touch" components of their strategy.

In addition to knowing your firm's constituents, part of a successful high-touch strategy involves managing them effectively. If the future is becoming clearer and brighter, then your firm is managing them correctly. Conversely, I have seen head sales people literally ignoring customers in the early stages of their firm's Organizational Adolescence. Such gaffes can kill an enterprise.

Crowded House

"Some of us are sitting on top of each other."

—Donna Willliams, Vice President of Marketing,
BigStar Entertainment

Depending on the pace at which the market blesses your firm's offering, you may or may not be headed for more grandiose digs. It is likely that you will be working in your humble (to say the least) digs for a lot longer than you had anticipated. If you set your expectations accordingly, you may be pleasantly surprised. Better to pleasantly rather than unpleasantly surprised.

If the firm really is on the takeoff ramp, it will be hiring people at a furious pace. Therefore, space will become scarce. Cubes will go up in the strangest places. Maintain your sanity. Hopefully you won't be in cramped quarters forever. Cramped quarters can heighten tensions at a time when your firm can ill afford to fumble the high-touch aspects of its game. You simply have to make sure you don't let it get to you.

Plugging the Holes: Executing on the "Eureka Strategy"

"The only way I know you're doing something right is when people are buying the product."

—Alan Kitty, President and CEO, LinkTank L.L.C.

Through fumbling around for precision, your firm may have reached that epiphany of strategy—the "Eureka Strategy"—that yields the road map for exactly how the firm will attain real financial success in spite of a competitive marketplace. Holes will need to be plugged to ensure that the ship arrives at its destination safely, but people will know what they are. Management has seen the light in the darkness, and now the company must get to the light, through executing well. Charging toward a light that is visible is far better than fumbling around for one that is not.

This time in the company's development will be an exciting one for you. If it executes properly, the firm will become far less dependent on venture capital to sustain operations. Management will start to anticipate with eagerness the prospect of growing sales substantially. Maybe an IPO is in the cards.

There may even be a vision of the company breaking even in the near future. At this point, your company's chief financial guru, who until now has been gazing into a crystal ball to develop sales and operating projections, can start presenting numbers that at least give the appearance that he or she is not smoking something funny. Now all those rosy financial numbers that you read in the company's business plan, which everyone believes are either somewhat exaggerated or truly a bunch of bull, can be dispensed with and real, meaningful numbers can be presented. Of course, the workload to execute on the strategy, which appears to be a winner, will be huge. You will continue to endure positive turbulence as you and your colleagues frantically work to plug the holes, fill in the gaps, and nail down open issues.

Increasingly, the Future Is Now

"You get great feedback from (customers) . . . good press . . . more prestigious companies come to talk to you . . . they take your call."

—Judy Schneider, formerly Vice President,
Content, Community, and Education,
Onhealth, now Consultant

As your firm has gotten traction around its strategy and goals, hopefully you are starting to see favorable developments in the marketplace. Namely, customers want to buy your product. There may be a few intermediate steps along the way, like customers lining up at your booth at a trade show to look at your firm's product or service and understand how it works and to see whether it is right for them. You begin to notice that more, rather than fewer, customers are interested.

There is no set timetable for how long this phenomenon can take. In the warp-speed software marketplace, it can be a matter of weeks or months. In the realm of the biotechs or new materials, it could be a couple of years or longer. The point is that you should be seeing a steady stream of increasing market interest in your firm's product or service.

Other telltale signs abound. Maybe your firm is getting more press. Maybe a news reporter is showing up at your firm's door to do an interview. Be on the lookout to see whether the heightened press coverage is the result of your own firm's PR efforts to generate press interest aimed at impressing would-be investors into yet another round of financing. You are looking for genuine external expressions of interest by objective outside parties here. Drawing the distinction between the two can sometimes be difficult.

Maybe the executives of would-be acquiring companies are showing up to meet with your firm's management. However, if your firm has a really solid concept, your venture capitalist investors will have no intention of selling off to anyone except the stock market, in an IPO. For the venture capital firms, the IPO is usually the ultimate return on their investment, and by far the most profitable one.

The momentum your firm has gained strategically and operationally should be paying dividends in a variety of ways. These dividends may initially manifest themselves in less tangible form, but at some point they should result in cash registers clanging away, as the firm closes sales. Increasingly, the future is now because everybody came on board in the first place to do business with customers.

FIVE POINTS YOU CAN USE TO MEASURE WHETHER A COMPANY IS AT THE OA STAGE

In this section we turn once again to the NETS Stage Factors. The differences between OA and OI are subtle, but they are important. They are especially meaningful to you as a techstart-up career searcher, because you will ultimately need to decide how much risk you are willing to take. That risk could mean the difference between whether you take a job at a given start-up or not.

Taking the factors in Table 5.1 in turn, you see that little has changed between the OI and OA stages. However, there are two directional key differences that are well worth discussing because they relate to what amounts to a sea change in the firm's momentum. The change occurs in the company's sales and financial picture and demand picture. As you talk to start-up firms, you want to see evidence of positive momentum that is driving the company toward success. The company is making progress in terms of being able to stand on its own for an extended period of time (two years) without having to take on more investment. Ideally, the company can or will attain this financial independence from the revenues it will generate. In other words, it will reach profitability, the true

Table 5.1   NETS Stage Factors: Organizational Adolescence (OA)

NETS Stage Factor	NETS Stage Indicator Questions	OA Stage Answers
Cash Position	1. Has the company raised venture capital money from investors?	Yes
	2. Is any nonfounder a full-time dedicated employee of this company?	Yes
Sales Status	Are the company's revenues and finances such that they will enable it to cover its costs within the next two years?	Yes
Business-Model Status	Is the company's business model documented as part of a business plan or other company document(s) that was used to motivate investors to finance the company?	Yes
Demand Status	If the company hires more marketing and sales people, will it sell more product?	Yes
Product Status	Does the company's product exist on more than just a piece of paper? (Note: Even if the product is not fully built or tested, if some part of it exists, answer Yes.)	Yes

hallmark of Organizational Adulthood. However, in some businesses, particularly in the biotech arena where development times are longer, companies will raise a significant amount of money up front to cover their financial obligations for several years to come. Many companies, including both biotechs and Internets, will actually go public through an IPO to raise money even before they are profitable.

Cash Position and Sales Status

The company's revenues and finances are such that they will enable it to cover its costs within the next two years. How much money does the company have in the bank? On the sales side, what is its annual revenue run rate? If this company did not raise another penny from investors, could it be financially viable for the next two years? It doesn't matter if the firm secures financial independence through investment it has raised or from healthy revenues, although you'd prefer that it be from the latter, as long as you know the company's viability is solid for the next two years. Why? Because within that two-year time frame, much can happen to improve the firm's future prospects. This is not to say that you should not join a company if it does not have its two-year costs covered. It just means that the firm is not an Adolescent. Therefore, the risk to you is higher if you sign on as an employee.

From an employee standpoint you would expect that in an Adolescent company a team of full-time employees has been working for the firm for some period of time, say, six months or a year. You would also expect to see that the Adolescent firm's ranks had grown over time as the firm raised money and hired more people. This is not a hard-and-fast rule for Adolescence, but it will be true more often than not.

Business Model Status

As did the Infant firm, the Adolescent firm has a documented business model. Although it may have undergone a process of refinement and improvement, it should be pretty much intact. A red flag should go up if you find yourself talking to an Infant or Adolescent start-up that has already raised venture capital investment but whose management does not have a high degree of confidence in the business model. At the OA stage, most of the questions relating to business model should have been addressed. Having said that, there are plenty of e-commerce companies out there, some of which are even publicly traded, that still don't know what their ultimate business models will be and continue to refine them. Such situations should raise for you the question of risk. You shouldn't necessarily rule out joining such companies, but you should know their risk to you is higher. Start-ups with proprietary technology that is guarded by patents, specific know-how, or preferential contracts can be in advantageous positions relative to those that don't enjoy such positions. The easier it is for you to articulate a given firm's business model and why it will succeed, the better off you are.

Demand Status

If the company hires more marketing and sales people, it will sell more product. At this point, you really know the company is taking off. Hopefully demand for your firm's product is jumping off the charts. Keep in mind, though, that this indicator is really based more on your feel or intuition than on hard fact. You may notice it during interviews as you walk around. Phones may be ringing off the hook. Sales and marketing people might look frazzled because they've been meeting with and talking to prospects or customers for the last five days straight. People are hopping all over the place, yet they seem happy. In such an environment, you can be pretty sure that if the firm hired another sales person tomorrow it would be selling more product. At this point, the only obstacle to the firm's growth is the firm itself, and the firm's ability to hire more people to service customers.

The unhealthy Adolescent tech start-up is the one that hires more sales and marketing people in anticipation of needing to serve more customers, but they never show up for the party. Such a condition can arise because the firm's product is not ready for prime time, or because there simply isn't that much real demand for it. In your interviews, if you sense that you are talking to an unhealthy Adolescent start-up, you will want to probe on customer demand and degree of product completion. You may want to ask someone to talk to you about the last customer the firm lost, and why. Look for trends. Obviously, if a product needs to be more complete, that is a more solvable problem than an overall lack of demand for the product in general. You will need to make a determination for yourself whether a firm is a healthy Adolescent. If you are interviewing with an Adolescent firm, its management may tell you that demand is exploding as a way of enticing you to join. You will need to be alert and observant. If you join a firm in a pre-Adolescent stage, you will need to be on the lookout for whether your firm is stalling out in the OA stage due to a lack of demand.

Product Status

As in the OI stage, the product concept exists on more than just a piece of paper. Directionally, you should expect an Adolescent firm to have a more complete product than an Infant one does. Hopefully, you will also see validation of the product in the form of greater numbers of customer orders and inquiries.

WRAP-UP

Organizational Adolescence is about the firm making the significant transition from Infancy to a new level of maturity. The OA stage firm is well positioned financially, at least for the next two years. The company's business model is validated to the point that if it hires more marketing and sales people, it will sell more of its product or service.

A subtle distinction between Infancy and Adolescence is worth noting: It is possible for a company to be able to cover its costs in the next two years and still be an Infant. In such cases, the funds will have been raised from investors, not generated from sales. This is especially true for biotechs and other firms where there are long development cycle times. The reason is that the "well funded Infant" may need at least two years' worth of cash in the bank to develop its offering. However, for such firms, the hiring of more marketing and selling talent will not generate more sales in the near future.

You will feel the positive momentum of an OA firm. As an employee of an OA stage firm, you are excited to go to work each day. You will probably feel exhausted but happy with your job and the direction of the company. In general, you will feel bullish about your future career potential with the OA firm.

6

SUMMARIZING THE STAGES OF A TECHNOLOGY START-UP

SUMMARY OF THE ORGANIZATIONAL STAGES

Let's take a moment to recap the organizational stages of a tech start-up from Birth through OA.

Birth Stage

At the Birth stage, the firm is either self-funded or backed by angel investors. At the time of receiving seed funding, perhaps the founders commence to work on the project on a full-time basis to produce proof of concept. Usually nobody but the founders will work on the project full-time until there is a proof of concept. A Birth stage firm has no sales and cannot cover operating expenses for a two-year period without raising more funding. A proven product does not yet exist. Seed funding was invested to enable a founder or group of founders to develop it. The status of the business model is probably developed to some degree, although it may just exist on a napkin. Although demand for a generic product like the one a start-up firm intends to make may exist, demand for the firm's product specifically does not exist yet because the product is unproven and incomplete.

OI Stage

At the OI stage, the firm has raised or will raise venture capital funding. Venture capitalists will invest money in the firm and will provide advice, expertise, and connections to the firm in exchange for a stake of ownership. Their stake of ownership and involvement with the firm will be greater than that of an angel investor. The amount of cash the firm has raised is usually not enough for the firm to cover operating expenses for two years. Even if the cash it has raised is sufficient to last two years, that alone does not meet the test for Adolescent status, because without the customer demand and revenues (as opposed to invested cash), the company still has its financial training wheels on. The product at the OI stage exists on more than just a piece of paper. A concept has been proven to some degree, and venture capital has been invested to help the firm complete that product. Demand for the product is not skyrocketing yet, but hopefully prospective customers are calling to check in.

OA Stage

The OA stage firm is at the point where a combination of its revenues and finances will cover its expenses for the next two years. It may have had to raise multiple rounds of financing, but demand for the product appears to be there, the business model is proven, the product is mostly if not totally complete, and the firm needs to hire more marketing and sales people to keep up with demand. Hopefully customer demand for the product of the OA stage firm will translate into sales of a sufficient level that sales alone will enable the firm to cover its operating expenses.

Table 6.1 summarizes the three key early stages of a tech start-up using the NETS Stage Factors.

Although there are other factors you can consider to help you pinpoint the stage of a given tech start-up, such as number of people in the firm, it is difficult to give reliable figures. Obviously, at a start-up firm's birth, there are only a few people. However, that number could be one or eleven, or any number in between. Similarly, there are Adolescent firms that, because of their attractive

Table 6.1 NETS Stage Factors: Summary

NETS Stage Factor	NETS Stage Indicator Questions	Birth	Organizational Infancy	Organizational Adolescence
Cash Position	1. Has the company raised venture capital money from investors?	1. No. Financing at this stage is from founders or angels.	1. Yes	1. Yes
	2. Are there any nonfounders who are full-time dedicated employee of this company?	2. No	2. Yes	2. Yes
Sales Status	Are the company's revenues and finances such that they will enable it to cover its costs within the next two years?	No	No	Yes
Business-Model Status	Is the company's business model documented as part of a business plan or other company document(s) that was used to motivate investors to finance the company?	Maybe	Yes	Yes
Demand Status	If the company hires more marketing and sales people, will it sell more product?	No	No	Yes
Product Status	Does the company's product exist on more than just a piece of paper? (Note: Even if the product is not fully built or tested, if some part of it exists, answer Yes.)	Maybe	Yes	Yes

operating characteristics, are ready to go public even though they may have only a hundred—or fewer—employees. Such was the case for Donna Williams at BigStar Entertainment, which, at the time of this writing, has fifty-five employees. In contrast, there are infant stage firms that may have twice that number of people but may still be at a point of trying to refine their business models, as was the case with Bruce Pomfret at Nets. In my own experience, HST was also an infant that stalled out while trying to attain Adolescent status. Demand never took off, and the product was never complete to a point that enabled the company to sell many units. It is better to focus on the operating characteristics of the firm rather than on the number of employees, which can be deceptive. That's where you can use the NETS Stage Factors to help you.

THE START-UP COMPANY AS MATURE ADULT

A tech start-up company that attains Adulthood—profitability— is a rare breed. We don't read about all of those that fail, but many of our interviewees recite the same information relating to the success rate of start-ups in general: ninety percent fail. Although you hope to sign on with a start-up that actually does go on to achieve Adulthood, it is more likely that your firm either will be acquired or will go out of business. Adulthood for a start-up firm is in some ways much like that at other more stable, established companies. One factor that will likely remain different for the new Adult firm for a while is its sales growth rate. Although the former start-up company may no longer be growing at eye-popping rates, its growth may still qualify as exceptional. If the firm has gone through an IPO, investment analysts may rate it a top pick as a growth stock. Hopefully the fast-paced culture will persist, although at this point it is rare for a single customer to represent a do-or-die situation for the company.

One key challenge that such firms have at this stage is attracting and retaining outstanding talent. Because so much of the risk is gone from the company at this point, the potential reward will be reduced as well. The firm may still grant stock options, but their total potential will be small compared to grants distributed to those who joined the company before it went public. However, depending on your personal risk profile, which we explore in the next chapter, this young Adult firm may be just the place for you to enter the new economy career marketplace. Much of the risk is removed, but you stand to gain excellent experience from the opportunity, and the stock options you are offered are almost guaranteed to be worth more a few years from now than they are today. You may also get paid more by a firm at this stage than at an earlier stage.

You'll find that company management changes at the Adult stage. Many managers with significant professional experience tend to focus on a particular phase or type of company where they have expertise, as well as having a great deal of passion for helping the company grow to the next stage. Once they have helped the company get to that next stage, they may prefer to move on to another opportunity. It is often said that the manager who is great at running a company of 50 people is not necessarily someone who can run a company of 500 people. Experienced managers usually know if they are one or the other and tend to be fairly explicit about it because they are usually not lacking in job opportunities. They can afford to be selective about the ventures they wish to pursue. Indeed, accomplished managers who specialize in a certain growth phase will tell a firm coming in that they intend to be with the company until a certain point, at which time their job will best be managed by someone else.

For you, it all comes down to the type of situations in which you feel most comfortable. Virtually everyone interviewed in this book has emphasized that you should not join a start-up if your intention is to get rich. You should join a start-up because you are passionate about an opportunity to contribute, grow, and learn. If you happen to attain wealth in the process, that's a bonus. The start-up experience will pay dividends over the course of your career. To maximize the value of the experience to you, it helps you to know the stage of start-up where you will be most comfortable and from which you would reap the greatest experience. Knowing your risk-tolerance profile will help you accomplish that.

WRAP-UP

You should now be familiar with the trigger points for the OI stage transition to the OA stage. You also have a good understanding of some of the basic conditions found in Adolescent firms or those firms that are transitioning from OI to OA. You know how to use the NETS Stage Factors to differentiate an OA stage firm from one in the OI stage.

There are only two key differences between OI and OA, and they are related. Unlike in OI, demand for the OA firm's product is taking off. If the OA company hires more marketing and sales people, it will in fact sell more product. Therefore, the company is gathering significant momentum towards being able to cover its operating costs from revenues and finances within the next two years. In fact, if demand proves brisk enough, the company may break even from sales alone within that time frame. Many companies will stall out between the OI and OA stages. Although you may see positive signs of momentum for the OI stage firm, it may actually never get off the launching pad.

You also understand that an OA stage start-up firm is on its way to Adulthood when you can know with confidence that the firm will break even within the next two years. Although this is a rare accomplishment for start-ups, it's what they're all shooting for. You are definitely looking to identify the tech start-up firms that appear to have Adult potential.

Although your risk is reduced once you join a start-up that is at the OA stage, your firm's security, and therefore that of your job, is greater. Knowing your personal risk tolerance profile is a key factor in determining what stage of firm you should seek to join. Your personal risk profile is the topic of the next chapter.

7

EXPLORING YOUR TOLERANCE FOR CAREER RISK

"Think about what you want to get out of {the tech start-up experience}. Understand your personal situation. . . . You've got to measure {the risks} yourself."

—ADRIANNA PARADISO,
FORMERLY PRODUCT MANAGER WITH NETGROCER,
NOW DIRECTOR OF MARKETING, E-STEEL

Are you comfortable taking risks? That's a bit of a loaded question. The reality is that most of us take risks quite regularly. Some of us take higher degrees of risk generally, while others of us are more comfortable with different types of risk. Take boating as an example. One person might consider kayaking down whitewater rapids a moderately risky experience. Another might consider a boat going more than five miles an hour on a calm lake a terrifying experience. In other words, what might seem very risky to one person might seem like a sure thing to another. Everyone has a unique personal risk tolerance profile that indicates the types of situations in which he or she is more or less comfortable. This risk tolerance profile extends to all facets of one's life, including work situations.

Your auto insurance company will tell you that you are taking a risk every time you get behind the wheel of a car. In fact, your auto insurer's people are so knowledgeable about calculating risk that they can tell you the precise probability that you will get in an accident in a given ZIP code over a certain period of time. They are willing to tolerate the risk of your driving because they charge you, and everyone else in their insured population, a premium that will help to cover the costs of any one person getting into an accident. That premium is typically sufficient to cover the accident costs for which the insurance company is responsible, as well as enable the insurance company to make a profit. The insurance company is taking a risk by insuring every customer, but the risk is a calculated one.

Similarly, health insurance companies employ legions of actuaries who can determine the probability that a person with a given demographic profile will suffer a certain type of disease and the age at which it is likely to occur. In such situations, calculating risk seems almost like rocket science, and in some ways it is. But it's made a whole lot easier for insurance companies by having a huge population base with an experience history to study.

Unfortunately, measuring the risk of tech start-up companies is significantly more challenging because tech start-ups don't have the same extensive history that other fields do. Although quantifying the risk of a given tech start-up may be difficult, we do have the frequently cited statistic that 90 percent of start-ups fail. Although it sounds pretty harsh, that statistic includes all kinds of start-ups: restaurants, dime stores, and numerous other types of family-owned-and-operated businesses. However, there's no inherent reason to think tech start-ups should have an easier time succeeding than family-owned businesses. After all, the goal of the tech start-up is to go public or get bought out, whereas that of the family-owned business is often simply to *survive*. It's probably more difficult for tech start-ups to succeed than most other types of start-ups simply because their goals are more ambitious.

Don't put this book down yet. Although tech start-up risks appear daunting, there is much you can do to reduce your risk in identifying tech start-up situations you would consider signing up for. You need to match your profile to the type of risk that's appropriate for you.

SELF-ASSESSMENT: WHAT DOES
TECH START-UP RISK MEAN TO YOU?

As you already know, technology start-up companies involve a lot of risk. However, we need to distinguish between company risk of the tech start-up and its risks to you and your career. This is a key distinction because, depending on the company's evolutionary stage and what you intend to learn and accomplish while there, it may not matter to you at all if the company in question ever takes off. Although this may sound selfishly Machiavellian, the reality is that the tech start-up is treating you in the same opportunistic way. The tech start-up may give you a base salary that is well below what you could earn elsewhere. You have been given an additional incentive of stock options, but you know that the probability of their ever being worth much is limited.

The risk you need to consider most is not actually that of the start-up company itself, which you already know is inherently high. Rather, you need to seriously consider what start-up risk means for your financial status, career, and personal relationships. Despite the high risk of the start-up's survival, your personal risks may be mixed and could even be quite low. It depends on what matters most to you.

Financially, the biggest risk you take in joining a tech start-up is the opportunity cost you incur. You could potentially earn much more money in the near term by pursuing another opportunity, say, working at a larger, more established company. Most people who join tech start-ups are aware of this reality, and it's still worth it to them, largely because of the rich start-up experience they will gain no matter what happens to the company. Such experience can greatly enhance a career. There is also the potential upside of those stock options, but don't take that to the bank.

From the standpoint of your personal finances, it's imprudent to join a tech start-up without having some savings put away so that you can live for a while if you need to search for another job. Bruce Pomfret and Adrianna Paradiso advise putting away six months' worth of salary at least. The worst thing that can happen to you is that you lose your job. It can and does happen with tech start-ups. Of course, it happens in corporate America as well. It could be that *you fire the company*—you quit, deciding that it's not worth your time to be there any more. In any event, you could find yourself out of a job at some point. To avoid being caught off guard, you need to be prepared for this possibility. That means having some money saved up to put food on your table and buy necessities like health insurance while looking for that next big opportunity.

Having a reserve of money saved does not apply just in the case of tech start-ups. You should save emergency money to live on all through your career, irrespective of the types of companies you work for. Because things happen so fast in the tech start-up universe, you could find yourself jobless quicker than you might in other situations. If you really enjoy working in start-ups, you may find yourself in a temporary jobless situation far more frequently than your parents ever did. However, such occurrences are more acceptable today to prospective employers than they ever were before.

From a career experience standpoint, you really have nothing to lose and everything to gain from joining a tech start-up. If you are selective about the type of start-up you join and the role you take on, the career risk of joining a start-up can be very low. In fact, depending on the field or technology, it may even be nonexistent. Because of the broader role and responsibility you are likely to have at a tech start-up, you will be attractive to other companies, start-ups and non-start-up firms alike, after your current tech start-up role. Your learning curve will be faster and steeper, and you will have done many more things than you might in a larger, more stable firm. As an example, Andrew Blake is Director of Developer Relations at Handango at age twenty-four. If he were in a larger firm, he might be reporting to an assistant director. The entrepreneurial experience Andrew is gaining is sorely lacking at many firms, and they are often willing to pay attractive salaries to people who have it.

You may be concerned about how a tech start-up firm's failure might reflect on you. Actually, rather than being a stigma, tech start-up failure is almost a badge of courage these days. Career-search candidates who have lived through the failure of a tech start-up are often more attractive to prospective employers than those who have succeeded all along. The reason is that those who have failed usually learn a great deal about why their company failed and can prevent others from making the same mistakes. Bill Demas and Bruce Pomfret note that you learn much more from failure than you do from success. The only note of caution I would add is that you want to try to avoid hopping around too many different situations in a short period of time.

The biggest risk to you personally of joining the tech start-up is the potential impact on your relationships. If you are married or seriously committed to someone, then you need to consider how your partner feels about your joining a start-up. Can you and that person tolerate the stress you both might feel if it doesn't work out? If you are in a secure situation financially, you can mitigate much of the stress you might feel in your personal relationships. Are friends and family supportive? You need your network to support you in a start-up effort. There can also be a potential social stigma of working in a tech start-up. Even though many people think of tech start-ups as very "sexy" these days, incredibly there are still those who turn their noses up at them. Of course, those aren't the people you want to work for after your tech start-up experience!

Another personal risk posed by the tech start-up relates to your psyche. Bruce Pomfret points out that it can be "psychologically devastating" to watch your company fail. You and your colleagues can work incredibly hard night and day only to be ignored by your customers, which can hurt your self-esteem. It can be a real letdown to go to job interviews after an aborted tech start-up experience and have to explain what happened. Why did you make the decision to go to that company, and why did you leave? I've had to do it before, and it can be intimidating. However, I was amazed at how genuinely interested most people were in what I learned from the experience and how it could apply to their businesses. They truly enjoyed talking about it and reveled in its challenges, almost as if they were living the experience vicariously. I definitely found that the tech start-up experience made me more attractive as a prospective employee, and if you position the experience well, it will do the same for you.

In the end, how you overcome the negative aspects of the failure of a tech start-up is up to you. But you can position the tech start-up experience in hugely positive ways to make yourself attractive to future employers. You should not allow yourself to get depressed over the failure of the tech start-up firm. You knew the risks of failure from the outset. If you had support from your network going in, then you will continue to draw support from it as you seek other career opportunities after the tech start-up fails. In fact, I believe the greater your network support going in, the more positively you will perceive the tech start-up experience afterwards.

HOW MUCH RISK CAN AND SHOULD YOU TOLERATE?

How much personal risk you can and should tolerate is a very subjective matter. Simply stated, you should not sign up for a tech start-up situation where you are highly uncomfortable. On the other hand, you may be in a situation where you are outside your normal comfort zone. If you're a first-time tech start-up prospect, then the tech start-up will definitely push your comfort envelope. However, in today's economy, taking calculated risks is becoming more necessary than ever. A tech start-up will help you learn to be more comfortable with risk, which can only benefit you no matter what type of company you join later.

Although you may be paid less than you would be at other companies, you should not have to dramatically alter your living habits just so you can take a job at a tech start-up. However, you may not be able to save as much money as you used to or would like to save. You should know before joining a tech start-up for how long a period of time you are willing to live under such circumstances. Maybe you can live that way forever, or maybe you are only willing to live that way for a year or two. If you haven't already considered your tolerance for financial risk in a tech start-up, think about it now. Figure out what salary you're willing to work for and over what period of time. Write it down and stick to it. You may or may not be taking a pay cut. I would not accept more than a 15 percent cut in base salary, but what you're willing to accept is a matter of personal preference.

You may find that some start-ups don't offer you enough of a salary for *any* period of time, even after negotiation. You should turn them down unequivocally. A company that fails to produce an offer that is attractive to you makes your job as a career searcher easier. When you are talking to many different companies, it can be helpful when companies self-select themselves out of the running. In today's tremendously hot job market, there's nothing wrong with saying "No thanks" to a prospective employer if you can't come to terms. When I was looking at tech start-ups in Seattle, several firms self-selected themselves out of the process because of base compensation. We parted on good terms, and their final words were: "Call us if you want to work together in the future."

You should expect to be given a great deal of responsibility and the latitude to make major contributions at a tech start-up. There should be very little risk in that. Know before joining the company what experience you expect to take away and how it integrates into your overall career plan.

Regarding future promotions, bigger salary, or other career benefits to you, if you don't get them in writing, assume they won't happen. So much within a tech start-up is outside your control that you need to be content with the job that you will be taking on a day-to-day basis. Assume that the role you are signing up for is the only one you will ever perform for the start-up in question, and be sure that it will provide you with the experience that you're looking for professionally. For example, if you join a company as a product manager, assume that you will not be promoted to vice president of marketing at this firm. If the company takes off, maybe you will be promoted, but even if it doesn't, you will have gained valuable experience as a product manager. After your stint as a product manager with this firm, perhaps you will pursue the marketing vice president role at another one. Andrew Blake of Handango notes that he intends to use his start-up experience at a higher level in another entrepreneurial situation later in his career.

Because of the high risks generally inherent in tech start-ups, your career is one area where you should have very low tolerance for risk. Conversely, you should have a very high degree of confidence that you will get out of the tech start-up the experience, knowledge, and skills that you want and expect. Fortunately, tech start-ups generally offer fabulous career opportunities, and most people who join them find that they reap enormous career dividends based on their tech start-up experience.

One risk that you run career-wise is that you may be unclear about the experience you will gain in advance. With a tech start-up, it can be difficult to know what you will learn and contribute before you actually take the job. To avoid this pitfall, learn as much as possible through the interview process. For every tech start-up you consider, gain a very clear understanding from your potential supervising manager and others about the experience you will gain and the contributions you will make. Know how you intend to use it in the future. Write it down for every tech start-up company you talk to, so you can keep score among the different start-ups you consider joining. Keeping score is one way you can ensure that you will get the best career tech start-up experience possible.

From a personal standpoint, you should tolerate as much tech start-up risk as will allow you to defend your choice of going to the company in the first place and taking the job that you did. With your interests at heart, your personal network of friends and colleagues should be the harshest critics of your prospective tech start-up. Ask them to play the role of devil's advocate in your discussions with them as you consider joining a tech start-up. Adrianna Paradiso at e-STEEL adds:

> Can you "sell" the company to friends and family? Do they believe your prospective firm is viable? If you can explain your decision to join to their satisfaction, then you will be able to explain it to future employers.

In these heady days of rocketing IPO tech stocks, many people are literally running off to join tech start-ups without doing any serious due diligence, only to find themselves in an untenable position later when trying to defend their career choice. A prospective employer is unlikely to consider "getting rich" a particularly great reason for your wanting to join a tech start-up, although it may be one of the reasons you joined. If you join a tech start-up on a whim and it tanks, friends may turn around and say "I told you so," and prospective employers may question your judgment, which hurts your ability to get future jobs. Therefore, make sure your rationale for joining a tech start-up involves your keen desire to make major contributions in areas where you can add value. Do those in your network agree with your logic? They should.

By consulting friends, family, and colleagues along the way in your decision process, you reduce the risk of straining personal relationships if you do decide to take the plunge. In fact, your relations will actually take a greater interest in your success and that of your firm if you consult them. They will feel a sense of ownership in your decision. That base of support should reduce considerably the stress you will feel inevitably over the course of your tech start-up experience. Knowing that you have many people rooting for you is a powerful feeling. In addition, by consulting friends and relations you will help yourself to make a more informed decision. Friends and family are assets to you in your career search. If you don't know the questions to ask about the company's business, get your friends and family to prime you with questions.

Ultimately, you alone have to weigh the mix of risks posed to you by the tech start-up experience, but you can and should get the input of others. At the end of the day, if you do your homework, you should see that the biggest risks to you of the tech start-up aren't really related to the firm at all, but rather are tied to what the experience means for your pocketbook, your career, and your relationships. Hopefully, you are beginning to see that you really can be in the driver's seat, even in a tech start-up. You have a great deal of control over the financial and career risks you accept, for how long, and what you will do with the experience going forward.

You may have made up your mind already that you intend to join a tech start-up company. You are hardly alone in making this decision. You are probably grappling with the question of *which* tech start-up to join. Perhaps you haven't determined that you are going to join a tech start-up company but feel that you would join certain types of start-ups. In either case, a key input into making the decision of whether to join a tech start-up is knowing your tolerance for tech start-up career risk, which you can determine by identifying the earliest stage of a tech start-up you will consider joining.

DETERMINING THE STAGE AT WHICH YOU SHOULD CONSIDER JOINING A TECH START-UP

The earlier the stage, the higher the career risk, and commensurately, the higher the potential reward should be. In contrast to the successful founding start-up entrepreneurs that you read about in splashy articles in the business media, maybe you don't sky dive or bicycle parachute off the sides of cliffs in your spare time. You are more risk-averse, but you are willing to accept some risk in return for potentially higher reward. Therefore, you want to know the earliest stage at which you will be comfortable joining a tech start-up.

There are three variables that you can combine to yield personal insight into this question: company profitability, your base compensation, and your overall career comfort level. Why these three factors? Because they relate to very basic, visceral feelings you have about what matters most to you in a tech start-up situation on a day-to-day basis. Your perceptions about these variables are neither right nor wrong. Rather, you can use them to inform yourself about the level of risk that you are willing to accept.

Company Profitability

If you don't expect a company to be profitable for a long time, that may influence whether you would join a given tech start-up company in the first place. Maybe you expect that a tech start-up should be profitable within one year. Maybe you don't care when it becomes profitable. Realistically, you know that the company needs to be profitable within some reasonable duration of time because its investors are looking for a return. The greater the time frame to profitability that you are willing to accept, the more risk you are willing to take with a tech start-up. Conversely, the shorter the time to profitability you are willing to accept, the less risk you are willing to take. Let's assume your time horizon spans from 1 to 10 years. Determine the greatest number of years you are willing to wait before a tech start-up becomes profitable. Write down that number now.

Base Compensation

Your base salary must be at some acceptable level because you need to cover your living expenses on a day-to-day basis. Although at some point you hope to reap the rewards of stock options, you won't realize that huge payoff right away. Indeed, you may never realize that huge payoff. You also know that you might earn a much higher salary at a larger, more established company, and that your stock options may end up being worth nothing. You need to think about the time frame in which you are willing to accept a tech start-up base compensation that you know could be less than that at a different type of firm. Perhaps you are only willing to accept it for one year. Depending on your function and expertise, maybe you stand to get paid even more in base compensation at a tech start-up than you could earn elsewhere, although this is less likely. But perhaps your base salary is such that you are willing to live with it for up to six or eight years. Within a time horizon of 1 to 10 years, write down the greatest number of years that you are willing to accept what you believe will be a tech start-up's base compensation offer to you.

Your Overall Career Comfort Level

Based on what you know about tech start-ups in general, how comfortable are you with the notion of joining a tech start-up? Consider how you feel about the experience that you can gain from a tech start-up relative to that you could obtain from other opportunities at larger, more established firms. Consider how confident you feel that you will be able to use that tech start-up experience in other jobs, quite possibly at other companies. How well do you feel you can position the tech start-up experience to recruiters you may deal with later in your career? On a scale of 1 to 10 , with 1 being low and 10 being high, how confident do you feel about the career experience you will gain from a tech start-up? Write down that number.

As you consider these variables, it is important to keep in mind that you seek to establish *what you are willing to accept* as opposed to *what you want* from a tech start-up. Obviously, you want to maximize your potential in any job situation, but this exercise is about finding the limit of your tolerance for career risk. The question you're trying to answer is: What is the highest amount of tech start-up career risk I am willing to tolerate? Of course, you would willingly assume lower risks.

Diagnostic Exercise: Determining Your Personal Tolerance for a Tech Start-Up Career Risk

Having given some thought to your tolerance levels for each of the three variables in Table 7.1a, combine them to determine the earliest stage of tech start-up you should consider joining.

The total possible score is between 0 and 300 points. Now that you have a score, what does it tell you? Use Table 7.1b to find out.

Note that these results are directional and are not meant to be strictly prescriptive. As an example, a score of 150 does not necessarily mean that you should go charging into any OI tech start-up. If anything, it suggests that you might want to join a late-stage organizational Infant rather than an early-stage one. Such a start-up is probably about to close one of its later rounds of venture capital investment. A score of 150 definitely tells you that you are comfortable taking on more career risk than someone with a score of 230. Similarly, it also indicates that you are unlikely to accept a level of risk that a tech start-up company's founders assume when they launch the new business.

Although the purpose of this exercise is to gauge your general level of personal tolerance for tech start-up career risk, so far we have not discussed how it applies to specific tech start-up situations that you may be considering. Generally, you may be most comfortable joining an OA stage tech start-up, but you may find a situation in which a specific OI stage firm is attractive. Such an exceptional situation may arise because of the company's particular

Table 7.1a   Identifying the Stage at Which You Should Join a Start-Up

Variable	1. Your Personal Rating (n)	2. Calculate (10 – n) x 10	3. Total Score (Sum of Column B)
Years to Company Profitability (1–10)	_____	(10 – ___) x 10 = _____	_____
Base Compensation in Years (1–10)	_____	(10 – ___) x 10 = _____	_____
Your Comfort Level: Subjective Rating (1–10)	_____	(10 – ___) x 10 = _____	_____

Table 7.1b   Your Personal Tolerance for Tech Start-Up Career Risk

Tech Start-Up Stage	Score Range	Your Personal Tolerance for Tech Start-Up Career Risk
Birth	0–100 points	Very high
Organizational Infant (OI)	101–150 points	High
Organizational Adolescent (OA)	151–200 points	Medium
Adult	201–300 points	Low

business or technology position, your knowledge or expertise in a particular field, or some combination of these types of factors. Therefore, you should refer back to this diagnostic exercise for each start-up opportunity you are considering because your perceptions about each will differ.

TEN KEY POINTS TO CONSIDER IN WEIGHING THE CAREER RISKS OF DIFFERENT TECH START-UPS

Many of the considerations you need to take into account in assessing whether to join a tech start-up are indeed the same as those you would evaluate in making any career decision. However, there are some key differences in job components between tech start-ups and other types of firms, and there are differences in the weights you should assign to them. Deciding the right career situation for you is an intensely personal decision, and I don't pretend to have all the answers. However, once you know the ten key points to consider in weighing the career risks of different tech start-ups, you can make a highly informed decision about which tech start-up opportunity you should pursue, if any.

The ten key points to consider in weighing the career risks of different tech start-ups are

1. Role
2. Responsibility
3. Potential experience
4. People
5. Opportunities for growth and development
6. Compensation
7. Company ability to execute
8. Company competitive position in the marketplace
9. Company environment
10. Personal comfort level

As you read through the discussions of these points, pay attention to how they should differ between the tech start-up and more stable firms. Also, if you've started to interview with tech start-ups, think about the situations you've encountered and how they differ from each other on these points.

Role

Your role is most likely going to be defined by your job title. Some people care a great deal about job titles; others don't. In a tech start-up, you should care about your job title more than you would at a larger, more stable firm, because at a tech start-up you seek to be a bigger fish in a smaller pond. You want to have broader influence than you would elsewhere, and that implies a title of a higher level than you would have elsewhere. You don't necessarily need to have a higher-level title, but at a minimum you should have the same title you could get at a larger firm. This is acceptable as long as you have greater responsibility.

Responsibility

Responsibility is one of the most important reasons you should consider joining a tech start-up firm. If you decide to join a tech start-up, a major contributor to your decision should be the larger set of responsibilities that you will have. You seek to make greater contributions, have greater influence on strategic direction, and generally have a greater impact on the tech start-up firm than you would at a larger, more stable enterprise. If you don't sense that you would be in this position with a given tech start-up firm, then you should question whether the opportunity is the right one for you.

Potential Experience

The experience to be gained from the tech start-up is one of the invaluable assets you will walk away with no matter what happens to the company itself. You should be able to trade on your tech start-up experience in subsequent career endeavors, whether or not they are at another tech start-up. Obviously, responsibility ties in with experience fairly closely, so if you go into a tech start-up situation assuming a high degree of responsibility, the odds are good that you will gain solid experience. However, your potential tech start-up experience encompasses more than just your direct job responsibilities. It involves learning the industry and its competitors, gaining an understanding of how the business works, and solving managerial challenges. The experience you stand to gain, as well as the speed and intensity of the learning curve, should be greater at a tech start-up than at a more established firm.

People

You are seeking to work with highly dynamic people in a tech start-up. Give major consideration to their education, prior work experience, management style, and team orientation. You want to ensure that you can learn from these people for as long as you are willing to be with the start-up. Moreover, you should seek people with whom you can work successfully. Ideally, you are looking to work on a day-to-day basis with higher caliber people at a tech start-up than you would in a more established firm. At a minimum, the caliber of people at a tech start-up should be at parity with those in other career situations you would consider.

There are several categories of people for you to consider within the tech start-up. Obviously, you need to consider your supervising manager. Then there are your peers within the firm, as well as those who report to you or your peer group. Finally, there is the firm's management team and board of directors. More so than in larger, more stable firms, the tech start-up's board is important for its experience in the industry, contacts, and reputation.

Another consideration is your fit with the organizational culture and ethical principles of the tech start-up. Will you get along with the people there? Do you agree with their philosophy and vision for the company? It's important that you do, not only because of how much time you spend there but because your motivation will drag if you disagree. You need to be inspired by the people you work with.

Opportunities for Growth and Development

Although theoretically you need to be content knowing that you may never receive a promotion or pay raise while at a given tech start-up, you are seeking out firms where the potential for such opportunities is high. Obviously, there are no guarantees, but you want to find situations in which potential rapid company growth will translate into faster professional growth and development for you than you could expect elsewhere.

Compensation

You probably know by now that you aren't joining a tech start-up for the base salary that you will be paid. You are signing up for some potential upside with tech start-up stock options. Of course, those may never be worth anything. Opinions vary widely about whether you should take a pay cut to join a tech start-up company and, if so, how much. If you expect to earn more at a tech start-up than you would elsewhere, be prepared to defend your thinking. My personal viewpoint is that you should be willing to accept a slightly lower base salary than you might be paid elsewhere, but in return you should get a healthy batch of options and potentially a signing bonus. Compensation is a fairly personal issue, but you have some insight based on your tolerance for tech start-up career risk: You've already considered your floor level of base salary at a tech start-up and for how long you are willing to accept it. Relative to the general compensation of more established firms, think of tech start-ups as representing greater risk and greater potential reward.

Company Ability to Execute

You are seeking to join a tech start-up that has a demonstrated ability to execute its strategy and plans. Consider the areas of product development, marketing and sales, and fundraising, among others. Depending on the stage at which you intend to join a tech start-up, the firm may not have a long track record, so you need to consider the track record of executing the firm's people have demonstrated in other jobs. In general, tech start-ups have a greater sense of urgency than more established firms and therefore seek to accomplish more in a shorter period of time.

Company Competitive Position

You want to assess the company's overall competitive position relative to others in the marketplace. Specifically, you want to understand the extent to which the company has distinct competitive advantages in the form of technology, intellectual property, an established customer base, a talented employee team, or other key assets. It may be difficult to get a full picture of a company's competitive position in a new or emerging market, but you should be able to cite compelling evidence as to why a given company will win.

Environment

You probably aren't joining the tech start-up firm because of its glorious ambiance. The general tech start-up environment is probably less appealing than that of more established firms. If you find a tech start-up where the environment is nice, consider yourself fortunate. Most tech start-ups will have decidedly casual work environments. Of course, their lack of stuffiness can be genuinely refreshing.

Personal Comfort Level

Your personal comfort level, as you've learned from determining your personal tolerance for tech start-up risk, is likely to be inherently lower than it would be if you were to join a more established firm. Of course, this is tied to the higher risk and higher potential for reward that you stand to realize from the tech start-up. If you are as comfortable within a tech start-up setting as you are elsewhere, then you are either more willing to take risks than most people or you've found yourself a start-up with a high probability of success.

WEIGHING THE TEN KEY POINTS AND DEVELOPING A COMPARATIVE FRAMEWORK FOR ASSESSING DIFFERENT TECH START-UPS

To help you decide which tech start-up situation might be right for you, use Table 7.2 to assign scores to each of the ten key points. The scores represent the weight of importance that you place on each of the ten key points. In column 2, I have suggested scores for each of the ten key points and provided some guidance for the types of inputs you should use in scoring each. At the end of the day, this is your personal decision tool. Therefore, you should assign your own scores in column 3 based on your personal preferences.

You now have your own scoring system for assessing any tech start-up. You have weighted each key point based on its importance to you. Using your scores as a benchmark, how does a given tech start-up compare? Your scores from Table 7.2 represent the highest possible rating for a given key point.

Let's say that you decide the highest possible total score for Role is 10. At a given tech start-up, you rate the role a 9 out of a possi-

Table 7.2   Comparative Framework for Assessing Different Tech Start-Ups

Key Point with Suggested Inputs and Scores	My Suggested Scores	Your Score	Suggested Relative Value of Tech Start-Up vs. More Established Firm
Role	10		Same to higher
Responsibility	12		Higher
Potential Experience	12		Higher
People	12		Same to higher
Supervisor (0–2 points)			
Peers (0–2)			
Firm Management (0–2)			
Firm Board of Directors (0–6)			
Industry experience (0–2)			
Reputation/Contacts (0–2)			
Your Perception (0–2)			
Opportunities for Growth and Development	8		Same to higher
Compensation	10		Same to lower base
Base Compensation (0–6)			Higher long-term potential
Long-Term Compensation (Stock Options) (0–4)			
Company Ability to Execute	12		Same to higher
Product Development (0–4)			
Sales (0–4)			
Fundraising (0–4)			
Company Competitive Position in Marketplace	10		Same to higher
Environment	4		Generally lower
Personal Comfort Level	10		Same to lower
Total Possible Score	100	100	Greater

ble 10 points, based on what you are looking for. Assess each key point at a tech start-up against your benchmark scores in this way to get a total score. Let's say you score a given tech start-up 85 across all key points. What does the score mean? Use Table 7.3 to find out.

Now that you have a framework for evaluating the career risk of different tech start-ups, you can compare opportunities to determine

Table 7.3   Is This Start-Up Right for You?

Score	Comment
90–100	Go for it; you definitely want to join this start-up and are not afraid of the risks involved.
80–89	You are pretty excited about this start-up; you may have some minor reservations, but generally, you're sold.
70–79	You have some reservations, but you're still leaning towards doing it. Think about the specific issues and/or concerns and see if you can't address any of them before joining.
60–69	You have a few significant reservations. The specific situation may not be right for you. Perhaps others are better. Maybe you can negotiate with the start-up on your role, title, or compensation to improve the scores.
50–59	You have several major reservations. It is probably best to pursue other start-up options.
40–49	You are definitely leaning against joining this start-up.
30–39	You are leaning heavily against joining this start-up.
20–29	The opportunity costs of joining this start-up are clearly large.
0–19	Why are you even asking?

which is the best one for you. By inserting columns into the comparative framework for each tech start-up being considered, you can line up the opportunities side by side to compare them relative to the ten key points. Let's say you've interviewed with tech start-up companies A, B, and C. To assess which is the best opportunity for you, assign a score to each along the ten key points. (See Table 7.4.)

What's great about lining up the opportunities side by side is that you can pinpoint precisely the benefits and disadvantages of each. You see the trade-offs of selecting one opportunity over another. Also, while you may have an intuitive "feel" about one specific opportunity, when you compare it to others in this manner you may find that it doesn't look as attractive as something else. It may be that you are undervaluing that particular tech start-up opportunity or that something else actually *is* more attractive. In either case, you may need to do some more homework on a specific opportunity if you still believe it is your best bet. You may also decide you need to change your personal weighting system after interviewing with a few tech start-ups, because you might discover

Table 7.4   Comparing Different Tech Start-Ups Using the Ten Key Points

Key Point	Your Score (Total Possible)	Your Score Tech Start-Up A	Your Score Tech Start-Up B	Your Score Tech Start-Up C
Role				
Responsibility				
Potential Experience				
People				
Opportunities for Growth and Development				
Compensation				
Company				
Ability to Execute				
Company Competitive Position in Marketplace				
Personal Comfort Level				
Total Score	100 out of 100	____ out of 100	____ out of 100	____ out of 100

that what you thought was more important to you is actually less so. As was the case with determining your personal tolerance for tech start-up risk, the ten key points are not intended to be totally prescriptive. You should use them as guidelines to help inform you about the right decision.

One item that is missing as a key point is strategy. The reason I have omitted it is that if a tech start-up company can't articulate a solid strategy to you, then you shouldn't waste your time pursuing it. A tech start-up's strategy does not need to be airtight, but it does need to be credible enough that you can see how the firm will make money. In the biotech, hardware, software, and communications sectors, the strategy piece should be straightforward, and frequently it will be. However, start-ups focusing on e-commerce can be much foggier on strategy. You need to be cautious about strategy and a firm's ability to execute in the e-commerce tech start-up sector.

You may have noticed from the scores that I suggested for the Comparative Framework that a majority of the weight in making a decision to join a tech start-up is given to key points that relate to your future career in some way. The only aspects that don't relate as strongly are those of your personal comfort level and the tech start-up firm's environment. The reason for such a heavy future orientation is that you need to consider seriously your career game plan for after your tech start-up experience. You might ask, "What do you mean? I'm considering my next job opportunity at a tech start-up firm and you're already telling me to be thinking about the job *after* it?" Absolutely. Thinking about your next career move after the tech start-up will help you reduce your tech start-up career risk dramatically.

REAL-LIFE EXPERIENCE:
THERE ARE MANY PATHS YOU CAN CHOOSE

In general, there is no right or wrong way to consider a tech start-up career opportunity in the context of your career. You determine how and under what circumstances it is right for you. The people whose comments you've read in this book have pursued various different career paths, all for good reasons, and all of them viable. Their experiences can be categorized into five different models. Exploring their career paths and seeing the tech start-up in that context may help you to formulate your longer-term career game plan. It may also help show you how to position the tech start-up experience within it. Different models work for different people and for different career stages, but you should be able to identify the approaches and people who most closely represent your situation.

First Build Experience at a Recognized Firm, Then Join a Tech Start-Up

The advantage of this approach is that you gain experience and credibility from working at brand-name companies. Bill Demas at

Vividence, Prabha Fernandes at SMT, and Donna Williams at BigStar fit this model. All worked for at least eight years within large, well-known companies before joining start-up firms. They believe this career approach has merit, not only because they themselves followed it but also because there is a definite logic to it. All are senior-level executives within their respective companies. Bill is Vice President of Marketing at Vividence, Prabha is President and CEO at SMT, and Donna is Vice President of Marketing at BigStar. Unless you've founded your own firm, you don't get to be a top executive in a company without building a track record. The prior career experiences of Bill, Prabha, and Donna have enabled them to assume positions of major responsibility within their respective tech start-up companies.

Bill Demas worked in sales at IBM straight out of college. He then went to Harvard Business School and joined Microsoft upon graduation. While at Microsoft, he worked in the Consumer Group and helped build a new digital dictionary business: Encarta. He was part of the team that grew Encarta from a concept into a $100 million business. That experience made Bill a very attractive executive candidate for a number of technology start-up companies.

In Prabha's case, she earned a Ph.D. in microbiology from Thomas Jefferson University in Philadelphia. After doing doctoral fellowships at the Institute for Cancer Research and Temple University, she moved into industry with Squibb Company. At Squibb, she conducted in vivo studies on the first antibiotic in a new drug class, Azactam. She then moved on to Abbott Labs, where she directed microbiological studies for Abbott's antibiotic, Clarithromycin. She then joined drug maker Bristol-Myers Squibb (BMS) as Vice President of Microbial Molecular Biology, which was a fairly new field at the time. She served in that role for ten years before moving to Small Molecule Therapeutics. Over the course of her career, doing pioneering work for major drug makers, Prabha learned literally all facets of the business of bringing a drug to market. She draws heavily from this critical experience at SMT.

Donna worked at Bankers Trust on Wall Street for seven years before going to Columbia Business School for her M.B.A. Upon graduation, she pursued a career in business development with the Mosby book division of the Times Mirror Corporation. After working in a big company for a while, she decided to join a start-up company, BigStar Entertainment, as Vice President of Marketing. BigStar went public in August 1999, and Donna has been incredibly busy ever since. In fact, she was pretty busy before the IPO as well.

Although some might disagree with this approach, clearly it has worked for Bill, Prabha, and Donna. If you aspire to senior-level positions in technology start-ups, it can enhance your position greatly if you have prior experience at a well-known firm. Moreover, once you have that brand-name company experience, it stays on your résumé no matter what you go on to do in the future.

Use a Start-Up as an Entrée to a Bigger, Better Opportunity

The complete reverse of the career path described above is to join a tech start-up first and use that experience to attain a position of seniority within a larger, more established firm. Adrianna Paradiso and John Lindsay have pursued this career path successfully. Although it is unlikely that you can work for a tech start-up and then be recruited as the CEO of IBM, you can gain valuable experience at the tech start-up that will enable you to make this career move to a higher level of responsibility. Because the learning curve is so steep at tech start-ups, you can leap from a tech start-up into such a position.

Adrianna, a Columbia M.B.A., until recently was Director of Business Development for Cendant Corporation, the diversified consumer marketing company. Cendant owns a number of online properties, ranging from Rent.net for apartments to Privacy Guard, offering online credit reports to Netmarket, an online discount offering warehouse. Prior to taking on her role at Cendant, Adrianna was a product manager for NetGrocer, the online mail order grocery vendor. Based on the experience she gained at NetGrocer in working with vendors and building an online brand, she was an ideal recruit for Cendant, which was then looking to build relationships with partners to grow its businesses. More recently, Adrianna has moved from Cendant into another start-up, e-STEEL, an online marketplace for the steel industry.

John Lindsay worked for USData for eight years before joining Microsoft. While at USData, John realized that he ultimately wanted to work for Microsoft. His experience is instructive:

There was a point at which I knew I wanted to go to work for Microsoft. Even several years before the opportunity presented itself for me to go there, I knew that I wanted to get there. I had the opportunity at USData to be the Microsoft [representative] there . . . in the product management group. . . . I was the one raising my hand saying, "I'll take the Microsoft platform" at a time when (Windows) NT was not considered something that you would run your business on . . . which was great because no one else really wanted to fool around with it. . . . But it allowed me to gain experience and to build relationships with Microsoft, and to build this portfolio of skills so that one day I could walk into Microsoft and have a lot to show that would enable me to get that job there, which was my plan.

John notes that you can afford to make more mistakes at a tech start-up because the company probably can't afford to lose you. Because there is so much to do, mistakes are going to be made anyway. What matters most is recovering from them fast. A start-up teaches you a great deal about recovering from mistakes. John also notes that in larger companies, you have more competition for jobs than you do at a tech start-up. In the tech start-up, you get the opportunity to play more roles because there's often no one else around to do them.

Although it might seem counterintuitive, start-ups really can propel you into bigger, better opportunities, both within other tech start-ups and at larger companies. I'm a classic example of the latter. After my stint at HST, I was recruited for a role in business development, where I work on deals, many of which have been with tech start-up companies. Having sat across from tech start-ups at the negotiating table, more than a few of my colleagues have noted that my start-up experience enables me to see the situation from the point of view of those on the other side and to understand their critical issues.

Use a Start-Up as an Opportunity to Switch Industries

Bruce Pomfret attended Northeastern University in Boston, Massachusetts, majoring in journalism. After graduating, he worked as an editor for a series of progressively larger local New England newspapers. Over time, Bruce realized that the publishing business is one in which you really have to "pay your dues" before you can get ahead. So when he was recruited for an editorial job at tech start-up Nets, Inc., Bruce leaped at the chance. Over time, largely on his own initiative, Bruce taught himself HTML and other programming languages, which enabled him to progress to higher-level positions. In his current role as a software engineer at Perot Systems, Bruce helps clients develop and manage their Web sites. Having worked his way into a role that is central to the Internet explosion, Bruce gets job offers just about every week, although he is happy where he is.

Andrew Blake is another example of someone using a start-up to switch industries. Upon graduation from Vanderbilt University, Andrew became a commercial real estate broker. He quickly realized that in spite of his hard work, he would also have to pay his dues in a more stable, traditional business for a long time before making really good money. After two years of working in commercial real estate, Andrew returned to his hometown of Fort Worth, Texas, and joined Handango, an online marketplace for software for handheld and wireless devices, where he manages Handango's relations with software developers. Andrew notes that in a tech start-up, he has a huge amount of responsibility and is learning more and doing so much faster than he would elsewhere. I completely concur that Andrew, at age twenty-four, definitely has more responsibility than he would in a more traditional industry and has learned a phenomenal amount in his five months with a tech start-up.

The experiences of Andrew and Bruce are very similar in that both identified where major financial opportunities were for younger people and actively pursued them. Obviously, the older you are, the more experience you are likely to have in one particular industry, and the less likely you are to want to switch to another. If you are in that situation, you know that you have much to lose if you decide to make the switch, and the challenge for you is to identify permutations of your current industry and leverage your years of experience in tech start-ups that require the knowledge and experience you have.

Choose Start-Ups as a Way of Life

Some people are truly bitten by the tech start-up bug. It happens to lots of people for various reasons. The speedy pace of tech start-ups is dizzying. The people in tech start-ups are generally smart and interesting, and that's appealing. Also, you usually know within a few years whether your start-up is destined for the big time. Of course, if you decide to pursue a professional life of working in tech start-ups, you need to be prepared for a great deal of stress. You could be out of a job at a moment's notice. You may not get great benefits. You may miss out on a paycheck every so often. However, there are those for whom the lifestyle is attractive.

Erin Hill is one such person. Although she did work for a while at Intel, most of her job experience after leaving Cornell Business School has been in the tech start-up arena. Erin is attracted to the fast pace of the environment, the technology, and the people of tech start-ups. She has seen a great deal over the course of three start-up experiences, and while not all of the results have been positive, Erin has learned a tremendous amount and will have plenty of career choice in her future.

Alan Kitty is another example of someone who has spent much of his career in tech start-ups. Formally trained as an actor, Alan spent thirteen years in New York City doing a variety of plays and acting jobs. Although acting was an enriching experience for him in many ways, Alan wanted to make more money and began to seek out opportunities to do so. He found he had incredible skills as a salesman, and he has worked for a number of tech start-up companies in the areas of sales and business development. Alan has enjoyed the tech start-up career experience because it's like acting in plays. "You do one play, and when you're done, you go on to the next," he notes. What can be a fairly transitory existence is nothing new to Alan because of his prior acting experience. Alan also found he really enjoyed the diversity of businesses he could pursue in tech start-ups, so much so that he is now a consultant precisely because he wants to be able to pick and choose a variety of projects to work on.

Although making a career out of tech start-up experiences has its attraction, it will not appeal to everyone. Many of the people who will pursue work in tech start-ups on an extended basis will do so because they have already succeeded professionally. If they are at one tech start-up and it fails, they will get right back up and go try it again elsewhere because they are financially and professionally secure. Not everyone is in that position. If you have kids and a mortgage, you may not be running to join a risky tech start-up venture. There may be a misperception that tech start-ups have lower risk these days, and my response is that they are still risky, and only you can determine how much risk you are willing to take with your career. I wouldn't pursue the tech start-up as a career way of life unless I had the financial security to do so.

Begin with Tech Start-Ups, Then Consult

Many of the people I've interviewed have followed more than one of the career paths outlined here. Over the course of your career, one start-up career path choice works at one point, and some other option may prove relevant later on. Such is the case with consulting. In the early 1990s, Judy Schneider worked for a venture, backed by Microsoft founder Paul Allen, called StarWave, the Internet online content site (now part of Infoseek). She then joined Microsoft for a few years, after which she worked as a consultant for ThirdAge, the San Francisco-based online destination for active older adults. She's just completed a stint in Seattle working for the health care Web site Onhealth, and is now consulting again. From Judy's experience, you see that you can actually move from tech start-up roles into consulting and back again. Similarly, although Bruce Pomfret and Alan Kitty are consulting to Web-based companies currently, both reserve the option to go back to working for a tech start-up company on a full-time basis.

Consulting after working at a tech start-up may be the right choice at a time in your career. It may be so enjoyable that you may never want to do anything else again. One reason that it may be the right thing to do after a tech start-up experience is that you can generate income temporarily while figuring out your next career move. Or, as in the case of Alan, you may enjoy the diversity of the work. Many independent tech start-up consultants these days get paid in stock options, so you can consult and still retain some potential upside in your client company. For Bruce, consulting for a larger firm provides the stability that he wants now that he has a family. Bruce doesn't have to work until midnight on an extended basis trying to fix holes in a piece of code, as he used to, but he's still working at the nexus of Internet technology and business.

WRAP-UP

You've explored your personal tolerance for tech start-up career risk, learned a framework for comparing tech start-up opportunities, and considered the career paths that the tech start-up experience affords. You are now ready to get down to the nuts and bolts of how to assess a tech start-up company. You need to focus like a laser beam on the critical success factors to determine whether a given tech start-up has what it takes to succeed. Many of them don't.

Your goal is to make the most informed decision possible. That process has to involve an understanding of how tech start-ups are financed and what the financial underpinnings mean to you. Understanding how a given start-up is financed and knowing the types of investors involved can help you gauge the risks and influence your decision.

8

TECHNOLOGY VENTURE FINANCE 101

Why do you need to know about tech venture finance and the people who provide it? Good question. You need to know about the investors in your tech start-up for a number of reasons. First, their philosophy will be a big determinant of how you are compensated. Second, their expertise and experience will be important in helping your start-up to succeed. Investors' track records are highly meaningful. If they have a proven record of success, that bodes well for your firm. If they lack a track record, there is definitely more of a risk in terms of their ability to help the firm succeed.

If you are granted stock options by a start-up, the financing process definitely influences your compensation. The developmental stage at which you join a start-up will influence the size of your stock option grant. The earlier the stage of the start-up at the time you join, the larger your stock option grant will be. Your risk will be higher, so your potential reward must be higher as well.

More than just the stage of development is important. You need to try to gauge the company's funding needs because future funding will *dilute* your share of ownership in the firm. Let's say that today you have a certain number of options on stock that is valued at $4.00 per share. If your start-up has to raise more money, perhaps it will offer a stake to an investor at $6.00 per share. On the one hand, that's good news: Now the shares on which you have options are valued at $6.00. However, the company had to give up a piece of equity or a percentage of ownership to secure that investment funding. So even though the number of shares on which you hold options has stayed the same, your percentage of total shares in the company has just decreased.

However, the total value of your shares is higher, and that's what you're looking for: value appreciation of your equity in the company. This simple example illustrates the process by which tech start-ups raise money to keep operations running until they really start selling their products and can go public. Management has to give up something, in this case a percentage of ownership in the company, to receive something in return, investment capital that is vital to keeping the company running in the near term.

In a start-up, you generally start to pay attention to things that have an impact on the value of your stock options. I know I did. Many people who have gone through the process of joining a tech start-up agree that they wish they knew more about how the financing process works. Although the decisions about how the company secures funding and at what price may be entirely out of your control, understanding their implications will help you assess whether or not you are getting a good deal before you join.

Over time, as the company goes through multiple funding rounds, your total percentage of shares of the company's stock will decline. Your goal is to try to ensure that you will realize the value of the increased appreciation in the company's share price over time. Judy Schneider at Onhealth recalls a friend who worked for a start-up where the management team was not forthright with its employees about the ownership structure of the firm. The start-up ultimately sold itself off to another company, and the ownership structure was such that the top people all made a decent profit but everyone else made little money. The goal of this chapter is to help you understand the fundraising process and learn how to ask the right questions so that you can avoid such situations.

Understanding the start-up financing process by stage of development will help you determine if your company's management team is looking out for your interests as well as theirs. By knowing the different types of investors and their motivations, you can see why they get involved in the process when they do. From a financial standpoint, the real genesis of the tech start-up begins with seed funding.

SEED FUNDING

Seed funding is defined as the early-stage financing provided to help a company cover costs of developing a business plan or working prototype of its product. Usually this money is used to cover time and materials costs as well as any consulting or outside design costs. Although the financial risks of a tech start-up at this very early stage are especially high, the amount of money required for developing the prototype is fairly low relative to the eventual financial requirements of the company. For our purposes, seed funding is associated with the Birth stage. At this stage, the company's founders are generally the only principals involved with the project, and they will use the money to prove their concept. Seed investments are typically below $2 million, although they can run as high as $5 million. Seed funding is commonly referred to as "Series A" funding because of its spot at the front of the line in the fundraising sequence.

Seed funding can come from many different sources: angel investors, the owners and founders themselves, friends and family, research centers, universities, communities, and governments. Because of the technical knowledge and understanding required to make tech start-ups successful, high-tech angel investors play a key role in helping many such start-ups get off the ground. Although it is difficult to estimate the total investment amount that angels contribute to start-up ventures, the U.S. Department of Commerce has projected the figure for angel investment in the United States as high as $20 billion per year. The lines between venture capitalists and angel investors have blurred to some degree, but there are key differences between angel investors and venture capital investors that still hold true. Specifically, angels invest smaller amounts of money into start-up ventures than do venture capitalists, and usually they are less demanding in terms of the return on that investment.

Angel Investors

A typical tech angel investor is someone who

- invests in emerging technology ventures,
- expects a lower rate of return on the investment than a venture capital firm,
- is typically "patient" with his or her investment, willing to wait for up to eight years to see a return,
- provides an investment amount that is lower than what will be required later,
- makes other angel investments periodically,
- is an expert in the technology and industry,
- likes to be involved in the start-up in some way, often in a mentoring role, and
- seeks to invest with other people.

It used to be that angel investors were predominantly retired technology executives who were looking for something to do with their spare time, money, and expertise. Many such people are still angels today. Increasingly, however, younger people who have amassed personal wealth at technology companies and who are still early in their careers are becoming angels as a way of helping others, while continuing to work in a day-to-day capacity at their own jobs.

Angels become involved in tech start-ups for a variety of reasons. They want to help other people with ideas in technologies that they understand and in which they have an interest. Having been successful themselves, they like to share their experiences with others who aspire to success. Although they don't always invest with other people, they often do, because investing with others enables them to share the risk. Angels enjoy contributing to early-stage ventures, but they aren't just investing out of the kindness of their hearts. They hope their investment will pay off many times over if the company goes public or gets bought out at a premium price. Of course, they recognize that there is a very high level of risk in their investment and that they may not see a payback. That's why angels are recognized as providing "patient money." However, there have been rumblings in the business press recently that angel investors are becoming more like venture capitalists. They are demanding more from their start-up companies, seeking a quicker and higher return on their investment, and are starting to get more involved than start-up managements would like.

Like venture capitalists, angel investors know the power of a network. Acting as an angel investor to an early-stage start-up with another angel is a way for someone to expand his or her network. Increasingly, angel investors are banding together to act as syndicates for angel investment and networking opportunities. There's even an angel group called "Band of Angels" in Silicon Valley, a hotbed of angel activity. Angel investor groups also have sprouted up all over the place, in Massachusetts around Route 128, in North Carolina's Research Triangle Park, in southern California, in Florida, in Texas, and everywhere in between. Such groups have also emerged in the United Kingdom, Australia, and parts of Asia.

Angel investors typically become involved with a tech start-up team at the idea formulation and Birth stages. The round of funding for seed capital is referred to as the "seed round," which correlates to the earliest stages of company evolution. At this time, angels can contribute the most in terms of their business and technology expertise. With this expertise and a modest amount of investment funding, they work with the founders at the formative stages to think through and address the critical business and technology issues that must be resolved to complete a working prototype product or business plan.

Angels may be growing more demanding in terms of their expectations, but they are usually *less* demanding than venture capital firms. As investors of "patient money," they typically have a longer time horizon for seeking a return on their investment. They want and expect to play a mentoring or advisory role to the founders of the start-up. Sometimes the extent of this role becomes confused between founding tech start-up entrepreneurs and angels. Angels may try to get too involved in an early venture, and founding entrepreneurs, eager for seed money, may neglect to define their expectations of angels at the outset.

Although angels recognize the risks in investing, they are hoping for a healthy return on their investment. Most angels would consider a return of six to ten times their original investment over a five-year period a superior investment. Such a return, of course, would significantly outpace that of the broader stock market, which is the point of early venture investing: to realize a higher return on investment for assuming higher risks.

Selected Angel Investor Networks and Companies They Have Funded

Most angel investors are part of a network of like-minded people. Some are informal groups or clubs, such as the Band of Angels in Silicon Valley. Others are community-based, nonprofit organizations. Most angels operate in an informal manner and their activities are often confidential in nature. As a result, information about angels and the companies they fund is more difficult to obtain than about the comparatively high-profile venture capital firms. Table 8.1 profiles a few angel networks and some of the companies they have funded.

In addition to matching start-up founders with investors, angel networks help to connect entrepreneurs to experts across many fields: bankers, lawyers, accountants, consultants, recruiters, trade

Table 8.1   Selected Angel Investor Networks and Companies Funded

Angel Investor Network/ Location/Web Address	Investment Emphasis	Selected Companies Funded and/or Mentored
The Capital Network (TCN) Austin, TX www.thecapitalnetwork.com	Software, medical devices, manufacturing, household products, durable goods	DAX Harvard Custom Manufacturer Savantage
Band of Angels Palo Alto, CA	Hardware, software, bandwidth, medical, other	Alere Medical, Inc. Sendmail, Inc. Znyx Corporation
garage.com Silicon Valley, CA, with offices in Boston, MA; Seattle, WA; Austin, TX; Europe; and Israel www.garage.com	Information technology and medical sciences	icopyright Startups.com Virtualis WebOrder
Mid-Atlantic Venture Association Timonium, MD www.mava.org	Internet, e-commerce, software, telecom, biotechnology	Amazing Medica, Inc. BioNetrix Systems Cerebellum Software, Inc. Earthwalk Comunications Mindbridge.com Neuron Therapeutics NovoVascular, Inc. SingleShop.com WomenConnect.com Zeus Wireless, Inc.
Southern California Biomedical Council Los Angeles, CA www.socalbio.org	Biotechnology, pharmaceuticals, medical devices, health information	Advanced Orthopedics BioDiscovery CancerVax E-radlink GenBasix MDProse Nova Therapeutics Systems Protein Pathways, Inc. Vialogy

associations, public relations specialists, and so forth. Some angel networks have Web sites that profile their activities, the companies they have funded, and their success stories. From those that have Web sites, you can definitely get a feel for the types of projects they pursue.

Based on the relatively recent success of many start-up companies, getting in early on a hot investment has become more important. As a result, angels have begun to see more competition from venture capital firms and other investors for early stage investments. Demand is growing in the matchmaking or "venture brokering" field of linking investors with start-up entrepreneurs seeking seed funding. Garage.com was a pioneer in the venture brokering field, but there are now many such services.

What does the involvement of angels mean for you? It varies. Generally speaking, the angel investor's direct role in determining your compensation package will be fairly limited. Because angels usually acquire a fairly small stake in the company for their seed investment, the founder owners will retain a major portion of ownership in the company. However, the involvement of angels starts the process of distributing pieces of ownership to different constituencies of the company. When venture capitalists enter the picture, the dollars and share of company equity involved are much higher than at the angel level.

VENTURE CAPITAL (VC) FUNDING

Venture capital is money that is invested in a start-up by a venture capitalist in exchange for a piece of ownership in the start-up. A venture capital investment is money placed against a high-risk opportunity with the potential for high reward. In addition to financial investment, a venture capitalist will contribute his or her "brainpower," in the form of experience, expertise, and contacts, to the firm and its operations. Venture capitalists will typically get fairly involved with a firm in which they invest. They will often sit on the company's board of directors and play a significant role in guiding the direction and strategy of the company. As a result, VCs have been known on occasion to drive the founders crazy. Venture capitalists usually ask for and receive a large percentage of ownership of the company in return for their expertise and investment. In recent years, with so much competition for attractive start-up investment opportunities, founders and entrepreneurs have been able to negotiate for more favorable terms. By playing venture investors against each other, they can negotiate for the money they need while giving up a smaller chunk of equity in the company.

The first round of VC funding is typically called the "First Round" or "Series B" funding. It is called the "First Round" because it is the first round to involve significant amounts of money. It is also known as "Series B" funding because the angel investor already received "Series A" stock. Bill Demas at Vividence explains:

> [Vividence] was started with Series A, which is basically the angel investor round. Series B was closed in the early summer, which is with Kleiner Perkins. And I joined shortly thereafter and we'll be closing Series C with a major venture capital firm later this year. So one thing I would say for people is that a lot times people think, " "Oh, Kleiner's in there at the beginning," and that's typically known as the first round, but almost always that's the *second* round. Usually, there's some sort of angel that you need just to get that initial seed money to get the concept off the ground and be able to pitch it to the VC community, if that's the route you choose to go.

Which fundraising round is a company in? The answer can be somewhat confusing, but it may help you to think about it this way: The A in "Series A" is for Angel.

Venture capital firms provide pools of money that they have raised from institutions and individuals to invest in new business ventures. Venture capitalists are competing directly with other investment vehicles, specifically the stocks of publicly traded companies, mutual funds, and bonds. In other words, venture capitalists are competing with other types of money managers. However, because the risks of their investments are so much higher, they require a higher return to satisfy their investors and pay themselves. Because many tech start-up ventures never succeed, venture capitalists have to diversify their investment portfolios, just as a mutual fund manager does, to lower their overall risk.

The goal for venture capitalists is to generate high returns for their investors, who will then allocate more money for them to manage. If they have the opportunity to manage more money, VCs then can make more money for their investors and themselves. Institutions and money managers will continue to allocate money to invest to those who have built a track record of success. Intense competition forces those that are not successful out of the market.

Typically, venture capitalists are veterans of technology companies. They will usually have specific industry experience and expertise in the fields where they manage investments. Most often, they have had highly successful careers in industry. Having built a strong reputation and contacts in industry gives prospective investors a high degree of confidence that these people will be successful in their investment approach. Many of today's successful venture capitalists spent time at companies with household names such as Apple, Compaq, Dell, General Electric, GTE, IBM, Intel, Johnson & Johnson, Lotus, Merck, Microsoft, Motorola, Silicon Graphics, and Texas Instruments. Bill Demas at Vividence and Prabha Fernandes at Small Molecule Therapeutics both observe that the industry experience of key venture investors on the boards of their companies has played a pivotal role in helping their companies.

Venture capitalists do what they do because successful venture capitalists make a lot of money. They also are generally very passionate about what they do. Indeed, successful venture capitalists typically thrive on the frenetic pace of their business and are often doing many things at once. Once you understand that venture capitalists are all competing against one another for funding and deals, you realize that the venture capital business is not for the faint of heart.

Venture capitalists typically become involved with a tech start-up *after* it has received its Series A or seed-round funding. In other words, they get involved with it *at or past* the Birth stage. Venture capitalists most often invest in a tech start-up in the OI and OA stages. Although the number of venture funding rounds may vary, venture capital investment is what always triggers the stage shift in organizational development from start-up Birth to Infancy. Throughout the start-up's evolution as an infant and up to and even during adolescence, there will likely be additional rounds of venture capital financing.

Most VC firms do not provide seed funding for start-up businesses because the seed round involves higher risk than the venture round. Moreover, because there is so much money in the venture capital business these days, venture capitalists are looking to invest fairly large sums of money relative to what is required at the seed round. A certain amount of due diligence, or analysis and evaluation, is required for any venture capital investment deal. It is usually not worth the time of VCs to try to determine if they should invest $500,000 in seed money for a specific venture. A VC would have a far greater preference for investing, say, $5 million in the company once the concept is proven and a company needs to be built around it.

The expectations of venture capitalists are high relative to other investors; they have to be. If a VC manages investments in ten companies, then he or she needs to have at least one start-up do really well to cover the losses of others *and* show a return that will be attractive to investors. Using an extreme example, if nine out of ten start-ups for a given venture investor fail, then to show an attractive return to investors, that one successful company needs to have a phenomenal performance. The life of a venture capitalist can be stressful.

Successful firms expect that any company they invest in will have a solid, proven, capable management team. In fact, no matter how great the idea, if there isn't a winning management team with a solid track record behind it, a venture capital firm will more likely than not pass on the idea. A VC firm expects great things from the management teams of their portfolio companies.

Selected Venture Capital Firms and Companies They Have Funded

Table 8.2 highlights a few venture capital firms and some of the companies in which they have invested. There are at least a few funded companies that are household names on this list.

You may have noticed that more than one of these firms backed the same tech start-up. Bill Demas's firm, Vividence, is a classic example, having received venture capital backing from both Kleiner Perkins Caulfield & Byers and Sequoia Capital. That is not a coincidence. In the increasingly competitive world of venture capital, companies are looking for great start-up management

Table 8.2 Selected Venture Capital Firms and Companies Funded

Venture Capital Firm/Location	Investment Emphasis	Selected Companies Funded
Austin Ventures Austin, TX www.austinventures.com	Information technology: applications and infrastructure, business-to-business services and e-commerce, business-to-consumer e-commerce and media, communications, and semiconductors	ActiveUSA.com Akili Systems Asset Works Benchmarq Semiconductor BenefitMall.com Celpage Deja.com ELaw.com Human Code iMark.com Living.com McData ShowSupport.com Silicon Laboratories TelOptica Vignette
Benchmark Capital Menlo Park, CA www.benchmark.com	Information technology: consumer devices, e-commerce, application services, networking equipment, semiconductors, software, and telecommunications services	1-800 Flowers Accept.com Ariba Ashford.com Broadbase Software Collabra Software Comcore Semiconductor E-Loan eBay ePhysician eShop Handspring Juniper Networks Keen.com Legato Systems MVP.com Palm Computing PlanetRx Red Hat Software Send.com Viasoft Webvan zipRealty.com

(continues)

Table 8.2   (*continued*)

Venture Capital Firm/Location	Investment Emphasis	Selected Companies Funded
Bessemer Venture Partners Wellesley, MA; Menlo Park, CA; Westbury, NY www.bessemervp.com	E-commerce, communications, optical communications and semiconductors, medical technologies, other	Airtech Arris Pharmaceuticals BabyCenter eToys Flycast Furniture.com InternetDiamonds.com ISIS Pharmaceuticals Summit Microelectronics Lightlogic Lightwave Microsystems Mindspring MotherNature.com PerSeptive Biosystems PowerTel PSI-Net SciQuest.com Sonus Networks Verio VeriSign
CMGI Andover, MA www.cmgi.com	Internet businesses: advertising/marketing; content and community; e-commerce; enabling technologies	AdForce AltaVista Asimba.com Engage Flycast Communications HotLinks Lycos MotherNature.com Oncology.com Productopia SalesLink Tribal Voice Vicinty yesmail.com ZineZone.com

(*continues*)

Table 8.2   *(continued)*

Venture Capital Firm/Location	Investment Emphasis	Selected Companies Funded
Domain Associates Princeton, NJ; Laguna Nigel, CA www.domainvc.com	Life sciences: biopharmaceuticals, drug discovery services, medical devices, instrumentation, diagnostics, advanced materials, healthcare information systems, healthcare services	Ablation Technologies, Inc. Advanced Corneal Systems Amylin Pharmaceuticals Aurora Biosciences Beansprout Networks, Inc. Carecentric Solutions, Inc. Creative Biomolecules, Inc. Dura Pharmaceuticals, Inc. Fusion Medical Technologies Microvention, Inc. Small Molecule Therapteutics, Inc. Trega Biosciences, Inc. U.S. Bioscience, Inc. Vivus, Inc.
Internet Capital Group, Inc. Wayne, PA www.internetcapital.com	Busines-to-business e-commerce: distribution, networks, strategic consulting and systems integration, outsourced service providers	Arbinet Autovia BidCom Breakaway Solutions, Inc. Collabria, Inc. Commerx, Inc. ComputerJobs.com Deja.com, Inc. NetVendor, Inc. PaperExchange.com Synrca Software Tradex Technologies US Interactive, Inc. VerticalNet, Inc. Vivant!
Kleiner Perkins Caulfied & Byers Menlo Park, CA; San Francisco, CA www.kpcb.com	Internet, enterprise software, consumer media, communications, semiconductors, medical devices and diagnostics, drug discovery and therapeutics, healthcare services and informatics	@Home Network amazon.com Brio Technology CalicoCommerce Cardima Cerent Citrix Systems Cypress Semiconductor Della & James drugstore.com eHealthInsurance.com

(continues)

Table 8.2 *(continued)*

Venture Capital Firm/Location	Investment Emphasis	Selected Companies Funded
		e-STEEL
		Excite
		Genentech
		Handspring
		Health Systems Technologies
		Healtheon
		Hire.com
		Homegrocer.com
		Homestore.com
		Intuit
		iVillage
		Juniper Networks
		Ligand
		Lotus
		MMC Networks
		Marimba
		MedRad
		myCFO
		Netscape
		Oncare
		Pharmacopeia
		Realtor.com
		Shiva
		Symantec
		Tivoli Systems
		TriQuint Semiconductor
		VLSI Technology
		VeriSign
		Vividence
		WineShopper
Sequoia Capital Menlo Park, CA www.sequoiacap.com	Information technology and life sciences: semiconductors, communications, software, Internet, computers, services, medical devices, health services, health software	3COM
		Actuate
		Applied Micro Circuits
		Amylin
		Apple Computer
		Banyan Systems
		Benefit Point
		C-Cube Microsystems
		Cardiac Pathways
		Chipshot.com
		Cisco Systems
		CV Therapeutics
		Documentum
		E-Loan

(continues)

Table 8.2   *(continued)*

Venture Capital Firm/Location	Investment Emphasis	Selected Companies Funded
		eToys
		Fusion Medical Technologies
		LSI Logic
		Medicalogic
		Netopia
		Oacis Healthcare
		Penederm
		Perclose
		PlanetRx
		PMC-Sierra
		Quote.com
		SangStat Medical
		Symantec
		Tandem
		VA Linux
		Vitesse Semiconductor
		Vividence
		Webvan
		Yahoo
Sevin Rosen Funds Dallas, TX; Palo Alto, CA www.srfunds.com	Communications, eBusiness infrastructure and solutions, Internet enabled business models, and others	ArQule, Inc. Bridgeway CIENA Corporation Citrix Systems, Inc. Compaq Computer Corp. Cyberonics, Inc. Cypress Semiconductor Lotus Development Corp. OnCare Sentient Networks Silicon Graphics Computer Systems Webridge

teams with great business ideas, which, as they will tell you, are rare. VC firms also like to share the risk with others. Often, when a blue chip name VC firm backs a tech start-up, there is no shortage of other VC firms who will line up at the door for the chance to invest in the same opportunity.

Although they often collaborate on opportunities, VC firms also compete directly at the same time. Not only are they competing to attract investment money from others, they are competing through the companies they support. An example of such competition is drugstore.com and PlanetRx, two online sellers of prescription medicine and pharmacy products. Drugstore.com is backed by Kleiner Perkins, whereas PlanetRx is backed by Sequoia and Benchmark. So although Sequoia and Kleiner Perkins are clearly working in collaboration to support Vividence, they compete in the online pharmacy marketplace. This simultaneous collaboration and competition, commonplace among Fortune 500 companies, is also quite typical for the venture capital community.

What does the involvement of venture capitalists mean for you? As it turns out, a great deal. Obviously, the best thing that can happen to a tech start-up backed by a VC firm is for it to go public. For the VC firm, as well as for all of the company's employees, going public will far and away deliver the highest investment returns. Every so often there has been the rare case of a privately held start-up being bought by another company for greater value than the public stock markets might have placed on it, but such an event is highly unusual. In most cases, everyone involved with the tech start-up—angels, venture capitalists, the founders and employees, and anyone else—would greatly prefer to see the company go public.

On the road to its IPO, the tech start-up's founders have had to give up equity ownership in the company to someone else, namely, the angels and VCs, to help get the company off the ground. The amount of ownership that the company's management gives to investors is that much less ownership to give to others, including you and all other employees. Typically the start-up will allocate a portion of its shares to be distributed to its employees in the form of stock options that will vest over time. The employee pool of options will stay fixed.

However, the company might at some future point issue new shares of stock to give to investors in exchange for funding. In that case, the shares you own or will own, once vested, will become diluted in value. This is part of the risk you take in joining a start-up. It is important for you to know how many fully diluted shares are outstanding when considering a stock option grant as part of a job offer. However, even if you know that total number of shares, it probably will change at some point.

MEZZANINE FUNDING

Mezzanine funding is a loan that often gives the lender the right to take stock in a company at some later point. This loan is usually "subordinated" to other company debt, meaning that the borrowing company's other lenders will be repaid first, although the mezzanine lender is senior to the company's equity holders. The conversion mechanism can take the form of convertible debt, convertible preferred stock, or warrants. In other words, the loan can be converted to common stock in the company in some way, at some price. A mezzanine loan typically has a term of five to ten years. Such a loan may require interim payments of interest only, with the principal on the loan due at the end of the term in a one-time "balloon" payment.

Mezzanine financing is also known as "bridge financing" because it fills a need for a company to "bridge" a period of time, maybe when the firm is still private but is preparing to go public. Why do companies use this type of financing? Depending on the terms negotiated, it offers both the company and the lender a higher degree of flexibility than a purchase of straight equity, which would cost more to the lender and would likely dilute the holdings of all of the company's existing shareholders.

The risk/reward profile of mezzanine financing is between that of straight equity and senior debt in the company. Clearly, straight equity represents the most risk one can take in a company, and senior debt represents the lowest. Mezzanine financing occupies the middle ground between the two. A start-up's management needs to be cautious about the terms it negotiates for mezzanine financing because of the nonfinancial terms that a lender might demand. An example would be a lender who demands a seat on the company's board of directors or other decisionmaking powers that might limit the company in some way.

Another important point about mezzanine financing is that mezzanine loans are usually made to companies who have or will soon have positive cash flow. The projected cash flow of a company, in other words, the money coming into the company, is what a mezzanine lender will use to assess the viability of the company. The more attractive the cash flow projection looks, the greater the likelihood that a mezzanine lender will want to participate. This is important for you because if you go to work for a "dot com" start-up that is losing money hand over fist and is expected to do so for the foreseeable future, you should not expect the company to have an easy time getting mezzanine financing.

There are many different types of providers of mezzanine financing. A variety of institutions, such as banks, funds, investor groups, and even some individuals, are among those who provide mezzanine financing. Often these entities will provide other types of financing to companies as well. The focus of mezzanine lenders can vary widely. They often have their own emphasis within a particular industry or collection of industries. Some, such as San Jose-based Western Technology Investment, specialize in financing high-technology companies.

Others focus on more traditional businesses, providing mezzanine funding as a way to help companies finance inventories or expand their manufacturing capacity. Also, as do venture capitalists and angels, mezzanine providers often have a geographical focus because they like to be physically close to their client companies.

Venture capital firms typically avoid providing mezzanine financing because it involves lower risk, but sometimes they will provide it to later stage start-up companies. Although VCs usually seek to deliver returns superior to those available from other investment options (like mezzanine financing), in some cases, such as when a company is preparing to go public.

Mezzanine lenders often manage institutional money. This money is looking for potentially higher returns than bonds would yield but at a lower risk exposure than owning equity. As an investment option, then, mezzanine financing often allows for the lending manager to have flexibility in terms of the preferred path for managing the investment: to be repaid on the mezzanine loan or to convert the financing into equity in the company at a predetermined price. From the standpoint of the mezzanine lenders, they are enabling other investors in a tech start-up to maximize returns on their equity by providing financial leverage. Because mezzanine financing is effectively a loan, it can be nondilutive or less dilutive to the equity investors in the company.

Mezzanine lenders typically become involved with tech start-ups at the late OI or OA stages. For many start-ups that are growing very rapidly, preparing to go public, or both, mezzanine financing has become an effective way to "bridge the gap." They need the additional capital now, and will repay it later with the proceeds from their expansion, public offering, or both.

Given that the term of a mezzanine loan is generally from five to ten years, the lender's expectation is that it will be repaid within the term period. The borrowing company often makes only interim interest payments until the end of the term, when it makes the one-time "balloon" payment to the lending institution. In the case of companies who are using mezzanine money on an interim basis before going public, they will repay the lender with the proceeds from their initial public offering.

Mezzanine financing can be creative, involving nonfinancial terms. Some of these terms will outline the expectations of the borrowing company. Perhaps a mezzanine lender will want certain decisionmaking powers within the company. Generally, mezzanine lenders expect that their borrowing companies will be successful in their endeavors, which is why they like to build a conversion option into the financing-deal structure, so they can convert the loan to equity at a preset price if they want to. In this way, they can participate in some of the upside by owning equity in the company if it delivers successfully on its plans.

What does the involvement of mezzanine lenders mean for you? Generally speaking, if your start-up is getting mezzanine financing, it's for good reasons. Your firm is probably expanding quickly or getting ready to go public. Although this is not always the case, it is more often so than not. By getting a loan instead of obtaining more equity financing, your company's investors are seeking to protect themselves, and you, from dilution. In other words, they don't want to give up a large chunk of ownership in the company at this stage, and mezzanine financing allows them to get the capital they need for the time being without doing so.

Each of the providers of mezzanine financing listed in Table 8.3 has a slightly different emphasis. As is the case with VC firms, the decisionmakers in these companies all have unique sets of expertise and prefer to finance companies in industries and businesses with which they are familiar. By financing businesses they understand, they are able to reduce their risk further.

TECH START-UP FINANCING AND NETS DEVELOPMENT STAGES

As you contemplate joining a tech start-up firm, you should be aware of how a company's funding and its sources influence the NETS Development Stages. The stage of funding of a given start-up will influence significantly your overall compensation package. Once you know the funding stage of the company as well as its NETS stage, you have powerful insight into whether your personal tolerance threshold is exceeded by the company in question or if it fits your profile. As you read about and talk to different tech start-up companies, you will quickly develop an ability to determine the financing stage and NETS stage of the company.

Table 8.4 illustrates the stages of tech start-up funding and the corresponding NETS stage of development.

Between Birth and Organizational Infancy, there is a direct correlation between the NETS stage and the funding stage of the company. The Pre-birth and Birth stages are funded by angel investors, the founding entrepreneurs themselves, friends and family, or some combination thereof. Typically, there is no venture capital investment at this stage. The Birth stage is also largely driven by the "sweat equity" of the founders, the hard mental and physical work that is so absolutely crucial to the venture at this point. A significant amount of thought and development goes into the

Table 8.3   Selected Mezzanine Funding Providers and Companies Funded

Mezzanine Financing Provider/Location	Investment Emphasis	Selected Companies Funded
Capital for Innovation and Development (CID) Equity Partners Midwest U.S., with offices in Chicago, IL; Columbus, OH; Cincinnati, OH; and Indianapolis, IN www.cidequity.com	Computer systems, software, telecommunications, medical technology and services, manufacturing, financial services, other	Allergenics, Inc. Alta Analytics, Inc. Bristol Corporation International Software Finance, Inc. SciCor, Inc. SPS Commerce The Wholesale Club, Inc.
TA Associates Boston, MA, with offices in Menlo Park, CA; and Pittsburgh, PA www.ta.com	Business services, consumer products and services, financial services, IT media, software, technology	AIM Management BMC Software Continental Cablevision Federal Express Network Associates
Western Technology Investment San Jose, CA www.westerntech.com	Hardware and software technology, life sciences	Banyan Systems Cell Genesys, Inc. Cytotherapeutics Idec Pharmaceuticals Infoseek MIPS Computer Novellus Systems Verisign, Inc.

product concept at this stage. If a prototype cannot be developed successfully, the venture will fail to receive further funding.

The first round of venture capital investment triggers the start-up's transition into Organizational Infancy. At this stage, the company can use the significant funds in its coffers, usually in the amount of several million dollars or more, to hire additional people. It can also purchase additional resources, such as computer servers, laboratory equipment, public relations expertise, office space, or whatever else might be required.

The key challenge to any tech start-up is to manage its growth effectively. This can be an enormous hurdle. Erin Hill saw one of her start-ups raise $25 million in cash and then hire over a hundred new people, only to be sold off at a fire sale price a year later.

Table 8.4   Tech Start-Up Funding and Corresponding NETS Stage of Development

NETS Stage			
Birth	Organizational Infancy (OI)	Organizational Adolescence (OA)	Adulthood
			Initial Public Offering Public equity markets
		Mezzanine Funding (if necessary)	
		Venture Capital Second, third rounds (Series C, D) Additional rounds (if necessary)	
	Venture Capital First round (Series B) funding		
Seed Funding (Series A)			

Bruce Pomfret saw NETs, Inc. ramp up with people, only to shed them by the dozens a matter of months later. Bill Demas at Vividence has noted the incredible emphasis his company has placed on being able to grow to scale and to do so at the appropriate rate.

A start-up's founders should only raise the money they need for a given period of time and no more. If the company is raising more money than it needs, it may not be getting a good deal. If the company has given up too much of its equity to raise more money than it needs now, it may have difficulty selling the appropriate amount of equity at the right price later. Moreover, if the company receives more money than it needs, it will have to put some of that money in the bank or in some short-term investment, where it will earn a low rate of interest. From the company's standpoint, this is not an efficient use of capital. If the company is doing things right and managing its growth effectively, it typically will need to go through multiple rounds of venture financing.

In fact, it is quite common for a tech start-up to go through at least three rounds of venture financing. These rounds, often known as "Series B, C, and D Funding" or "First, Second, and Third Round Funding," correspond to the NETS stages of Infancy and Adolescence. For each round, the company identifies the specific purposes for which it will use the money, usually detailing such information in a presentation or prospectus. New investors will conduct their own due diligence on the start-up, similar to the way you will from a career search standpoint, to assess whether the investment represents an attractive opportunity. The purpose of such due diligence is to verify that the company has represented itself appropriately and to identify unknown risks to the company. In addition to the generally high levels of risk that start-up businesses inherently represent, there can be other risks associated with start-up ventures that investors need to be aware of. Such risks can include lawsuits, patent issues or disputes, or unforeseen financial issues.

Assuming that a VC firm completes its due diligence, it then puts together a valuation, or an opinion about what the company is worth at that point in time. For each round of financing, this valuation figure is what is called a "pre-money" valuation, because it relates to the value of the firm before the new investment is made. The "post-money" valuation relates to the value of the firm immediately after the new investment.

FINANCING TERMINOLOGY YOU NEED TO KNOW

You need to be aware of a number of tech start-up financing terms. They relate to the process by which the value of the company is determined by prospective investors, and ultimately, what the impact is for you and your stock options. You will undoubtedly hear some of them in the course of your conversations with start-up companies.

Valuation

This is the dollar value assigned to the company at a given point in time. A start-up is headed in the right direction when its valuation gets higher with every round of funding. However, by no means does a higher valuation guarantee the company's success, because if the company runs out of cash, then what the last investor paid for the company's shares of stock hardly matters.

Pre-Money Valuation

This is the valuation of a start-up before a given round of financing. VCs will typically assign a pre-money valuation to a start-up in which they are about to invest.

Post-Money Valuation

The valuation of a start-up immediately after a given round of financing is its post-money valuation. A VC firm will typically assign a post-money valuation to the firm based on the pre-money valuation plus the new infusion of capital.

Over time, however, the value of the company will increase due to the improved prospects for the company as well as the new VC expertise and capability. In other words, over time, 1 + 1 does not equal 2, it equals more than 2. As an example, let's say that a company has a pre-money valuation of $20 million. A VC invests $10 million, giving the firm a $30 million post-money valuation. Six months later, the company has signed four deals with partners that substantially enhance its prospects. Additionally, it has grown revenues by 300 percent. This company will no longer have a $30 million valuation. Maybe it now has a $50 million pre-money valuation for its next fundraising round. In other words, the next investor who wants to back the company will have to acquire shares on the basis of the $50 million valuation, not $30 million.

Dilution

In the context of privately held tech start-ups, dilution refers to the devaluing effect of certain events on ownership of a company's stock. The key event that causes dilution of ownership in a tech start-up is the issuance of new shares of company stock. When new company stock is issued, the total number of shares increases. Therefore, if you have 20,000 shares before new stock is issued and the same number of shares afterwards, then your percentage of ownership in the company has been *diluted*. Hopefully, however, the value of your shares has *increased* because the pre-money valuation of the company when you received your shares was much lower than the current post-money valuation. So, although everyone in the company has experienced dilution in their percentage share of company ownership, hopefully the total value of their ownership is greater because the company's valuation is higher now than when the employee shares were distributed.

For publicly traded companies, dilution can also refer to the devaluing effects that certain events may have on the share value of a company's stock. Such events reduce the company's total earnings and, therefore, the value of the company's existing shares. As an example, let's say a publicly traded company acquires another company (often called the "target" company because it is the target of an acquisition) for cash, and that the acquiring company pays some amount above the actual book value of the target company's assets. That incremental amount of money is referred to as *goodwill*. Goodwill has a dilutive or negative effect on the acquiring company's shares of stock because it has to be accounted for on the acquiring company's income statement over time in the form of *amortization*. Having said all of that, many acquisitions in high technology are ultimately not dilutive to the acquiring company's shares of stock because the target company is growing sales and earnings so fast that the total earnings of the combined company are not negatively affected on a per share basis. Often, such acquisitions will actually increase the earnings per share of the acquiring company, in which case they are said to be *accretive*.

Antidilution Protection

Some people within the company, and potentially the early venture round investors, will be given antidilution protection. In other words, their total ownership in the company cannot be diluted, or it will be diluted less than the holdings of others. So, if a founder owns 4 percent of the company and he or she has antidilution protection, then as additional shares of stock are issued, he or she receives additional shares to keep the same percentage of ownership position.

Preferred Stock

Preferred stock has a higher priority in the company's ownership than common stock. Typically, all company employees and founders are given options to buy common stock. Investors will almost always get preferred stock because doing so avoids a tax liability of having to recognize a profit on the increased value of their share ownership based on higher company valuations in later financing rounds. Preferred stock is converted into common stock at a predetermined ratio at the time of the company's IPO.

One other comment about preferred stock is crucial. Venture investors may have secured terms on their preferred stock such that if the company is acquired, they will be guaranteed some level of return beyond their original investment. In other words, if a VC firm invests $10 million, it may have deal terms under which if the firm is acquired, the firm will receive some multiple of its original investment. As an example, let's say that multiple is 2 times. What this means is that your company would have to be acquired for at least $20 million before any of the employees would receive any compensation for their equity in the company. Make absolutely sure you ask start-up management about the terms on the company's preferred stock. You can see that depending on whether a start-up is acquired or goes public, the outcome can have a different result for you as an employee.

Stock Option

The option to acquire stock is granted by the company to its employees. An option is the right to purchase a share of company stock at a preset price, typically called the "strike price." Options vest over a period of time, known as a "vesting schedule."

Strike Price

The strike price is the price above which a stock option is worth money. In other words, an option to purchase a share of stock at a strike price of $10.00 per share is worth $5.00 if the share is trading at $15.00.

Lock-Up Period

The lock-up period is a specified amount of time agreed upon by company management and the underwriters of the company's stock (investment banks) as to how long shareholders must retain their shares of stock before selling them in the open market. It is put in place to show faith by existing company shareholders in the prospects of the company. A typical example of a lock-up agreement is the stipulation that employees must hold their vested options for at least six months after the company's IPO. Underwriters will often ask companies to put in place lock-up stipulations in the event of a company merger as well.

Vesting

Vesting is a measure of ownership of stock options. Options "vest" or become owned over a period of time.

Vesting Schedule

The vesting schedule is the timetable that specifies when the options to acquire company stock are owned by the employee. A three- or four-year vesting schedule is quite common for tech start-ups. Using four years as an example, your options might vest at the rate of 25 percent per year. At the end of one year, you would own 25 percent of your option grant. If you have been granted 20,000 options, under this scenario you would own 5,000 options at the end of year one.

Often, however, the vesting schedule is back-end loaded to encourage people to stay with the company. As an example, let's take your 20,000 option grant from the prior example. Maybe only 22 percent of your options vest per year for the first three years, with 34 percent vesting in the final year. The goal of such an arrangement is to encourage you to stay on for that last year, and this type of schedule puts the economic incentive in place to achieve that end. However, in an increasingly competitive career market, companies are finding they must offer ever-more-favorable vesting terms to employees to recruit them. A three-year vesting cycle is fairly common in 2000, but it was uncommon as recently as 1998.

Convertible

Any source of financing that can be turned into common shares of the company's common stock is said to be convertible. The preferred stock of the tech start-up's investors is convertible. Very often, mezzanine loan financing is also convertible.

WHAT THE TECH START-UP FINANCING PROCESS MEANS TO YOU

In simplest terms, think of the total ownership of the firm as a piece of pie. You own a piece of that pie. As the start-up goes through its process of fundraising, your percentage of that pie will gradually become smaller. However, if the total size of the pie is expanding fast enough, which it should be, then your total piece of the pie will in fact be larger than it was before. This is the underlying philosophy of tech start-up financing.

Let's take your hypothetical option grant of 20,000 options and see what will happen (hopefully) to its value over time. Refer to Table 8.5 to see how the shares of a tech start-up grow in value over time.

Assume that you join a tech start-up at the middle of the OI stage, after one or two rounds of venture financing. Table 8.5 shows that after *all* rounds of venture financing the start-up has a valuation of $80 million. But let's say that you joined when the valuation was $40 million. As part of your job offer, you were given a grant of 20,000 options. Given the valuation of the company at the time you joined, your options have a strike price of $2.00 per share. Your options become valuable, or "in the money," at the point when the company's shares of stock are valued at more than $2.00 per share. In this hypothetical example, if you are granted options at $2.00 per share and the company goes public at a price of $15.00 per share, your options are each worth $13.00 to you at the time of the IPO.

Table 8.5   How Start-Up Ownership Changes with Funding Rounds: An Example

CONSTITUENT	BIRTH Post-Seed Funding Round Shares Owned/ Percent of Total	INFANCY & ADOLESCENCE After All Venture & Other Financing Rounds Shares Owned/ Percent of Total	ADULT Post-IPO Shares Owned/ Percent of Total
Angel Investors	200,000/4%	200,000/1%	200,000/0.9%
Founder Owners and Employees	4,800,000/96%	4,800,000/24%	4,800,000/20.9%
Venture Capitalists	N/A	11,000,000/55%	11,000,000/47.8%
Other Investors	N/A	2,000,000/10%	2,000,000/8.7%
Options Outstanding	N/A	2,000,000/10%	2,000,000/8.7%
Options Available	N/A	N/A	500,000/2.2%
IPO Shares	N/A	N/A	2,500,000/10.8%
(Offered at $15.00 per share)			
Total	5,000,000/100%	20,000,000/100%	23,000,000/100%
Valuation	$1,000,000	$80,000,000	$345,000,000

In all probability, future rounds of financing will dilute your relative percentage of ownership of the company. In other words, the percentage of the company that you own at the time of your original stock option grant will *decrease* with additional rounds of financing. Table 8.5 illustrates that point. Notice what happens to the relative ownership percentage of the angel investors or the founder owners and employees. Although at the seed round, they own the entire company; after the IPO they own a fraction of what they owned at the beginning. Of course, if you're the employees, owning 21 percent of something that is worth $350 million is a lot more attractive than owning 96 percent of something that is worth $1 million!

A disclaimer is in order here. The preceding example briefly outlines what *should* happen with a tech start-up. Most start-up employees will probably agree that the greatest financial achievement to which the tech start-up firm can aspire in its early years is that of an IPO. However, one recent estimate projects that fewer than one in ten venture-backed start-ups actually go public. So, if you join a tech start-up and it is venture backed, there is still at least a 90 percent chance that something other than going public will happen to your company. That's one of the reasons why picking the right tech start-up is so important.

You can learn a lot about management's financial expectations through your interviews. Ask top managers what valuation they expect the company will receive when the company goes public. Ask them their projection of the company's valuation if it is acquired. Ask them how many more rounds of funding they expect to go through before going public or being acquired. Their answers to these questions will help you calibrate your expectations. Although they may avoid giving you specific figures, they should have a point of view. If they don't have "snappy" answers to these questions, then that should tell you something: They don't care as much as you do.

WRAP-UP

You now have an idea of how the process of financing a tech start-up works. Knowing how the process works does not mean you will become a millionaire. However, it should bolster your chances for negotiating a better deal for yourself. You are now in a position to ask the critical financial questions about a given start-up to determine if it's the right place for you. Understanding the financial implications of a tech start-up is imperative. The business fundamentals of the company in question are every bit as important. Investigating the business fundamentals of a tech start-up is the topic of our next chapter.

9

DOING THE RESEARCH

*"Who are you going to work with? What's their philosophy?
Do you agree? What's their product? . . . Take a look at where
the money's coming from. Who's on the board? What kind of
clout do they have? . . . See who you're working with.
. . . How do your work styles mesh? What is going to be your
compensation package?"*

**—JUDY SCHNEIDER, FORMERLY VICE PRESIDENT
OF CONTENT, COMMUNITY, AND PERSONALIZATION,
ONHEALTH, NOW CONSULTANT**

The challenge of pursuing jobs at tech start-ups is that you have to
do much more homework than you would if you were interviewing
with large, well-known companies. The latter are generally household names and there is a wealth of information available about
them. With tech start-ups, this is not at all the case. There is hardly
any available information about them, and their markets may not be
understood with any accuracy. Maybe they have a business model
that's "never been done before." The work required to make a thorough assessment about a given tech start-up is substantial.

Although sizing up a tech start-up can be daunting, you will find
that you get better at it quickly. The interview questions you need
to ask will become routine to you. You will learn to differentiate between a compelling response and a faulty one. Even by just learning
the diligence process for assessing tech start-up companies you ele-
vate your professional capabilities to a higher level. The ability to

perform due diligence on a tech start-up will help you make business decisions quicker, whether or not you ever go to work for one.

GOING IN WITH YOUR EYES OPEN: DOING YOUR DILIGENCE ON TECH START-UPS

What does going in with your eyes open mean? Isn't that how you should approach any interview or career-search process? You bet. But your sensory antennae need to be even more keenly aware for assessing a tech start-up. As you walk through the halls of a tech start-up, take note of everything. Watch the people. How do they talk, move, interact? What is happening?

Going in with your eyes open also refers to your research process. Develop your own point of view about the markets that your prospective tech start-up serves. Is your market projection in line with that of the tech start-up? Why or why not? Talk to as many people as you can about a prospective tech start-up, its markets, and your potential role there.

Before the Interview: Who's Betting on Your Horse?

It goes without saying that you need to prepare for any job interview or negotiation, regardless of the type of company. But in the case of a tech start-up, you want to find out who is backing the firm and its concept. You want to know what the collective marketplace is saying about your prospective tech start-up before you even walk in the door. If you find that the prospects for the company are poor or are too risky for your liking, you don't want to waste your time going through the interview process.

More likely, after doing some research you will find some favorable attributes about a given company but also that you have questions. Doing up-front research enables you to prepare questions that will make you appear knowledgeable about the tech start-up and its marketplace, which, in turn, will make you a more attractive candidate. Moreover, these are key questions to which you need answers to make a more informed decision.

Know Thy VC Firms

"You want to look at who's backing the company. . . If you are some-what risk averse, or want to have a greater degree of success . . . you do reduce the risk profile if you're with a major VC firm . . . venture capital firms like Kleiner Perkins, Benchmark, or Sequoia. . . . Let them do the work for you. They look at hundreds of deals a month and then they . . . pick a few which they want to invest in."

—**Bill Demas, Vice President of Marketing,**
Vividence Corporation

If a tech start-up company has venture capital backing at all, then the firm in question will very likely promote that fact. Such back-ing represents credibility and means that someone believed enough in the firm to be willing to put up big bucks—usually several million dollars—to fund the company, in exchange for a large chunk of ownership, of course. A tech start-up may also seek to impress you and everyone else with the *name* of the VC firm(s) in question to further emphasize its credibility.

Getting information about the VC firms that have funded your prospective firm is valuable for several reasons. First, if the VC firm has a track record, you can check it out, online in most cases. When I considered joining HST, which, like Vividence, was funded by Kleiner Perkins Caulfied & Byers (KPC&B), it was easy for me to dig up information on the firm as well as its track record, which is highly accomplished. I was able to read up on the members of the firm who served on my prospective com-pany's board, as well as various other companies that KPC&B had funded. The list was impressive. KPC&B had helped launch such successful technology companies as Compaq, Intuit, and Genentech.

Second, you can learn about a VC firm's relevant industry expe-rience. Again, much of this information will be available on the Internet from many VC firms. You want to see VCs who have rele-vant industry experience on your prospective firm's board. Having prior industry experience is extremely important because it can save your firm major pain and aggravation if it has access to the high-powered expertise and contacts of its board members. If board members don't have relevant industry experience, then they are less likely to add value.

This brings us to another topic that is important for you to understand: "smart money" versus "dumb money." "Smart money" refers to money that is supplied by people who add value to the company in some way other than just contributing capital. High-tech VC firms are smart money. Ideally, the smart money backs a tech start-up earlier than the dumb money, because the players who understand the opportunity are "smart." The venture investors who bring a company into the Organizational Infancy stage are usually "smart money." In return for their smartness, these earlier-stage investors command a disproportionately large stake of the company relative to investors who join later. These smart investors will add greater value to the company through their experience, expertise, and contacts.

The "dumb money" invests later on. Dumb money refers to capital invested by those who lack the same insight and network as the VCs in the high-tech arena. Many of the major U.S. retail banks and other financial institutions have venture arms that invest in high-tech start-ups, usually at a later stage, and therefore are dumb money. Lacking the expertise, these investors are content to let the "smart money" identify the opportunities for them, and they are willing to take a commensurately smaller slice of the equity pie for their investment. If the company takes off, the dumb-money investors will still profit handsomely, although they will not do as well as the high-tech VCs who are taking on greater risk and contributing more.

The "lead" VC in a given start-up is the firm that makes the initial VC investment and takes on the most risk. It will therefore own a large slice of the company. Regarding the lead VC, a word to the wise comes from our friends on Wall Street: "Past experience is no guarantee of future performance." Often applied to picking stocks, this disclaimer has relevance for VC firms as well. That a blue chip VC firm has backed a bunch of successful companies previously in no way guarantees that its next pick will be a home run. There is a tendency in the career search marketplace for people to assume that because a blue chip VC firm is backing a given company, its success is assured. This is not in any way true, and the VC firms themselves will be the first to confirm that. If a blue chip VC is the lead investor in a given tech start-up, that's a positive sign that should give you confidence as a potential employee and investor of your time and effort in the firm. However, you still need to do your own homework to determine that the start-up in question represents a good opportunity for you and your career.

One helpful insight on VC firms is to know how they think and how they approach their investments. They are betting on numerous companies other than yours in many fields of technology. Your firm represents one of a total *portfolio* of companies: maybe ten, maybe a hundred, maybe more. Just as a rational investor seeks diversification of his or her stock portfolio, so the prudent VC firm diversifies its resources as well.

A fairly common characterization of the VC approach to tech start-ups is as follows. A typical VC firm will invest, say, $30 million in a total of ten start-ups. Each start-up receives an investment of $3 million. Of that portfolio of ten start-ups, the VC firm expects that five or six will go out of business. It expects that three or four will succeed on a mediocre level, which means maybe doubling or tripling the investment of the VC firm. Maybe one start-up will hit a home run, resulting in a return of fifty, sixty, or even hundreds of times its original investment.

VC firms that have been around awhile will have a track record as good as or better than that described above. They have to be incredibly diligent in identifying attractive tech start-up opportunities and management teams on which to place their bets. Moreover, they are often competing with other VC firms for the best opportunities. However, success does breed success to some degree; if your prospective tech start-up's lead VC is a blue chip firm with a great track record, then it will be more attractive to tech start-up entrepreneurs.

There's another important truth for you to know about VC firms: "They're financially driven," notes Prabha Fernandes. "They're there to make money for the people who invest in them. So it's important for people, when they start, to realize that [investors] have put money into you because there's money coming out . . . at the other end of the road." This is a critical point that cannot be overstated. VCs must make a living from their investments. Earning a return on their investments is how they and their investors get paid. Just as the tech start-up has pressure to succeed, the same is true for VCs.

Although this background may seem cautionary or sobering, the fact is that everyone is looking to minimize his or her risk. That's why you bought this book. Having insight into the VC firms who are backing your start-up will reduce your risks as you contemplate joining the firm.

One final comment on reducing risk. Many high-tech investors have a specific approach to investing to help them reduce their risk. In the case of Silicon Valley-based Kleiner Perkins, the approach is that of a "keiretsu," or group of companies that are affiliated through KPC&B and its funding. As a result of being part of the keiretsu, these companies are customers of each other and are able to harness the collective experiences of keiretsu member firms. There are other variations on the keiretsu. The holding company approach is one. Examples of companies taking this approach are publicly traded CMGI Ventures and Internet Capital Group (ICGE). There are doubtless many others taking similar approaches. Being a part of a keiretsu or holding company to be able to leverage the experience of a broader group of companies has big advantages, so be on the lookout to see if the tech start-ups you are considering are a part of any such team of companies.

Your action items regarding VC investors in a given tech start-up are:

1. Identify the lead VC investor in your prospective tech start-up, if any.
2. Learn as much as you can about the VC firm's track record and industry experience.
3. Evaluate the VC firm for reputation and contacts *in the industry.*
4. Evaluate the VC firm based on the perceived level of congruence between the VC firm's track record and expertise and the mission of the tech start-up.

What's the Press Saying?

"You should look . . . in the trade press and see if there's any hype or buzz around either your potential start-up or the idea that they have. It

could be that you're coming on board with a start-up that is being de-
liberately secretive."

—**Bruce Pomfret, formerly Web Programmer,**
Nets, Inc., now Software Engineer,
Perot Systems Corporation

Pay attention to the press and any other public relations releases
that relate to your prospective start-up, its technology, or its markets. To Bruce's point, if the market category is very new, a given
start-up may be somewhat secretive about its approach. However,
in such cases the trade press should have identified some type of
market. From there, you may find out about competing firms.
What you hear, or don't hear, can tell you a lot. Read your prospective firm's press releases and those of the competition. Although
"vaporware" or only partially complete products are commonly
over-hyped in high tech, silence about a product or company, conversely, can be deafening.

Tech start-ups will use press releases for a variety of strategic
reasons. They use press releases as a way to signal a firm's inten-
tions in a market, possibly as a scare tactic to frighten off potential competition. They will also use them to cement the firm's
credibility in a marketplace with prospective customers, competitors, and investors. If your firm competes in a marketplace
that is potentially attractive to giants, you will want to pay particularly close attention through the press to the moves of those
giants.

It can take you a while to get your arms around a marketplace
that is new to you. Reading as much as possible about it will help
you. Bill Demas notes that it takes him about "three to six months
until I feel like I have some sort of intuitive or visceral feel for the
market." That doesn't mean you should do three to six months'
worth of reading before you feel comfortable approaching tech
start-ups about career opportunities, but it does mean that you can
expect to learn on the job.

Your action items in doing your advance homework about a
given tech start-up are:

1. Identify the top three sources of information on your
   prospective tech start-up company.

2. Identify the top three trade sources of information on the firm's market (they may overlap with sources you find for #1).
3. To the best of your ability, identify the three most significant events that have happened to the firm in the past three to six months.

What's the Market Saying?

"You have to . . . do a reality check. . . . To the best of your knowledge, stress test the idea."

—Adrianna Paradiso, formerly Product Manager with NetGrocer, now Director of Marketing, e-STEEL

The market, specifically the customers and competitors of your prospective start-up, will say a lot of things. Your customers want the tech start-up to solve their problems. The competition also wants to solve them. By gathering data from customers and prospects, you can gain insight into the competitive landscape. If a prospective customer is using a competitor's product now, then your firm can gain valuable insight into how your product needs to better address the requirements of the customer in question. However, turnabout is fair play, and your competition is probably doing the same type of diligence against your firm's product.

The market also talks at trade shows and seminars. At such events, competitors may give demonstrations of their products or talk about upcoming products, new features, and enhanced performance. If the industry issues awards, find out who is winning them and why. Similarly, find out who is winning customers and why. You can also learn about the market through trade publications and Web sites.

One final important point regarding the market for the technology itself. Prabha Fernandes observes: "For a product that is first in its class, there is no market. . . . So you've got to realize if you come up with a novel product, you will create the market." It is incredibly important for you to remember that just because you aren't finding much in the way of press or trade buzz about a given product or market, that doesn't mean there isn't a huge opportunity. It may just mean that the giant hasn't awakened yet.

Your action items from a market standpoint are:

- Identify the potential top three customers or groups of customers for the tech start-up's product or service.
- Other than "speed to market," identify the top two or three determinants of success in this marketplace.
- Identify the top three sources for information on this marketplace.

Know Thy Competitors

"You've got to understand your competitors. What do they have over you? How easy is it to duplicate? How well funded are they versus you? What makes them different? Why would you go with [a given tech start-up] versus a competitor?"

—Adrianna Paradiso, formerly Product Manager with
NetGrocer, now Director of Marketing, e-STEEL

Before you decide to join a tech start-up, you need to know a few key details about the firm's competitors to make an informed decision. How many are there? Do they have deeper pockets than the start-up you're considering? What are the key differences between your firm's offering and that of the competition? Can you explain to yourself why a customer would buy your product rather than that of the competition? That's one I wish I had asked myself in retrospect. The firm's business plan may disclose information about the competition, but it may be limited.

In many instances, competitors may be publicly traded companies, in which case the information about them is readily accessible. Publicly traded companies must file documents with the Securities and Exchange Commission (SEC) at regular intervals, and they are required by law to provide this information to anyone who asks for it. You can access the SEC filings of a publicly traded company on EDGAR, the SEC Web site (www.edgar-online.com). You can also call publicly traded companies and request an investor packet containing their annual report and latest 10-K form.

The 10-K form discloses all kinds of valuable information about a company's business, strategies and technology. What a great way to get the inside scoop on the competition! Recognize, of course, that if the market is very new, there may be very limited information available publicly.

Your action items in assessing the competition are:

- If possible, identify the top three competitors of your prospective start-up.
- Identify the advantages your prospective firm has over its competitors.
- If possible, determine how well funded other competitors are versus your firm.
- If possible, find out what customers are saying about your firm versus the competition.

What Do the Industry Trends Tell You?

"Look at other start-ups in this industry. You've got to look at trends."

—**Alan Kitty, President and CEO, LinkTank L.L.C.**

From targeted industry sources such as trade journals, newsletters, and other industry publications, you can gain insight into the industry trends that directly affect your prospective tech start-up firm and its product(s). Additionally, the *Wall Street Journal* and other national newspapers such as the *New York Times* are good for stories on specific industries. The business media can be a good source of information as well. Obviously, the Internet makes literally mountains of information available on your industry, and it is available at your fingertips.

Typically, large and powerful constituents within the industry can influence trends by driving them or attempting to do so. Within your industry, you should familiarize yourself with these constituents, because presumably one of them is your customer base, another is a competitor or a key group of competitors, and another very well may be the government. Other start-ups may be competition for your prospective firm, but you may find a more attractive opportunity at a competitor as opposed to the firm that is recruiting you. Be open to such possibilities.

Your action items on industry trends are:

- Identify the top two to three trends that are driving the growth of your prospective tech start-up's market.
- Identify, if any, the potential competing technologies or companies that could make your company's offering and those like it unnecessary or obsolete.
- Determine whether your tech start-up has the agility to seize a significant piece of the market and to respond to competing technological threats.

What Is the Investment Community Saying?

"We started having investors and analysts coming in."

—John Lindsay, formerly of USData,
now with Microsoft Corporation

Until you actually get inside the doors of the tech start-up in question, it may be difficult to assess whether bankers and prospective investors are roaming its corridors every so often. However, even before you interview with a tech start-up, you can learn what the investment community is saying about a given class of technology or market opportunity. Although in some cases information on a particular firm may be difficult or impossible to obtain, more often than not there will be a publicly traded competitor of a given tech start-up company. If you can identify those competitors, you can check out any of dozens of financial and investor Web sites to see what analysts are saying about those companies.

Investment banks publish equity research reports on various companies and markets that are of interest to investors and to the companies that compete in those markets. At every opportunity you should read those that pertain to your start-up's market or competitors. If you can, get yourself on the mailing lists of banks that produce them. Not all banks will send them out freely on a regular basis, but some will. Many financial institutions are making their research available on the Internet, so this type of information is more widely available than it ever has been before.

One way investment houses make money is to help new firms in an industry like yours go public. That is, they help manage the IPOs of companies, including tech start-up firms. Because banks compete for the right to manage a company's IPO, they also compete in researching various industries and strive to distinguish themselves for high-quality, accurate reports. If they succeed in doing so, they will attract more IPO candidate firms, and therefore earn more money. However, the important take-away for you is that banks have a vested interest in producing *accurate* research reports on nascent firms and their industries. If you have access to information that discusses the dynamics and trends in your industry, you are in a much better position to evaluate the prospects for your firm and its competition.

If you do join a tech start-up, you can take it as a good sign if you see people dressed in expensive suits walking through your company's halls. Most likely, these people are prospective investors in your firm. The heads of these entourages usually have authority to make an investment in your company. Their fancy attire may look out of place in your firm's offices, where most people are wearing blue jeans. Smile at these people anyway. Some of them are paying your bills.

Your action items regarding the investment community are:

- If possible, develop some sense of what investment analysts are saying about the market and companies in it, if any.
- Research publicly traded companies that are either in the target market or the closest thing to it, and assess what investment analysts are saying about them.
- During your interviews, ask what investors or prospective investors have said they like and don't like about the company.

What Are Prospective Partners Saying?

"Make sure the players are respected, well known."

—**Alan Kitty, President and CEO, LinkTank L.L.C.**

As you review the press, trade literature, and press releases about a given marketplace, pay attention to what prospective partners are saying in general. More specifically, see what they are saying about your prospective tech start-up. Figure out the types of firms yours would be likely to partner with. Identify the value that each partner brings to a potential partnership.

Realize, of course, that if you don't know much about the industry in question, you may have no idea who the right partners are or why they might be attractive. However, if you consider where your tech start-up is in the value chain, you can quickly determine some of the areas where a firm might need partnerships. In software, it's other software products, because they have to talk to each other. In biotech, it will usually be a large pharmaceutical company that has a marketing and sales infrastructure to sell products. In e-commerce, it will be a range of software and other e-commerce companies. In materials sciences categories, it will be key suppliers and downstream producers of hardware products.

Because prospective partners have their own interests to look after, they will be struggling with many of the same partnering issues as your prospective firm. They will be trying to figure out who is the best partner for a particular need. To some extent, they are trying to pick the winner of a certain category, just as you are. If your firm already has a few strategic partnerships in place by the time you come on board, so much the better.

To Alan's point above, you always want your prospective partners to be the best possible candidates. Obtaining the best partners in an industry is just one more measure of validation of the tech start-up. To the extent that your firm lands partnerships with well-known, highly respected firms, it enhances its attractiveness to potential investors, customers, and new recruits.

Your action steps on prospective partners are:

- If possible, identify the ideal partners for your firm in key areas.
- Assess the strengths of these partners.
- Evaluate the companies these prospective partners have chosen to work with: your start-up or a competitor.

What Are Colleagues Saying?

"Talk to as many people as you can. Get objective viewpoints."

—Erin Hill, Product Manager, Loudeye.com

What do your friends and associates in the industry say? You may even want to seek counsel of people *outside* the industry. It can be surprising how dynamics in one industry can mirror those of another. Conversely, it can also be informative to understand how and why dynamics in one industry do not work in others. Do these people have insights about current conditions or past events that have a bearing on your firm's industry or situation?

Ask your friends if they have contacts that might have insights for you as well. Getting referrals will augment your knowledge base of the marketplace as well as expand your network. Also, be open to insights from unexpected resources. I once received a call from a headhunter who had a deep level of knowledge of my start-up firm and had a strong opinion about it, which he shared with me. He had served the industry for years and had significant expertise, so his opinion carried weight. In retrospect, his viewpoint was prophetic.

Your action items for talking to colleagues are:

- Get the input of as many people as possible.
- Talk to at least a couple of people you consider experts in the industry.
- Talk to at least one person outside of the industry.
- Ask all of the above to challenge the business model of the tech start-up firm in question.

WRAP-UP

Because most start-ups are not household names, you need to do more research to understand start-up firms and the career opportunities that they represent. Although this research can be cumbersome, you can draw on many different resources to help you with the task: information about VC firms, the business press, the market and competitors, industry trade resources, the investment community, prospective partners, and colleagues in industry. You should treat the challenge of assessing each start-up as a learning experience, one from which you become sharper each time through the process. Hopefully your learning curve will be fast and steep, and very quickly you will identify the key attributes a company needs to present if it is to be successful. Similarly, you will develop a battery of questions that will enable you to determine quickly whether or not a start-up has what it takes.

10

THE INTERVIEW
PROCESS

There's a great deal you can do in advance of your interviews to prepare yourself. Not only can you educate yourself about the firm and its markets, but also, by taking the actions steps I've identified, you should be able to develop a list of follow-up questions. You should cover these in your interviews. You will come across as especially well informed to your interviewers based on these crucial questions you've identified. I appreciate insightful questions from job candidates, and I think most people do.

Although you can develop an "outside-in" view of the tech start-up firm on your own, you really can't develop a totally informed opinion until you meet with the company's management face-to-face. From the interview process, you will gain critical information that would be virtually impossible to obtain any other way. Therefore, the interview process represents a massive opportunity for you. Make the most of it.

Your goal for the interview is to validate the firm's thinking against your own. How does the "inside" story of this tech start-up compare to your "outside in" view? If you've done thorough advance homework, the interviews will help to sharpen your picture of the company and its opportunity. If you find that there are major disconnects, you should either seek to clarify them or move on to other, more attractive opportunities.

BUSINESS PLAN

"What business are you in? How are you going to make money? What's your unfair advantage?"

—Erin Hill, Product Manager, Loudeye.com

Read the company's business plan. They should have one. Ask to borrow a copy. You may have to sign a confidentiality agreement to do so. If the company isn't willing to lend you a copy of its business plan, then you aren't willing to work there. It's that simple.

Assess the business plan for quality. Is it logical and easy to understand? Is it obvious to you that there is a market for the company's product? Do you follow the business model? Does it make sense? If you can't understand it, then you certainly shouldn't sign up to support it. Also, if company managers can't convince you of the viability of the plan, then they most likely won't be able to convince investors, either.

After reading various sections about the company, the product, the market the company intends to serve, and the management team, you will see a bunch of numbers in the business plan, most likely some type of pro forma (read "estimated") revenues, expenses, and earnings for several years into the future. Do the numbers look realistic? It may be difficult to tell. You can only begin answering this question by answering those listed above. You also need to know how the product is priced, information that should be contained in the business plan. Then you need to determine if the previously described market would actually buy this product at the price given. Your answer should be based on what the business plan says about competing products and your understanding of the marketplace.

A cautionary note is in order here. Adrianna Paradiso observes that you have to test the company's financial projections and that it's always going to take longer than you think it will for the company to generate sales. This is a highly relevant observation. When I joined HST, I took the business plan sales forecast and lowered it to *one-half* the level of the stated sales forecast. My assumption going in was that we would deliver half of the sales projection in the same time frame. As it turned out, even half was too high an expectation. My recommendation is that you reduce the sales projection of any tech start-up you deal with by one-half to two-thirds. Then see if the firm's sales growth will be sufficient to keep the company up and running, either from its own sales or because even the lower sales projection would still attract new investment. If you believe this would be the case, then the sales projection passes your stress test. I have seen many, many tech start-ups with ridiculously over-inflated sales projections. A healthy sense of skepticism will always help you when reviewing start-up sales projections.

The business plan will also describe key managers within the company and their backgrounds in some detail. The connection between their past experience and their current roles should be highly evident to you from reading the plan. If it isn't, that should raise a red flag.

Your action items regarding the business plan are:

- Get a copy of the company's business plan.
- Read it and determine whether you understand it and believe its assumptions.
- Perform the reduced-sales test: Even at your lower projected revenue growth rate, does the company represent an attractive opportunity?

MANAGEMENT TEAM AND BOARD

"How do they compare with others in the field? How do others regard their abilities? What does their track record look like? If someone has done something successfully . . . fifteen times, I wouldn't be hesitating too long."

—Alan Kitty, President and CEO, LinkTank, L.L.C.

Hopefully you will gain greater insight into the management team by meeting with several of their ranks over the course of your interview process. You should expect them to talk in fairly forward-thinking terms about "when" the company reaches various milestones, enters new markets, and acquires other companies. Although these notions may seem ludicrous to you while sitting in a cramped, unglamorous room or cube that houses one of the company's ranking execs, they will discuss these events as foregone conclusions, and they should. That's why they were hired. The odds are good that they have grown companies much like yours from the ground up before. They've seen the movie before and they liked it, so they came back to see it again.

Your conversation will resonate with them if you engage in similar, forward-thinking dialogue about how you will help the company achieve the success they have already painted in their minds. The management team was hired to guide the company up a steep growth curve, and they seek to hire people who share their view of the future. Look for clues about management chemistry. Alan Kitty and Judy Schneider point out that it's incredibly important. Poor management chemistry can kill a company.

Learn about the past roles and track records of your firm's management team. Look for consistent themes of success: executing against plans, delivering results, and generally building successful companies. More than anything else, the grand prize for a tech start-up is to become a long-term, sustainable business *that makes money*. When that happens, the success is usually bigger than anybody thought it would be.

Ask your prospective firm's managers what their biggest failures have been and what they learned from the experience. If they're good, they won't even hesitate when they respond to your question. They will tell you very specifically what they or a previous company did wrong and what they personally took away from the experience. The response may almost seem rehearsed, and that's no coincidence. They've probably had more than a few opportunities to share their learning with others. Be prepared for tech start-up managers to ask you about your past failures and lessons learned as well. Although these are fairly standard interview questions at almost any company, their meaning carries more weight in a tech start-up, where the learning you take away from a mistake is hugely important.

Although everyone wants to avoid making mistakes in a tech start-up, be wary of managers who seem intolerant of mistakes. Any technology veteran will know that mistakes are inevitable in a tech start-up and that the speed with which you respond is what makes the difference. Every person quoted in this book agrees that you learn more by failing than you do by succeeding in your first efforts. In a tech start-up, you generally get a second chance to get the right result. You should seek managers who believe strongly in second chances.

Pay attention to different personalities and behavior styles as you go through the interview process. Bruce Pomfret and Erin Hill offer the useful observation that the people whom you like the most initially may not be the ones with whom you get along with best later on. In fact, both have observed that some of the people whom they liked least in their interviews turned out to be some of their best coworkers, people whom they grew to respect a great deal. This does not mean you should set out to work with people who rub you the wrong way. Rather, it implies that the degree to which you like someone in the interview process is not a great indicator of how well you will work together. If you focus your questions on work styles, hopefully you can reduce your risk of ending up with a lemon for a management team.

You also reduce your risk if you join a management team that is older and more experienced. Your opportunities to learn from a highly seasoned management team are great in such a scenario, but your financial upside may be lower. If you are considering joining a tech start-up for the first time, that trade-off may be well worth making. You'll be getting to learn from a whole bunch of other peoples' experiences, which you'll get to use for the rest of your career. Not a bad deal.

To ensure that you align yourself with a start-up management team that has what it takes to succeed, Adrianna Paradiso and John Lindsay advise that you probe for management's ability to adapt and their understanding of the firm's technology. Adaptability is important to react and respond to quick and potentially unforeseen changes in the marketplace that could threaten your start-up's technology or business model. Management's understanding of the technology is critical to know what is possible in the event of sudden market changes. John notes that he's seen companies run aground whose management teams did not understand the technology thoroughly enough. The board should add value in these areas as well.

As for the tech start-up's board of directors, you already know that there will probably be a few venture capitalists among the ranks. They should be contributing the same degree of value as the firm's management team. Their past experiences and contacts should show demonstrable benefits to the tech start-up. As you know, their track records as eminent players in the industry are important.

The board will also have at least one manager from the tech start-up firm in its membership. Find out who from the tech start-up management team sits on the board. At a minimum, the CEO of the company will be on the board. If he or she isn't, find out why. Such a situation is highly unusual.

It can be helpful to have non-venture-capitalists on a firm's board, especially if such people have deep industry experience. They can often help bring a dose of reality to potentially antsy VCs who panic every time a sales projection is missed. Sometimes a tech start-up will establish an "advisory board," comprising not the firm's investors but rather an outside group of industry experts or "opinion leaders" who lend credibility to the firm. In exchange for associating with the tech start-up, these people may hope to gain consulting or speaking deals and possibly some direct compensation from the firm.

Your action items regarding the management team and board are:

- Rate the quality of the firm's management team as a whole.
- Envision yourself working with this team: Does this situation work for you?
- Evaluate the track record of top managers. Have they achieved past successes? Have they learned from their mistakes?
- Understand how the firm's board of directors is adding value to the firm.

COMPETING COMPANIES
AND TECHNOLOGIES

"[The company] may be doing better than their competitors, but they may be in a dying industry."

—Bruce Pomfret, formerly Web Programmer, Nets, Inc.,
now Software Engineer,
Perot Systems

You already know there is much you can do to assess the competition before you even show up for the interview, but it is also critical for you to know how management views its competitors. Find out whom they view as their top three competitors. Are the competitors they name the same ones you found in your research? At least a few should be. Management should be able to talk in depth about their strengths and weaknesses. This is the kind of stuff you won't necessarily be able to pull off a Web site. Do your interviews with management augment your understanding of the competitive landscape? They should.

Beyond the firms identified as existing competitors, are there other technologies or product concepts that have emerged that could make those of your tech start-up obsolete? Tactfully find out what your prospective firm's managers know about other potential competing technologies and how they intend to keep the firm on top. You may learn things from this conversation that you did not know. Have you heard anything that changes your outlook for the company or its marketplace? If this firm has its act together, then you will be favorably impressed and feel more reassured about its prospects. However, recognize that some interviews may lead you to a different conclusion: that the company lacks a compelling case.

Your action items on competing companies and technologies are:

- Do you agree with management's perceptions of who their competitors are?
- If possible, determine if there are risks of this company's technology being made obsolete by that of another.

- Determine if managers' track records show flexibility in dealing with constantly evolving market dynamics.

MARKET LEADERSHIP

"If you look at [new technology] markets right now . . . basically there's a number one and a number two player and everybody else is, on a relative basis, not nearly as successful. Can the company be the number one or two player in that category?"

—Bill Demas, Vice President of Marketing,
Vividence Corporation

Beware the tech start-up manager who says, "It's a huge market out there. All we need is to capture a very small market share and we've got it made." For most markets, this statement is generally inaccurate. In tech start-ups, it's even less accurate. The lion's share of market dollars, especially in tech start-ups, is allocated by customers to the one or two top competitors in a marketplace because these competitors are doing the best job of meeting customer needs.

Therefore, your goal is to identify companies who have an excellent chance at being first or second in terms of market share. Ideally, these will be big markets, in the billions of dollars in size. Although it is an oft-used trick in corporate America for business entities to define their markets in a way that makes them appear to have a leadership position, most people aren't fooled. The reason you want the market potential to be huge is so that as the market evolves, if it does become segmented to some degree, your firm will still be able to carve out a large piece of it.

Your action items for assessing prospects for market leadership are:

- Determine if the company has the potential to be a number one or two competitor in its market.
- Understand why it has market leadership potential and why competing companies may not.

SELLING

"In the end, you're not going to get big contracts because you know somebody. . . . I was the person . . . put in front of these people . . . to sell them on the technology."

—John Lindsay, formerly of USData,
now with Microsoft Corporation

Selling is absolutely mission critical to the tech start-up. Your firm could have the best technology in the world, but absent a capable sales force to sell it, the firm will flop. Conversely, your firm could have inferior technology, but as long as it has the better sales force, it can compete successfully. To sell successfully, the sales force has to understand the needs of the customer. In high tech, it can be tough to stay on top of customer needs because businesses and technologies change so fast.

It's incredibly important for you to understand the customer needs of your potential start-up and the degree to which the firm meets them. During your interviews, find out what management believes are the priority customer needs for this class of technology. You may find that this company is the odds-on favorite to win in a given market, or you may find that someone else has the lead.

Your action items for determining the firm's selling capabilities are:

- Determine what management believes to be the three top customer needs in this market.
- Determine how effectively the firm can deliver against those needs, and if it has a lead on the competition.
- Understand the track record of the company sales force, or what its hiring strategy will be when it gets to the point of needing one.

ASSESSING WHAT YOU LEARN — AND HOW TO USE IT

Going through the interview process at a tech start-up company, you will learn much about the firm, its prospects, and its marketplace. As you near the end of the interview process, consider whether the start-up in question has presented a compelling case and if it really excites you. Although of course you can't turn a company down if you don't have a job offer, you need to make a quick mental "go or no go" decision about whether you want to pursue the opportunity.

When a tech start-up identifies an attractive candidate, it usually moves very fast to make an offer to try to close the deal. Hopefully, you will have lined up many interviews simultaneously so you can try to manage your pipeline of job leads, ideally landing several job offers at once to give yourself a few options. Beyond giving yourself a choice, interviewing at many firms offers you three benefits: You get very good at interviewing, you learn about a number of different companies and business models, and you sharpen your ability to determine what works and what doesn't from a business standpoint.

ASSESSING THE CONSISTENCY OF WHAT YOU'VE LEARNED IN YOUR INTERVIEWS

"Have them lay out for you what their plans are. How are they going to get from here to there? What other companies have done this and how successful have they been? I think that if you do your research . . . you know walking out of a place whether you feel good about it."

—John Lindsay, formerly of USData,
now with Microsoft Corporation

Seek to check the consistency of what you learned in your interviews in two ways. First, you want to compare what you heard and what you learned about the company with what you learned in your own advance research. Second, you want to check the consistency of the feedback you received from each person at the start-up with that of each person's coworkers. These two checks will help you a great deal in assessing whether the start-up in question is attractive to you.

First, have the interviews validated what you already knew from your advance research? Have they filled in missing details about the company that help give you a clearer understanding of its over-all potential? If they do, that's a good sign. You had a hypothesis about the company going into your interviews, and what you learned validated what you already believed and gave you greater insight into the opportunity. You are now convinced that you read the situation correctly.

Conversely, if you are confused by the interviews, and what you learn from them is inconsistent with what you knew about the company beforehand, then you need to reconsider your assessment of the company. It may be that you had developed a negative view of the company from your advance research, and through the inter-views, many of the reasons for that were dispelled. In that case, the company has exceeded your expectations. However, if you have a fa-vorable view of the company going into the interviews and become confused about key aspects of the company during the process, then the company has fallen short of your expectations. It happens.

You should not be afraid to upgrade or downgrade your opinion based on what you learn during the interviews. It happens all the time. Don't doubt your own abilities to make such judgments. This is your career, and you're in the driver's seat. It may be that although the category of technology you are exploring is highly at-tractive, the particular company with which you are interviewing is not the odds-on favorite.

OTHER COMPANIES: IS THERE A MORE ATTRACTIVE SITUATION?

"Be willing to read and learn about the marketplace, and be willing to change with the times, because the marketplace changes very rapidly."

— **Prabha Fernandes, President and CEO,**
Small Molecule Therapeutics

Other Companies in the Same Category

Consider other companies in the same technology category. Perhaps there is a specific category of technology to which you are attracted, or maybe you have a specialization in a particular field. If you have a strong interest in one technology category, then be open to exploring different companies in that category. Just because one tech start-up looks like it lacks the winning formula doesn't mean another will. If you have identified a technology category that you are convinced is going to explode, then you need to find the one or two companies that will become the market leaders.

Be open to the idea that the odds-on favorite in a given technology category could, in fact, be a larger, more established company. Bill Demas is quick to point out that many large technology companies, such as Microsoft, IBM, Intel, and Dell, pursue new opportunities internally through "intrapreneurial" efforts. In fact, you can gain tremendous experience from such opportunities. There are more than a few managers at tech start-ups today who cut their teeth building new businesses while working for larger companies.

But, you say, if I go join a larger company, then I lose out on all that potential upside in stock options. That may be true, but you may also be paid a significantly larger base salary and stand to gain phenomenal experience that you can take to a start-up later. If you really are leaning towards the start-up, and you know that there are some larger companies getting into the same market, then you need to consider carefully how and why your tech start-up will survive. If it can't, your stock options won't be worth anything anyway. I'm not trying to dissuade you from joining a start-up when you know your company is going to go head-to-head with large, deep-pocketed competitors. Tech start-ups can and do win against larger companies in many David versus Goliath battles. However, they also lose, and when they do, you are looking for a new job.

Other Companies in Other Categories

Consider other companies in different technology categories. Another piece if knowledge you may take away from your interviews with tech start-ups is that there is a different technology category that has great appeal. Perhaps there is a different company that everyone is raving about. The interview process is about far more than you looking for a job. It is a golden opportunity for you to gather and assimilate information about new opportunities. It's also fun. Make the most of it.

Just as you shouldn't be afraid to revise your opinion of a given company after interviewing, neither should you be afraid of deciding that you'd rather pursue another company or category of technology. From the interview process, you can learn much about why a certain product or technology will or won't win. If you decide one company or technology is not destined for success, you become that much smarter when you go to subsequent interviews and can articulate what attracted you to that next company. It also shows that you take your career seriously and are being selective about the types of opportunities you will consider.

WRAP-UP

The interview process affords you the opportunity to drill down on the firm's business plan and to explore its management team and board, competing firms and technologies, market leaders, and selling dynamics. From what you learn, you can paint a picture of the firm's prospects. The interview process also helps you to identify whether there are more attractive opportunities with competing firms or with other firms in different fields altogether. By going into the interview process with your eyes open and doing some diligence on prospective companies up front, you can develop a hypothesis about a company and its marketplace. The interview process gives you an opportunity to test your hypothesis, as well as to determine if the role and responsibility of a given opportunity are right for you.

Sizing up a start-up involves a lot of work. However, if you are willing to put in the effort to identify the best opportunities for you, the experience will prove richly rewarding. The career benefits you can gain from the tech start-up experience are difficult to quantify, but if you are selective in the opportunities you pursue, you will reap the dividends. The tech start-up experience will benefit you over the course of your career.

11

NEGOTIATING THE JOB OFFER

There are a few important things you need to know before engaging in any serious discussions to work for a technology start-up. First, know beforehand the general terms you are looking for in an offer. Consider the salary range you want, possible bonuses, and other benefits. Also consider what type of stock option package you believe you are worth. Consider other personal matters as well, such as whether you will you be relocating for the job. Although it may be difficult for you to know exactly what you are looking for, you do yourself a disservice by not thinking about it beforehand. The saying, "If you don't ask for it, you won't get it" applies to all job offer negotiations, especially those involving tech start-ups. You need to set some mental guidelines to know whether you are getting an attractive offer or one that you can't live with.

Second, defer any discussion of the terms of a job offer until you *have* a job offer. Get the job offer in writing. Unless you have a letter in writing, you don't have an offer. The negotiation from your end starts once you have a letter of offer in hand, and not before. You will probably be asked questions such as "What salary range are you looking for?" before you get an offer. Simply defer the discussion by saying, "I'm looking for a package that is commensurate with what other start-ups in this industry are offering someone with my skills and experience. I'm sure you have a good sense for what that is." If the interviewer responds that he or she doesn't know what is commensurate with the industry, then you may not want to waste your time with that company. A start-up's team should know what it takes to be competitive in their market. If they don't know that much, then there may be much more that they don't know. If you have to educate the firm on what they need to pay someone like yourself, then you probably have an uphill battle in front of you.

When the offer is presented to you, graciously listen to it, then ask for some time to consider it. If a letter of offer is not presented at the time the offer is made to you verbally, ask for the letter. You don't have to negotiate a reply date with the company until you actually have the letter in hand, because once again, until you have a letter, technically you don't have a job offer.

For positions that are not top-level management jobs, a firm should be willing to give you at least a week to consider the offer. You may even ask for two weeks, although in the world of tech start-ups, that's a long time. If the position in question is a senior-level management position, two to four weeks is quite reasonable, especially because you may use much of that time negotiating the offer, and attorneys may be involved. You always want to buy yourself some time when considering a job offer, not only to think about the offer itself but also to see if other offers will materialize in the near-term or to compare offers.

From a timing standpoint, you need to be sensitive to managing your decision process. Although you want to delay responding to an offer too quickly if you are still waiting on another, you want to avoid stalling for too long. If you receive an offer and are waiting on another, ask that firm's recruiter if the company can expedite the process. If they are genuinely interested in you, they will try to accommodate your request.

IS THERE ROOM TO DISCUSS THE ARRANGEMENT?

There's more than just a salary to negotiate. There is at least as much as if not more room to negotiate a job offer with a tech start-up than with a larger, more stable firm. Although a tech start-up may have less latitude to work with than a large firm purely in terms of salary considerations, they often have more flexibility to negotiate bonuses and other non-cash items to attract good candidates. Therefore, think of a job offer from a tech start-up as an opportunity for you to be creative in structuring a job offer that is attractive to you. You may not get what you ask for, but you may be amazed at what is possible. People have negotiated for flexible work schedules, days off in the middle of the week, and all sorts of different arrangements at tech start-ups.

Compare the offer to your expectations. Once you have the offer, think about what you had considered as reasonably acceptable. How does this offer stack up? Think about its different components. How does the base salary look? Depending on where the base salary is relative to your expectations, decide how you want to address it. It may be fine where it is, or you may simply need to ask for 5 or 10 percent more. However, if the salary offer is substantially lower than what you are hoping for, you may need to consider whether you want to negotiate the offer with the company at all or turn it down outright. I have turned down such offers before. It happens. Provided you do not have an extravagant lifestyle, you should not have to materially change the way you live on a day-to-day basis to take a job. It's that simple. Most people would never be happy in such a situation.

Consider a potential signing bonus or possible performance bonuses. What a tech start-up firm is not willing to give you in base salary it may be willing to give you in the form of a one-time signing bonus or on the basis of achieving performance targets. The practice is quite common in tech start-ups. There is a lot of opportunity for creativity here. Think about your specific situation to determine what might be reasonable in terms of either a signing bonus or possible performance bonuses.

Consider other elements of a package. Are you expecting the firm to move you for the opportunity? For anything below senior-level management positions, this is fairly uncommon. What are you offered in terms of health care and other benefits, such as vacation days? Vacation is a good leverage point to use when negotiating salary. If the firm is unwilling to give you what you had hoped for in terms of base salary, you can use that as a justification for getting more vacation days. This is not to imply that you'll get to use all of your vacation days at a tech start-up, because you probably won't. However, it's nice to know you have the extra time if you want it. If you are a highly prized candidate, you can be very creative in terms of setting your work schedule. Maybe you want Tuesdays and Wednesdays off instead of Saturdays and Sundays.

For senior management positions, you will probably need to get yourself a lawyer to write up an employment contract. If you're a highly valued executive, you will need an agreement with teeth because your opportunity costs are especially high. Among other things to consider in an employment contract, you should demand, and get, a salary guarantee for some period of time if you are terminated without cause. You will also want to negotiate for an equity stake in the company appropriate to your position and industry. Even though market conditions are always changing, a good attorney familiar with employment contracts should be able to help you determine normal practices for the industry at the time. There may be other considerations if you are in this situation, and an attorney familiar with employment contracts should be able to give you the guidance you need.

There's plenty of room in which to discuss an arrangement if you land several offers at once. Although it is great to be in the position of having more than one job offer, you don't want to escalate the situation into a bidding war. It is okay to let firms know that you have multiple offers, but although you may go through one or two rounds of offers and counter offers, it is unwise to keep going around in circles because it will annoy people. Also, when you get to a point where you have negotiated the package that you want and can reasonably expect, or even potentially more than that, that's a good time to end negotiations.

If you know one firm is unable to compete with others for your services, let the company know that. Don't keep it on the line. You are potentially helping the firm in two ways: You are showing it that it may not be competitive in the marketplace, and you are saving it from wasting time and energy trying to recruit you when there is no way it will win. Another bonus for you is ego satisfaction: A company couldn't afford you? Don't let it go to your head, but yes, you can look especially valuable to companies when you tell them politely that you can command far more than they are offering.

JUST HOW MUCH STOCK SHOULD YOU PUT IN THOSE STOCK OPTIONS?

Stock options are a special topic in the tech start-up universe. They're one of the big draws. You read all the time about people joining tech start-ups and getting rich from stock options in IPOs. There's part of you that is magnetically attracted to the potential of those stock options. You're hungry and you want to get rich, too. That's good. You're a card-carrying member of the new economy capitalist system, which is all about taking risks and realizing a handsome reward for those risks—and for your hard work, of course. How much are those stock options worth? Nobody knows, nor would anybody within a firm want to be held to an estimate. But you owe it to yourself to make an intelligent guess about what they could be worth.

One thing that amazes me about some people I've talked to who work at tech start-ups is that they haven't bothered to try to figure out the potential value of their stock options. They have *no idea* of their potential value. This is perplexing to me. If the stock options represent the single largest component of your economic upside at the company, don't you owe it to yourself to estimate what their value could be?

Bill Demas has recently gone through the offer negotiation process at Vividence Corporation. His insight on the topic of stock options is enlightening:

> Down in Silicon Valley, there's a real understanding that most of your compensation is going to be based in the equity and not in the salary. As a start-up, you need to conserve cash so the salary that you get at a start-up is going to be below maybe what your skill set would [command] at a Fortune 500 company. The issue becomes the equity: What percentage of the company is that? So one piece of advice I have is that as you're looking at a company, ask for the number of fully diluted shares. . . it's not so much the number of shares

[now], you want the *fully diluted* shares in the company . . . [including all] pools of stock. So typically this turns out to be a bit of a longer conversation. You also need to understand the risk profile of your company.

Bill underscores a number of important points about stock option compensation that are totally relevant anywhere, in Silicon Valley and beyond.

First, there is a salary-equity trade-off in a tech start-up. Although it is not a rule that you will be paid less at a tech start-up in base salary than you would at a larger firm, it is true more often than not. This does not mean you have to accept a pay cut to work at a tech start-up, but you probably could earn a higher base salary somewhere else. The issuing of stock options is designed to compensate you for that opportunity cost.

Second, a key question you need to ask of your prospective tech start-up is: What is the total number of fully diluted shares outstanding of the company's stock? Within the company's capitalization structure, in other words, the combination of funds that the firm has raised, there may be different classes of stock, including preferred shares that are convertible into common shares. The company may have debt that is also convertible into common shares of stock. You don't need to know all the vagaries of financing, but you need to find out the firm's total number of fully diluted shares. How many shares of common stock will there be if all classes of stock and debt are converted into common shares? Once you know that number, you then have a basis for determining what percentage of the company you will own through your stock option grant. Calculate your percentage of company ownership by taking the stock option grant the company has offered you and dividing it by the total number of fully diluted shares outstanding in the company:

$$\text{Your Percentage of Company Stock Potential Ownership} = \frac{\text{Number of Stock Options You Are Offered}}{\text{Total Number of Fully Diluted Company Shares Outstanding}}$$

The ownership figure is *potential* because you don't own your shares yet. Moreover, those shares will probably become diluted, as you know. You have been offered options to purchase them, so they have been earmarked for you. The percentage of potential ownership calculation is fundamental for you to consider once you have received a job offer from a tech start-up. Depending on your role within the organization and the stage of the start-up, your percentage will vary. If you are a senior executive, your stake of potential equity ownership may be 5 percent or more. If you are employee number 125 in the company, your percentage will be smaller, possibly in the tenths, hundredths, or even thousandths of a percentage. Even an ownership stake of this size can be worth a significant amount of money if the company goes public at a large market valuation.

In part, your stock option grant will be based on how much risk you are taking in joining the company. Bill Demas refers above to the company's risk profile, and as you already know, the earlier the stage of the tech start-up when you join, the greater the risk you incur. Therefore, the greater your share of equity ownership is likely to be. If you join later, there is less risk, and therefore your option grant is likely to be a smaller percentage than that of those in a similar position who joined the company before you.

Let's assume that you were offered 50,000 options in a company. Let's also assume that the total number of fully diluted shares in the company is 50 million. Your percentage of potential ownership in the company would be:

$$\frac{50{,}000 \text{ options}}{50{,}000{,}000 \text{ shares outstanding}} = 0.001 \text{ or } 0.1\%$$

You should also estimate the market valuation of the company. To do this you need some estimate of the company's potential in either sales or earnings. For many tech companies, the sales figure is the more relevant variable to use, because many do not have meaningful earnings yet, nor will they for at least a few years. Let's take a time horizon of four years, because at that time you may be in a position to cash in some of those stock options.

Let's say that you expect that four years from now the company will have revenues of $50 million. By looking at the way the stock market is trading stocks in the same or comparable industries as your tech start-up, you see that it places a value on similar types of companies at ten times sales. Using that multiple of ten times sales, you project that the firm's market valuation will be

$$\$50 \text{ million} \times 10 = \$500 \text{ million}$$

You realize that this is only an estimate, but there is some logic in your method for calculating it.

Using the results of these calculations, you can now estimate what your options might be worth. The value per share under these assumptions is:

$$\frac{\$500 \text{ million}}{50 \text{ million shares}} = \$10 \text{ per share}$$

So, at $10 per share, your options would be worth:

$$\$10 \text{ per share} \times 50,000 \text{ shares} = \$500,000$$

Of course, your options will have some cost, which will be the *strike price,* the price at which you can exercise your option to purchase shares of the company's stock. In this example, let's assume your strike price is $0.10. That means your option value net of cost would be:

$$\$500,000 - (\$0.10 \times 50,000) = \$495,000$$

$495,000 plus whatever annual salary you earn over a four-year period? Not bad, eh? But keep in mind that this option value number changes dramatically under a less optimistic scenario.

Ideally you want to develop a range of potential outcomes to give yourself a weighted average potential value of your options. Let's say the firm will be doing only $8 million in sales in four years. In that case, at ten times sales, it would have a market value

Table 11.1   Calculating Probability-Weighted Option Value

Market Value of Company	Implied Share Price	Option Value	x	Probability	=	Expected Option Value
The company market value . . .	Gives you an implied price per share . . . (Take market value and divide by number of fully diluted shares outstanding.)	Which you use to calculate the value of your options at this market value (Take price per share and multiply by your number of options.)		Which, multiplied by a probability . . .		Gives you an expected or probability-weighted option value
$2,000,000,000	$40.00	$2,000,000		0.05		$100,000
$1,000,000,000	$20.00	$1,000,000		0.05		$50,000
$500,000,000	$10.00	$500,000		0.05		$25,000
$200,000,000	$4.00	$100,000		0.05		$5,000
$80,000,000	$1.60	$80,000		0.05		$4,000
$0	$0.00	$0		0.75		$0
TOTALS				1.00		$184,000

of $80 million, and your holdings would be worth $80,000. And, of course, the value of your options will be zero if the company's market value is zero. The range of possible outcomes means there is a similar range in the potential value of your stock options.

Table 11.1 is a hypothetical look at probabilities of those stock options that provides some idea of the weighted average value of those options.

Based on a range of potential outcomes, and attempting to assign some probability to those outcomes, you see that the probability-weighted average value of your stock options under this set of assumptions is $184,000. Does this guarantee that your options will be worth $184,000? Absolutely not. As you can see, there is a very good chance that your options will be worth zero. A 0.75 probability that the company is worth zero means that if you have a four-sided die, three times out of four, or 75 percent of the time, the roll of the die will yield zero. Only in one out of four rolls, or 25 percent of the time, will it yield something other than zero.

Based on this hypothetical scenario, the weighted average of potential outcomes equals $184,000. What this weighted average number gives you is some sense of the order of magnitude that the value of your options might achieve. To figure your net option value, you need to remember to subtract the cost of exercising your options (your strike price times the number of options). With just a 5 percent chance that your options will be worth $2 million, you probably shouldn't go out and buy a mansion and assume you will make the down payment with the windfall from your stock options. By performing this probability-weighted option value analysis, you will be able to frame your expectations of what your options *might* be worth someday.

If your company is acquired rather than going public, the same calculations apply. Let's say your firm is acquired for $80 million. In this example, the windfall on your options would be $80,000 less your purchase price. Start-up companies typically are acquired for lesser values than those at which they go public, although this is not always the case. However, for the lower market valuation figures in your range, you might assign higher probabilities, assuming that the likelihood of being acquired is greater at a lower price. So, in the example above, you might assign the $80 million valuation a probability of, say, 10 percent, and reduce the probabilities of some of the higher valuation figures to account for the possibility of being acquired.

How does this example square with the twenty and thirty-something billionaires you read about? The reality is that those people are the statistical outliers. They are the exceptions to the outcomes realized by the vast majority of people. That's why they're news. They took very high risks, and joined, or more likely founded, a tech start-up company very early on. For taking enormous risks by joining a tech start-up at a very early stage, they were granted a large number of options. In contrast, by ending up with an option value of zero or some dollar figure that is relatively small compared to $1 billion, you are not news. That's what happens to most people.

If we change our hypothetical example and assume that you were a very early-stage employee at a senior management level, maybe you received an option grant of 1 million shares, or 2 percent of the company. In that case, using the market values and probabilities above, your probability-weighted average option value would be significantly higher: $3.7 million. Understand, however, that such opportunities do not grow on trees, and that at least as of this writing, most people are not offered option packages like this one.

Remember that stock options have "vesting schedules." Each option grant vests over a period of, say, four years. That means your options are *fully vested* after four years. If you leave the company after two years, then only some part of your options will have vested. If, after each year of working with the company, you are given an additional option grant, those options will likely have a vesting cycle as well, the term period for which will likely match that of your first option grant. In addition to back-end loading vesting schedules, companies use incremental option grants over time as a way of keeping valued employees around longer than the initial few years. This practice is where the term "golden handcuffs" comes from.

There are two classes of stock options that you may be given: nonqualified and incentive stock options (ISOs). From an employee standpoint, the nonqualified option is taxed as regular income when you exercise the option and doesn't result in any tax advantages for you. That could mean that the tax comes due on the options before you realize any benefit from exercising them. In other words, if you exercise the options but don't sell your shares immediately, you could be stuck with a large tax bill on the income, in the form of stock options, that you would have to report.

In the United States, ISOs are taxed at the capital gains rate, and the tax on the gain isn't due until you sell your shares. You can exercise your option to buy the shares and you will not be taxed until you sell them. If you're an executive in a high tax bracket, the tax rate on your ISOs could be significantly lower than it would be if the options were taxed as regular income. However, because there is a cap on the absolute dollar value that one can receive in terms of ISOs, their use is somewhat limited. Generally, ISOs are reserved for executives, and even then, the absolute dollar cap limits their utility. More than likely, most, if not all, of your options will be nonqualified.

If you don't remember anything else from this book, remember to find out exactly what percentage of the company you are being offered with a stock option grant as part of a job offer. I've seen too many people disappointed at the realization that their option holdings were in reality far smaller than they expected them to be. This happened because they failed to calculate the relative percentage of company ownership. Everyone I've talked to has heard of instances where people thought they were getting a good deal when in fact they had absolutely no idea whether it was a good deal or not. If you haven't calculated your percentage of company ownership based on the total number of common shares outstanding, then you have absolutely no way of knowing whether it is a good deal or not.

Given that the stock option grant represents your biggest economic upside by far at a tech start-up, don't you owe it to yourself to find out exactly what percentage you are being offered? You bet you do. You are going to work long, hard hours for a potentially lower salary than you could earn elsewhere, so you better make sure you're content with your situation. Many people have awakened to the fact too late that they are working way too hard for far too little reward.

What's the "right" amount of options for you to be offered? Only you can determine what a fair deal means to you. Let's say you are being brought on board as the CEO and are not an original founder. In this case, if you are offered 5 percent, that's a darn good deal as of this writing. If you are a middle-level manager or associate-level manager joining at the OI stage, one-tenth of 1 percent is pretty generous. These are only guidelines, and, as with everything, they are certainly subject to change, so check with friends and colleagues in the marketplace at the time you contemplate an offer to figure out the going rate for a person in your situation.

Even after you calculate your percentage of potential company ownership and decide that it's a fair offer, remember that your options may never be worth anything at all. Indeed, there's a high probability that they never will be worth anything. That's why the experience of what you will be doing is so important. In fact, it's much more important to your working career than any amount of stock options. If you strike it rich on your options and never have to think about working again, more power to you. But for most of us, the tech start-up experience is what counts.

FOUR NEGOTIATING POINTS

There are four key points to consider in negotiating a job offer with a tech start-up:

- Base salary
- Signing and performance bonuses
- Stock options
- Benefits package (health care, vacation, etc.)

Think of each as a lever that you can push and pull in negotiating your job offer with a tech start-up firm. If you don't get everything you want on one point, communicate that you were hoping for more and demonstrate your willingness to work with the firm by asking for more on another. You will find yourself horse-trading on each issue with the person who has made you the job offer, and over the course of your discussions, your goal is to find out where the company has the most flexibility to raise the offer.

Base salary can be a tough compensation component to raise because the start-up needs to conserve its cash. However, a one-time signing bonus may be a way for you to bridge the gap between what you want in base salary and what the company is offering. Because the company will only pay it to you once, it is able to keep its cash flow lower going forward.

Performance bonuses are fairly specific to your function, but if the overall package is close to what you want, see if you can bridge the gap with performance-related bonuses. You will need to get the entire revised letter of offer in writing, and you need to ensure that any performance bonuses are accurately defined in writing to your satisfaction. You want to avoid any possible doubt about what triggers payment of those bonuses.

You may find that the option grant is one component where the tech start-up will definitely be able to go higher. After all, stock options are free to the tech start-up, and the only thing that limits their ability to give you more is what's available in the employee option pool. In other words, if they give you more options, they have fewer to give to others.

Benefits plans, vacation days, and other benefits will be unique to your preferences. Remember that these points are also levers to use in your negotiations. The relative importance of each part of your offer is obviously a highly personal matter, but in general, great benefits and vacation packages aren't adequate substitutes if the rest of the offer is significantly below what you were seeking. If the rest of the offer is close to what you want, this is an area where you can push the company to give ground and get yourself a deal you're happy with.

Over the course of your negotiations, do not be deterred if the company representative hints that something is difficult. Within any job negotiation, there's a difference between something that is difficult and something that is *impossible*. Let's say that you've reviewed the company's letter of offer and you've asked for a higher base salary. The company agrees to a slightly higher base salary but is still slightly short of where you want it to be. You counter by saying you'd be willing to accept that base salary if the firm raised your stock option grant by 30 percent. Don't be cowed if your counterpart says something like: "I'll have to see if I can get that approved by the CEO," or "I'll have to go to the board of directors to approve a higher option grant." This may just be an intimidation tactic on the part of the company to try to get you to back off a request. Tell that person to get the necessary approval. If you are asking for terms that you consider reasonable, stick to your guns. If you've done your homework, you know what the market is willing to pay you for your services, and you've probably already figured out the places where the company has flexibility in negotiating your job offer.

Once you've conceded a certain point, do not give further ground. If you feel you are caving in on all of your reasonable requests, you won't be happy if you join the company. There is a huge difference between giving ground and caving in. Over the course of your negotiations, you may come to know what each feels like.

DOES THIS JOB INVOLVE EVENINGS AND WEEKENDS?

It probably will. In most cases, the tech start-up experience will involve many, many hours of work. Speed is absolutely critical to the success of most tech start-ups, and because there's so much that has to be done in a highly compressed time frame, there's no substitute for putting in more hours per week than you would elsewhere. It is for this reason that tech start-ups are not for everyone. Not everyone wants to put in the long hours without getting paid on a steady basis commensurate to his or her efforts, especially when the potential exists to make a higher base salary elsewhere.

Judy Schneider cautions that in joining a tech start-up, "You better be prepared to work your butt off. It's just the nature of the space." Of course, in large part because of those extra hours of hard work, your learning curve will be much faster. That learning is one of the assets you will take away from the experience, so working at a tech start-up is not a one-sided proposition.

Generally, people at tech start-ups will be honest with you about what the routine will be like. Bruce Pomfret notes that they aren't shy about telling you that the experience will involve a lot of work and that the company may not succeed. Bruce also notes that it's important to have a strong affinity with the company's purpose and mission, because if you don't, it is much more difficult to keep yourself motivated putting in those long hours. If you sincerely believe that you are changing the world, that's a much more powerful motivator than trying to figure out when your stock options will start to have tangible value.

To some degree, tech start-ups are flexible about where and when you put in all those hours. Some people like to come into the office and work all night. Some prefer to take time off during the week. Others can do much of their work at home. As long as you are producing at the level that you need to be and are accessible to those who need to contact you, you can have at least some flexibility. Of course, the company's flexibility with you will depend on your job function and when you need to be in the office. If you are involved in meeting with customers on site, then your hours will, by necessity, correspond with theirs.

FOR THE EXECUTIVE

If you are joining a tech start-up for the first time at an executive level, there are a few special considerations you need to keep in mind. You will be taking on significant responsibility, and the career risks are potentially higher to you. Having to explain why a start-up failed when you were responsible for strategic decisions is different from being the middle-level employee who is executing plans made by senior management. Even at an executive level you can market failures—just look at Abraham Lincoln's track record—but you have the added challenge that your name may be closely associated with your start-up's failure if it tanks.

At an executive level, there is probably not someone else doing your job full-time. Someone else may be trying to do the job in his or her spare time, but you will likely be the first person to come in and do the specific role on a full-time basis. As a result, others in the start-up may not know the full job description for your role or what it really entails.

Educate people about what has to be done. You may have to educate the firm's founders or other top-level managers about what has to be done in your area. The amount of time you need to spend on education will depend on the amount of experience of other top managers. If they have years of industry experience, then less time will be required. However, you should assume that you will spend an inordinate amount of time in the interview process educating others about the role and responsibilities of the job in question.

You also may need to educate others about the budget required for your area. Although the size of your budget may not be open for discussion, you should be able to give other top managers a menu of budget options. A world-class effort in your area would cost $X. To achieve half of that level, the company will have to spend $Y. Over the course of this conversation, you can demonstrate your knowledge and expertise and show that you know how to get the biggest bang for your buck. In exchange for your experience and expertise, you should ask for a lot from the start-up, because the opportunity costs to you are especially high.

Ask for an employment contract. Start-ups will often try to avoid giving employment contracts. However, in today's incredibly competitive job marketplace, you should ask for one. If you are an experienced executive, a start-up should be willing to do what it takes get you on board. Your career risk is high; therefore, you should ask for conditions such as guaranteed paid salary for some period of time if you are terminated without cause. You should also ask for antidilution protection for your stock options, meaning that your relative percentage of ownership of the company stays the same, no matter what. You may not get it, but if you don't ask, you definitely won't get it.

Interview with several start-ups simultaneously to get a feel for the "going rate." In terms of the percentage of the company that is appropriate, check SEC 8-K filings for ownership of companies that were private and have gone public. These will give you the ownership positions of top managers in company stock. Look at people in comparable positions to that for which you are interviewing and determine how much they own.

If you are a nonfounding executive, you may be given less ownership than the founders. However, what you don't get in company ownership you should get in base salary. For early start-up employees, a significant amount of their compensation may be tied up in stock options. For high-level executives who join the company at a later stage, it is common for vice presidents to earn more than the CEO if they joined the company at a later stage. They are given a higher base salary because they do not have as much upside from equity ownership.

For executive-level jobs, it is common to interview with a start-up's investors. Major investors usually have board representation, and the fit of key hires with them is as important as it is with other company employees. As an executive interviewee, you want to meet the investors to determine firsthand how much value they bring to the table. If you are interviewing with other start-ups simultaneously, you can determine which investor teams have the most smarts and offer the greatest prospects for success.

Rolling up your sleeves and doing is as important as setting direction and strategy in a tech start-up. Whereas executives in larger companies have more of a hands-off role in their activities, as a senior manager in a tech start-up you will both set strategic direction and roll up your sleeves and execute. For many, this is no problem. Indeed, hands-on managers are quite accustomed to operating this way. However, managers who are more hands-off may find this a change to their current routines.

WHAT IS YOUR EXIT STRATEGY?

"I think the biggest thing you're going to have to explain is why you're leaving after less than a year. . . . When Nets went bankrupt, there were people who were pretty shocked that suddenly they were out on the street. . . . But you've been on the cutting edge of your industry. . . . You can market failures."

—Bruce Pomfret, formerly Web Programmer, Nets, Inc.,
now Software Engineer, Perot Systems

Always have an exit strategy in mind when joining a tech start-up. You need to have an idea under what conditions you might leave the tech start-up voluntarily and what you will do with the experience after you leave. You never know when you will be out on the street looking for that next opportunity, and it's much better to have thought about it in advance than to be caught off guard. Although you will have much more control over your sphere of activity within a tech start-up setting than you might in larger companies, there is still a great deal that is outside your control. Having an exit strategy means that you can and will exercise some control over your situation if necessary, and that you know what you will do next from a career search standpoint, no matter what happens.

Defining the conditions under which you will leave the company voluntarily is key to your exit strategy. A few potential determinants of an exit strategy are:

- The company fails to hit a sales target within a given time frame.
- The company fails to raise funding of a certain amount within a certain time frame.
- The company is acquired by someone else.
- You stop learning in your job, or you've learned what you wanted to learn.
- The company fails to go public within a given time frame.
- You plan to be at the company for no more than some number of years, no matter what happens, and then you will leave.
- You are offered a more attractive job elsewhere.

Many of these variables are tied to company performance. They should be. Your tech start-up needs to deliver for you. After all, you're putting very serious effort into it.

The other key element in determining your exit strategy is developing a plan for what you will do after you leave. You already know that the tech start-up experience, new knowledge, and expanded skill set are key assets that you will take away from the experience. Therefore, you should have an exit plan, which gives you some idea going in what you will do with those assets once you have them. In general, it will take one of four approaches. You intend to use this experience to get a more attractive position at another tech start-up or company within the

- same function, same technology category;
- same function, different technology category;
- different function, same technology category; or
- different function, different technology category.

At a conceptual level, specific exit plans may look like the following:

- You will pursue career opportunities at one of your firm's partner companies that values the skills and knowledge that you will gain from this experience.
- You will move into another field where having this type of experience is important.
- You will seek a higher-level position with a company in this category or another closely related one.
- You will become a consultant to companies like this one, advising in a specific area of expertise.

Your exit plan is specific to you, your interests, and your aspirations. The more you know about what you will do with the experience after leaving the tech start-up, the better off you are.

Although the need to formulate an exit strategy may seem Machiavellian, having an exit strategy does not imply that you *intend* to leave the company. It simply gives you a road map for the conditions under which you will leave the company and what you will do afterwards. You may hope that you never have to leave the tech start-up and that it will be your employer for the rest of your career. That's fine. But you have to be realistic. Having developed an exit strategy in advance will help you get over the unpleasant surprise if your tech start-up goes out of business. Having an exit strategy also means that you take your career seriously and are not willing to put up with undue risks.

WRAP-UP

In negotiating the offer, it helps you immensely to know what the start-up market is paying for someone with your experience and skill set. Although stock options offer potentially enormous upside, the rest of an offer package has to work for you, and you should not have to materially change the way you live to join a tech start-up. Use the negotiation points we discussed to get a job offer that is attractive to you with a company that excites you.

12

GETTING STARTED
AT A START-UP

"I did not know what a start-up meant."

— ADRIANNA PARADISO, FORMERLY PRODUCT MANAGER,
NETGROCER, NOW DIRECTOR OF MARKETING, E-STEEL

You now have a pretty decent idea of how to size up a start-up in technology. But when you sign on with a tech start-up, as with any company, you need to know what you have to do to succeed in your role. Your decisionmaking process *must* involve whether you can do what it takes to succeed in a given start-up. In the course of your interviews, you will be "parallel processing" people's responses to your questions. On the one hand, you will evaluate the company's prospects for success. Does it have a defensible business model? Can it execute correctly? On the other hand, you will take notice of how people behave and interact. You will look for common attributes among people in terms of their attitudes, background, and experience. Do you share those attributes? It's important that you do. This chapter is not about how the firm will succeed, but rather, about how *you* will succeed once you're inside a tech start-up.

Although every tech start-up will be different, seek to identify those with values and behaviors that you can relate to. You will be uncomfortable enough as it is setting sail in the uncharted territory of tech start-ups, so you may as well be doing it with people you can identify with. As with anything, different situations will require you to respond in different ways in a tech start-up. Furthermore, you will almost surely be confronted with less-certain situations in a tech start-up than in an established firm, and more of them. Therefore, knowing some general guidelines for how you should behave in a tech start-up is helpful. I offer these insights as guidelines rather than rules, because there is no "one size fits all" solution in tech start-ups. However, these behaviors and attributes in tech start-up settings have been helpful to me and the others quoted in this book.

KNOW WHAT YOU HAVE TO BE TO SUCCEED

"It really helps if you're working long hours to be fully committed to what you're doing. You've got to truly want to build something."

—Adrianna Paradiso, formerly Product Manager, Net Grocer, now Director of Marketing, e-STEEL

You may find yourself swamped because five other people are relying on you all at the same time to provide them with something . . . now! In such a case, having a few clones of yourself would be helpful. Knowing what you have to be to succeed implies many things. It means knowing what is required of you and when. It involves molding yourself to match the needs of a given situation. It means you need to prioritize deliverables. It also means you know what success *is*. Is success getting the right answer or giving people the answers they want to hear? Even though in tech start-ups there is perhaps a lesser degree of politics than in larger, established companies, they still exist. Some of the insights in this chapter will apply to just about any work situation, but all are specific to tech start-ups.

Move Fast

Although larger companies claim that it is imperative for them to move fast, many in fact do *not* move fast. That's why their markets are being invaded by smaller, more nimble start-ups. Tech start-ups really do need people to move fast. Unlike large established companies, there is no other business generating cash to fund the start-up's operation. Investors funded the start-up, and they are considerably less patient than large company bureaucracies to see a return on their investment. The new economy is demanding that all companies move faster than ever before.

You have to move fast in a tech start-up. In everything you do, you must do it with speed. You should not do a sloppy job, but speed should take priority over accuracy. If you get a result only half right, if you move fast enough, you have a chance to correct it the next time around. In contrast, if you don't move at all, somebody else may beat you to the punch. The phrase "Internet time" refers to the speed of change in the online economy. Depending on whom you talk to, one year of calendar time equates to anywhere from four to seven years of time on the Internet. Alan Kitty sums it up this way: "In Internet time, change comes like a starving animal on the Serengeti plain and you're the meal."

Two ideas are worth highlighting here: first-mover advantage and learning on the fly. Being a first mover enables you to learn on the fly. If your company is setting the standard in the way it addresses a market and is being copied by competitors, it is in a position of strength because while competitors are trying to duplicate what you just finished doing, your firm is literally blazing the trail. Blazing the trail in a new market gives a firm the flexibility to learn on the fly by testing new ideas and concepts. If they don't work or only partially work, there is still enough time to refine them. If your firm is ahead of the pack, you can learn valuable lessons from failures that will stymie the rest later.

Have a Bias for Action

Having a bias for action goes hand-in-hand with moving fast. You need to think and move fast so that you can act fast. A bias for action means that you follow some sort of 80/20 rule. Acting now with 80 percent of the information you need will probably be more effective than acting later with that extra 20 percent. Time is simply too precious. Admittedly, it can often be a challenge to determine exactly what information is most crucial to a decision, and your boss may have a different perception of the problem than you do. You don't want to make a decision in isolation, but if you have input from colleagues and can defend your point of view, no one can fault you for not consulting with others.

Be Flexible with Workload Demands

Many people are fond of the expression "If you don't like what you're doing, don't worry, it'll change." Although you won't take a job that you know you will dislike, you may find yourself having to pitch in on projects and tasks that have very little relation at all, if any, to the role that you signed up for. You already know that you will put in long hours. During of those long hours, you will be doing things that you feel are totally outside your realm of expertise. That's good. That's part of what you signed up for: the opportunity to learn. Even after a few short months of such activity, you will be amazed at how much you've learned.

Being flexible and pitching in demonstrates that you are a "get it done" type of person. You are not concerned with whether something is or isn't your job. This attitude underscores your desire to move fast and your bias for action. Such an attitude will reflect highly favorably upon you with your boss and colleagues. The other benefit of being flexible is that when you pitch in to help others, you build capital with them. You have a bank account of favors with other people, so when you need to call one in, someone will very likely hustle to your aid.

Be a Chameleon

What's this, more Machiavellian philosophy, changing your colors to fit the situation? You bet. Being a chameleon means that you mirror the behavior of others. You act more like them. Not in a blatant way, mind you, but we all like people who are similar to us and who see the world the way we do.

Be assured that you will not always see the world the same way other people do, but being a chameleon means that you tell others the bad news in a way that they can hear it. You can raise questions in a nonconfrontational manner so as to lead someone to a different conclusion. You won't always win, but by being a chameleon you will become more comfortable raising questions that are tough to address. You will surely encounter plenty of highly charged debate in a tech start-up setting, but chameleons are better able to defuse a stressful situation.

Also, try to avoid pointing the finger at others. Everyone is going to make mistakes in a tech start-up. There will be plenty of mistakes to go around. Imperfections will flourish everywhere. Don't get hung up about it. Figure out what has to be done to fix the situation. That's where the real learning takes place.

Being a chameleon helps you to surface key problems and challenges, or "showstoppers" as they are often called. Those will be of highest priority for you and your team. In the face of trying to solve such challenges, everything else will be a distant second. Again, by figuring out what has to be done to fix the showstoppers, you demonstrate that you know what it takes to be successful. This holds true not just inside the company but outside as well, as John Lindsay learned when trying to help customers in the early days of Windows NT while at USData.

Don't Be Afraid to Stand Up for What You Believe

Don't shy away from putting your opinion on the line about issues that are important to you. Bruce Pomfret notes that you may not win every argument, and you may find yourself obeying orders that you philosophically disagree with. However, if you take a well-reasoned stand on a position, you won't be faulted for being a stick-in-the-mud. You may be proven right in the future, or you may be right in this instance, and everybody recognizes that, but your solution involves trade-offs the company can't afford to make right now.

Pick Your Battles

Although you should not shy away from taking a stand on an issue, you shouldn't take a stand on everything. Choose your fights wisely. Many, many issues involve trade-offs or compromises in a tech start-up setting; it's the nature of the beast. You have limited resources, and you have to do what you can with what you've got.

Everyone is going to have his or her pet projects or issues, and you will have yours. Others will ask you to pick a side in a debate in an effort to build support for their case. Here again is where those chameleon skills come into play. You may find yourself caught between two sides of an issue that doesn't matter to you. Be careful about how you respond in such situations, especially if you will need to enlist the support of others at other times.

Look and Listen Carefully

Judy Schneider advises you to be aware of how other people feel generally. Understand their emotional equilibrium. Such sensitivity will help you to "chameleonize" your responses to different situations. In the often-stressful atmosphere of a tech start-up situation, tempers will run higher than they do in more stable organizational settings. Try to avoid letting the high-running emotions of others interfere with your ability to succeed.

Pay Attention to What You See and Don't See, Hear and Don't Hear

Are sales closing? If not, maybe that's why the VP of Sales is in such a crummy mood. If engineers are feeling "up," maybe they just nailed a development test. Over time, you can put together a road map of the emotional high and low points of others. Take a step back and check the emotional road map you've plotted every few weeks. Are people's moods changing, and for better or worse? By being keenly observant, you can gauge whether the company is making progress or not.

Become the Expert at Something Important

Although your goal in any job is to become indispensable, it is even more so at a tech start-up. Very likely, you will become the expert at something important in a tech start-up whether you like it or not. Having mastery over an important domain in a tech start-up gives you power and authority. People will solicit your viewpoint and listen to you. Your opinions will carry weight.

More than being effective in your current role at this tech start-up, you want to become an expert so that you can trade on that expertise in future job experiences.

While he was at Nets, supposedly in a content and editorial role, Bruce Pomfret taught himself HTML programming. Then, when almost everyone else in the company was laid off, Bruce was one of the select few who were asked to stay on to keep the site up and running. Bruce then traded on his HTML experience to get his next job at Perot Systems.

John Lindsay built an expertise in Windows NT while he was at USData. His plan all along was to get a job at Microsoft, so by the time he went for the interview, he was literally an expert in Microsoft's Windows NT operating platform. John identified an area of expertise that he knew he could trade on later.

Two other examples, the career paths of Bill Demas at Vividence and Prabha Fernandes at SMT, are relevant. Each built a base of expertise, in software development and drug development respectively, on which to trade later in his or her career. From their experiences, you can see that building expertise in something important eventually translates into an executive-level role, which is what you should be shooting for long-term if you're not there now.

Share your expertise to free yourself up to do other, more important things. Once you've gained expertise in an area within a tech start-up, there may come a point when you need to relinquish it to pursue other responsibilities, ideally of higher importance. If the firm isn't growing, this need is less likely to arise, in which case you could be the expert in one area for longer than you would like. It can happen, and it's one of the reasons why many people leave a start-up.

When sharing your expertise, make sure other people know that you are the person teaching that expertise to others within the company. You want to get credit not only for having mastered an area of competence yourself but also for teaching that knowledge to others. Smooth transitions of role are fairly rare in the rag-tag world of tech start-ups, and to the extent that you help transition smoothly, you should be recognized for it.

I don't want you to get the impression that you will be changing roles often in a tech start-up. However, your responsibilities can change significantly in a relatively short period of time. As an example, while serving as a product manager in the marketing group of a tech start-up, you may actually manage three different products in nine months. You haven't been promoted, but your responsibilities certainly have shifted quickly in such a scenario. The same potential for shifting in role and responsibilities exists everywhere in a tech start-up, from product development to operations to sales to finance.

Establish Rapport with Key People

Adrianna notes that it's important for your success to build solid relationships with key people within your tech start-up. This isn't to say that you have to become best friends with them, but you want to have good working relationships with them, and you want them to think of you as highly competent. A huge part of your career success is your personal network, so try to build a rapport with these people so that you'd feel comfortable calling on them in the future, whether you're working together or not. People very often look to hire people they know because the risks of such hires not working out are far lower.

SELF-PRESERVATION REIGNS SUPREME

"Everybody has a place where they have to make a stand."

—Judy Schneider, formerly Vice President Content,
Community, and Education, Onhealth, now Consultant

Most of us experience career success in a progressive fashion, not in the instantaneous, explosive manner of the select few who become overnight multimillionaires from stock options. Most people never know exactly where success is going to come from. There is almost always a component of luck to career success. The goal is to put yourself in a position where luck can happen to you more often. That means you must constantly be on the lookout—not only in terms of your current situation, but for your future as well.

By self-preservation, I mean that you are looking out for number one. Upon joining the tech start-up, you will ask yourself, Under what conditions should I leave this company? You may tell yourself that you will stay with a given start-up for a period of at least three years, but if the bottom is about to fall out at the end of year one, your timing may change.

Even if the company is not tracking to your expectations and timetable, you may elect to revise the performance metrics by which you evaluate the company and stay on. As an example, let's say that upon joining, you expect a company to close $1.0 million in sales during your first six months, $3 million in your first year, and $9 million in your second year. In reality, the company closes only $100,000 in your first six months. Okay, you say to yourself, we're still on the take-off ramp. We had a few glitches on the way, so I'll reduce my first-year sales expectation from $3 million to $1 million. Then, at the end of the first year, the company does $200,000 in sales. At this point, you may have a difficult decision to make: You were expecting the company to have revenues of $3 million and it only has $200,000. Do you stay on or do you leave? You look for other clues that reveal prospects for the company's success. The company is having difficulty raising more cash. You decide that this start-up is not going to make it. What do you do?

Self-preservation in this case is about making the choice that is best for you. From his experience at USData, John Lindsay asks, Is there still more to learn at this start-up? Can you ride the ship until it tanks, or have you learned basically everything you can? Your goal is to optimize for your career experience. If you can get better experience elsewhere right now, then you should leave. If you can learn more in this setting, even though you know the end is in sight, then you should stay longer. Of course, other factors may soon come into play, such as how badly you need the paycheck. If the financial consideration is more meaningful to you than the incremental learning, then you know what you have to do.

Be on the lookout for runaway trains. Runaway trains in companies happen when a negative situation turns worse. Much more than your average bad news type of stuff, I'm talking about bad situations *that can kill your company*. They can happen for all sorts of reasons. However, their consequences will invariably lead to one result: the company's death. Failing to address a key deficiency in your start-up company's product could cause it. So could a lawsuit, over, say, a patent infringement. A series of poor decisions by management definitely can and often does do it. You need to be alert to identify these problems when they happen.

Generally, you will not just walk into work one day and see a runaway train careening off the tracks. The signs and symptoms are usually more subtle, although not always. As an example, you may notice the signs of a train destined to run off the tracks as you sit through a series of quarterly announcements by management detailing your company's performance. Your company has missed revenue and earnings targets significantly: not by just a little bit, but by a lot; not just for two quarters in a row, but for four. You might connect the dots to build a case that the train is off the track or is well on its way to being so. Drawing from his NETS experience, Bruce Pomfret notes that the dots get very easy to connect once the company is seriously spinning out of control.

A runaway train will most often happen when a management team convinces itself that it is making the right decision but in fact it is making a wrong one. Although the same thing happens in corporate America, it is usually a good number of quarters, if not years, before that bad decision reveals itself to a broader audience. In a start-up, there is very little room to run or hide. The fact that a poor decision was made will usually become evident quickly. The fact that such a decision has just moved you much closer to being sans paycheck will also occur to you with similar speed.

The challenge in identifying whether or not a company is indeed a runaway train is that few things, if any, will go off flawlessly within a tech start-up. It's often difficult to know whether some adverse event is just the start-up hitting a speed bump, or a powder keg. That's where collecting data points can help you. But you need to collect more than just a few data points, and ideally, they should be from a number of different sources. The same data points will also be your clues to whether the company is succeeding.

Don't overanalyze or overreact. John Lindsay notes that it's easy to get caught up in the rumors of what's going on with the company. He's seen it happen before: "One thing you have to be really, really careful about is rumors and talk. You can let yourself get sidetracked from reality by it." He also notes that you should avoid interacting with negative people who propagate such gossip. He has seen people leave their jobs who would be multimillionaires today had they stayed on. But because they were swayed by the rumor mill and believed that what they heard was true, they left. Such decisions can indeed be costly.

It can also be difficult to discern the real meaning or impact of key events within the company. As an example, let's say your company fails to obtain funding from a well-regarded venture investor. You could interpret that event, or rather, nonevent, in isolation and come to the wrong conclusion. You might think that your company is doomed because some really hot investor passed on it. However, in reality, perhaps that investor has no focus or expertise in your company's business. In that case, would you really want that VC on your board anyway? Given how much a VC's involvement could dilute everyone's share of ownership, you only want VCs on your board who will truly add value.

Bail out if the ship takes on too much water. What's too much water? Just as everyone has his or her own tolerance for tech start-up risk, so too will people differ about when to throw in the towel. Although you should have a planned exit strategy, the conditions under which you decide to exit may change, and you may decide to leave sooner or later than you originally planned. Then again, you may never leave. However, you must be prepared for just about anything. The timing of events may surprise you.

You will experience organizational turnover in a tech start-up situation, more so than in a more stable organization. Such events are not necessarily due to a person's lack of performance. More likely they will be caused by personal or philosophical differences in setting strategic direction for the company. Such events may affect you. If there is a change in company strategic direction with which you disagree, that could cause you to re-evaluate your exit strategy and might even cause you to leave the company. If the issue is one about which you are neutral, you probably won't change your exit strategy.

In any event, personal turnover can be unnerving, and ideally you will see less of it rather than more in your tech start-up.

Deciding if and when your ship has taken on too much water is difficult. However, knowing your risk profile will help you make this decision. You don't have to convince anybody but yourself that the time is appropriate to leave. Don't get too hung up on talking about it with other people, especially other people at the company. If and when you leave, be confident in your decision. Don't look back. There's far too much excitement in the future to dwell on the past.

HOW'S THE FIT?

"We're trying to develop a specific culture."

—Bill Demas, Vice President of Marketing,
Vividence Corporation

When you join a tech start-up company, you will undergo an orientation, much the way you did at college, high school, or summer camp. In fact, a tech start-up is like all three in some ways. Maturity levels will actually span a range even broader than that, if you can imagine such a thing. I found that it helps to remember that adults are just big kids. Although this truism is also evident in larger, established companies, it will become even more pronounced in a tech start-up situation.

Even a small start-up organization develops a culture fairly quickly. Although it can change fairly dramatically in a short space of time, it probably will have its factions, much the way your high school and mine did. You may notice the equivalent of high school bullies, cool people, nerdy types, and smooth talkers, among others. You will have to fit in and work with these people. This can be disconcerting, but it is a major opportunity for you as well.

The People Fit

The tech start-up's community is the sum of the personalities of the organization and how they interact with each other. You will need to be sensitive to the personalities of the organization and to learn how to get things done within the framework they make up. This can be challenging. The collective population of a tech start-up will always be changing, if for no other reason than that there are new people joining the company practically every time you turn around. People will be constantly learning about each other and figuring out how to work with one another. The tech start-up organization really is a soup recipe in process. New ingredients are being added continually. Learning how to succeed under such conditions is perhaps one of the greatest interpersonal challenges you can face. It is also one of the best parts of the tech start-up experience. If you can succeed there, you really can make it anywhere.

Part of the challenge is that when you are trying to change the world, which is what many in your start-up will consider to be the company's mission, it leaves practically no time to help others get oriented to their new environment. Admittedly, if your company is crammed into one room, it takes just a few seconds to get to know the four walls. However, more pertinently, the process of acclimation encompasses learning *how* things work: who does what; what, if any, the routines are; what the interpersonal dynamics are like; and so forth. You will have far less time to learn these dynamics in a tech start-up than you would in any other job.

New Employee du Jour.   During the Organizational Infancy and Adolescence phases, your start-up will be hiring lots of people rapidly. The organization will be a whirlwind of activity. New people will see it as a merry-go-round moving at warp speed. As new hires, they will have to hop on very quickly to start contributing. Such a situation can be very challenging. You in fact will be the new employee du jour at some point if you join a tech start-up, and you will be looking around trying to get a general sense of direction from people. Maybe it will be in trying to prioritize a feature set for the company's next product release or just looking for the restroom.

Generally, people who seek to join start-up companies are bright, capable, high-energy people, so they don't necessarily need a whole lot of oversight or direction. However, those first few weeks can be disconcerting for new people as they try to learn others' roles and responsibilities, strengths and weaknesses, and working and management styles. Help provide some context to these people in your tech start-up. You will look to others to provide the same for you. In fact, the start-up's success depends on people working effectively together, and it all starts with new people walking in the door. How an organization integrates new people and provides them with an organizational context can mean the difference between success and failure. So be on the lookout for the new employee du jour in your organization and lend a hand when possible.

Organizational Blend.   Sounds like a coffee, doesn't it? As new employees du jour are coming on board every day, the start-up as soup metaphor is appropriate because of the new ingredients being tossed into the pot at frequent intervals. People have to get used to each other, a process that extends well beyond the newness of being the employee du jour. Some of the people who will become close colleagues to you in your role may not even have joined the firm yet, or perhaps you haven't really interacted with them in your first six weeks on the job.

Although in any new job situation you must go through this process, in a start-up, because of its relatively small size and short tenure as an organization, virtually *everyone* is going through this process to some degree simultaneously. All of the firm's employees are getting to know new hires while still trying to figure out the "veterans" who may have been with the firm only twelve or sixteen months.

Ultimately, the challenge for people in a start-up is to "blend" organizationally, to understand areas of defined responsibility and identify the gaps where responsibility is undefined. There will be many. Similarly, there is a need for people in start-ups to understand the level of competence and industry expertise of their colleagues to know where to fill in knowledge gaps and to identify the appropriate resources that can provide insight on particular business or technology issues. Part of the blending process, then, is a diffusion of the collective knowledge and talents of the firm.

The organizational blending process for start-ups can take a while because many start-up firms grow in spurts. During its first year in business, a firm may grow slowly while refining and developing its technology. Once the product is complete to a point where it can be promoted and sold, the firm will grow dramatically as it ramps up its infrastructure to enable support of its sales growth. Bill Demas's plans for growing at Vividence recognize the need for this staged approach to growth.

Another noteworthy observation about blending in start-up organizations is the extent to which strategy can be affected by it. As the start-up gains greater expertise through hiring a diversity of people with different sets of experience, the knowledge and insights of these people can influence strategy greatly. Such strategic re-orientation happens in larger firms as well, but its impact on overall firm strategy in the context of a start-up is greater because the firm's survival is at stake. Large firms have the luxury of trying lots of different approaches to determine what works, and because they are diversified, they can abandon unsuccessful approaches and redirect resources to other opportunities. In start-ups, scarce resources, both financial and human, limit the number of such efforts and create a sense of urgency and resourcefulness that is unparalleled in business. This learned resourcefulness is one of the most valuable opportunities a tech start-up offers you.

Ultimately, the result of the start-up organizational blending process is the firm's "corporate culture." When you interview with a large, stable firm, you learn about its corporate culture, which encompasses work habits, behaviors, attitudes, and the values of its people. In companies with a long history, it is easy to identify their defining characteristics. This is not so in the start-up. The good news about a lack of formally defined culture is that you have an opportunity to help mold and create that culture. You can put your stamp on it in a way that you might not be able to in a larger firm.

The Cultural Fit

Adrianna observes that you need to fit culturally with any start-up that you would consider joining. Your beliefs, values, ideas, and perceptions about the marketplace need to be closely aligned with those of the tech start-up. If they aren't, that's a big clue that a start-up is not the right place for you.

Looking back to the framework for assessing tech start-ups, the degree to which you fit culturally with a start-up will ripple through many of the key evaluation points. Your personal comfort level, perception of the company's competitive position in the marketplace, assessment of the firm's people, and outlook on the potential experience you stand to gain are but a few of the key points that will be affected by the degree to which you identify culturally with the firm and its people. Of course, the framework cannot guarantee that you will join a firm where you are completely aligned with the culture, but it can help you assess whether you think you fit culturally. No matter what, there will be cultural determinants outside your control in a tech start-up, and you need to know what some of them are.

Gauge the Stage.   A big determinant of company culture in a tech start-up is the stage of the company. The earlier the stage, the less formed the culture will be. In other words, the earlier the stage, the more changeable the culture. Bruce Pomfret makes the important observation that the motivations of people who join the start-up at different stages can vary widely. Similarly, their impact on company culture can differ significantly.

Watch for the Actions of Factions.   Although it may seem amazing, factions really can and do crop up even within a small organization. Indeed, a tech start-up may have been started by a group of people who used to work together at another company. Groups of like-minded people who have a point of view about some aspect of the company or its strategy can help or hinder, depending on how much influence they have and whether they are on the right track or not. Factions are not necessarily bad things; you just need to be aware of their existence.

The Strategic Fit

Understand the strategic value you will bring to the firm. Ask yourself if you are seeing the opportunity in the same way as the firm's management team. Just because a firm is successful at fundraising, that does not mean that it will be successful in determining its strategy. You need to take a good hard look at the strategy and determine whether you believe in it and can sign up for it. More than just believing in it, you should feel passionate about it.

The Career Fit

Hopefully there will be at least some overlap between your past professional and or academic experience and what you are doing in a tech start-up. You will be stretched in many different directions, but you will want to have a foundation from which you can draw. You also need to know how the experience will play into your long-term career plan. Beyond having an exit strategy, you should know how you intend to use new skills in a subsequent role.

WRAP-UP

It is impossible to know exactly how to succeed when setting sail in uncharted territory. Every situation will require something different. The one thing you can do to ensure that you are in the best possible position to succeed is to be prepared. Knowing what you have to be to succeed is a learning process. A big part of your first thirty days once you've joined a start-up is to find out what you have to be to succeed.

With a view towards self-preservation, be sensitive to any runaway trains, but don't overanalyze any single given event and its significance to the company. You should monitor the firm's progress by connecting the dots over a period of time to paint the picture of perspective. You should also monitor how the firm fits with you—and vice versa—in terms of people, culture, strategy, and your career.

13

MAKING THE MOST OF A START-UP CAREER

"There's a lot of opportunity. It's out there for you to prove yourself and grab it. You can write your own ticket. If you find your thing, and you want to run it, and you prove you're good, chances are you'll be making it happen, and then, hopefully, you'll get to run it."

—ADRIANNA PARADISO, FORMERLY PRODUCT MANAGER, NETGROCER, NOW DIRECTOR OF MARKETING, E-STEEL

When you think about it, so much about a tech start-up opportunity is big. In fact, it's bigger than big. It's huge! The market opportunity is vast. The potential for growth, for the firm as a business, and for you professionally, is huge. The odds are in your favor that you will learn new skills and become more valuable than you are today to either your existing company or a future one. This is the "glass-is-half-full" outlook for a tech start-up.

In contrast, so many things about a start-up are *small*. It can almost be depressing. A tech start-up has a few dozen people, maybe more, maybe less, depending on the stage when you join. The company's offices are located in a couple of rooms in some unglamorous location. Quarters are cramped. Cubicles may be a luxury your firm cannot afford at present. You can practically hear people breathe. This, of course, is the "glass-is-half-empty" view of a tech start-up.

If you're even thinking of joining a tech start-up, you should think about how to make the most of every aspect of working there. Tech start-ups give you incredible opportunities to learn about technology, business, and people. Your learning curve will be dramatically accelerated in a tech start-up, putting you at a tremendous advantage in the long term.

REPORTING FROM THE SCENE:
CAREER SEARCHING ON THE
NEW ECONOMY FRONTIER

The job outlook for technology in general is very bright indeed. Seeking a job with a technology company is a great idea because it positions you on the new economy frontier. That frontier is where technology companies, the growth engines of the future, are doing the heavy lifting, carrying the economy to new levels of productivity and performance. New economy technology companies require higher levels of skill sets than many other industries, and by getting in, you guarantee yourself further on-the-job education that will increase your value as an employee.

The high level of skills required by many technology companies has meant that there simply aren't enough qualified people to fill these jobs. Even so, unemployment levels are near their all time lows in the United States. The competition for qualified people is intense. The people quoted in this book get calls practically every week from recruiters about new job opportunities.

As of this writing, some job sites on the World Wide Web boast over 2 million job openings in technology fields *alone*. Indeed, it is a fantastic time to be seeking a job in the new economy. Whether you are looking to make a move into a technology start-up company for the first time, switch from a start-up back to a more established firm, or switch from one tech start-up to another, the opportunities are unprecedented. Because the opportunities are so great, however, the challenge for you is to be even more selective in your decision. It is highly gratifying to your ego to receive numerous job offers. In some respects, choosing to accept an offer might almost be a letdown, because at that point you actually have to stop looking at so many other great opportunities. Therefore, it is important that you be confident in your choice and feel good about your decisionmaking process.

Here a Job, There a Job

One of the benefits of working in the new economy, and more specifically, new economy tech start-ups, is that the average job lasts for a shorter period of time than it does in other settings. Indeed, most likely you'll know within a fairly short period of time whether your start-up is going to take off. If you're joining at the OI stage, three years is probably on the lengthy side of how long you'll be in suspense. In most cases, you'll know before then what the fate of your firm will be.

In spite of an incredibly hot job economy, you still have to be careful about switching jobs too often. Prospective employers will understand why you had a job that lasted ten months if your start-up tanked, but you should avoid hopping from one job to another for short stints of time. Even in a hot job market, prospective recruiters will interpret a history of such moves as flightiness. Given the time and money employers invest in hiring people these days, you want to avoid the "flighty" label.

Even for people who are "start-up junkies," moving from one start-up experience to another, a difficulty can arise from the fact that you worked for, say, four different companies in five years. Let's say that all of those start-ups tanked. Such a history will raise questions among recruiters: Is this person thinking seriously about his or her career? What was the objective? Is there a long-term game plan here? Your judgment could be called into question. Do you have bad business sense to keep joining doomed companies? It's one thing if you have the Midas touch and worked for three different start-ups in three years, all of which were bought out by someone else, at which point you took your profits and decided to go elsewhere; it's quite another if your companies all went bust shortly after you signed on.

Having said all that, unbelievable things can and do happen. I've seen people explain successfully why they had six different jobs in seven years. However, your goal is to avoid negative perceptions and build positive ones. Having learned by failing is a great asset. However, at some point you need to be able to take the learning from failure and translate it into success. Having joined a string of unsuccessful start-ups makes it more difficult to prove that you learned from those previous mistakes.

The opportunities in today's economy should enable you to build a track record of achievement and stability in shorter periods of time than might have been possible previously. Within a two-year time frame, you might get promoted twice at a tech start-up. This is not to say that you should expect this to happen or even to suggest that it's normal; indeed, it isn't. But such possibilities exist in the tech start-up universe, whereas they are more rare in larger organizations. Both Bruce Pomfret and Adrianna Paradiso note that the possibility that you could build a whole organization from a fledgling department is one of the big attractions of tech start-ups. When growth happens to tech start-ups, its people literally ride the elevator up with the company to a new level of management and responsibility.

Similarly, demonstrating success within one start-up enables you to assume a position of higher level and or responsibility at another start-up, if that is the path you choose to take. Let's say you join one start-up as a product manager. Over the course of a year and a half, you are promoted to director of marketing. Let's say your start-up tanks at some point after that. Based on your experience and insights about what went wrong, you may well be qualified to join another start-up as a vice president of marketing.

When the Call Will Come In: Any Time

Because today's job market is so hot, you never know when you might get a call about another job opportunity. It could happen any time. Even if you're not in the job market when the call comes in, you should listen to it for at least a couple of reasons. First, maybe it's an incredible opportunity. If you don't take the time to hear someone out about it, you may be blowing the opportunity of a lifetime, literally. Second, although you may be content where you are, perhaps you can refer a friend, which helps you build goodwill and expand your network with both friends and recruiters. Third, it's always good to have your finger on the pulse of the career marketplace, whether you're looking for a new opportunity or not. Knowledge is power, and having insight into what's happening in the career marketplace helps you not only in your career but also in recruiting others to work for you.

If you become known for being talented at something, you will invariably get a lot of calls. In fact, depending on how much of a reputation you build, you will get calls for jobs, referrals, investment opportunities, and possibly interviews with newspapers and television programs. Your goal is to put yourself in a position where these things happen to you. In other words, you want to put yourself in a position where luck happens to you more often.

If you look at the careers of many of the people interviewed in this book, you can see very clearly how their career paths have built on their past experiences. Over the course of their working lives, these people have learned about industries, established expertise and track records in them, built a base of contacts, and put themselves in situations where luck could happen to them. This is not to say that they didn't work amazingly hard to get to where they are. In fact, they've all worked incredibly hard. However, it is through hard work in combination with developing an expertise and having a passion for building a network that they have gotten where they are.

The call about a new opportunity can come in at any time. Be ready to listen. If for no other reason, use such opportunities as a way to learn about your industry or marketplace.

Try, Try, Try

One of the greatest benefits of tech start-ups is the extent to which they allow you to try new things. With the generally recognized understanding that few people today will spend their entire careers at one company, there is more career flexibility today than there has been at any other time in history. Start-ups, more so than most organizations, will give you the opportunity to assume responsibility for areas that may be well outside your realm of expertise.

Although such situations present challenges, you can capitalize on them and demonstrate your ability to learn new skills and accomplish projects with less than complete information. Such abilities are becoming a bigger part of career currency in the new economy.

Tech start-ups definitely offer you greater chances for assuming a higher level of responsibility and trying a new function. Adrianna Paradiso, Donna Williams, and John Lindsay are proof of that. A start-up opportunity will almost definitely require you to try new things. If you demonstrate solid capabilities through your meaningful contributions to the firm, people will probably be receptive to your assuming responsibility for other areas that would otherwise be neglected.

Although a tech start-up does not give you carte blanche to decide whatever you want to do, it can come pretty close. In terms of career content, it will certainly offer more flexibility than most other situations. As long as you are covering your key areas of responsibility and doing a good job with them, no one will stop you from assuming more ownership, especially if it involves work that isn't already being done.

BIRD'S-EYE VIEW

Although much of working in a tech start-up involves heads-down, get-it-done execution, it really does pay for you to keep a strategic eye on what's happening in the broader marketplace. In working for a tech start-up, you are working on the cutting edge of both business and technology. As a result, you can position yourself to take advantage of your situation in many ways. In addition to working on exciting projects and learning about technology at warp speed, you are also learning about business and market trends that will play out over the next five to fifteen years. Although technology cycles are becoming more compressed all the time, the trends that you are learning about, which will shape the business and technology landscape early in the twenty-first century, will still take *years* to produce their full impact. That's plenty of time for you to capitalize on them.

Find the New Industry Trends and Companies That Will Shape the Future

Let's take a quick look at two broad categories where market trends are causing explosive growth: information technology and health care. These are two broad topics, but it's important to consider them from a macro level because they are two of the major areas in which a great deal of investment is being made. More pertinent to this book, they're also the areas where *venture capitalists* are targeting a majority of their investments. That means these are highly fertile areas for tech start-ups. It's really up to you to determine the business and technology trends that are of personal interest, but you'd do well to focus on tech start-ups in these areas.

There are all sorts of directions you can go with analysis of different markets and trends, so let's take two really big, really simple ideas. Starting with information technology, consider the fact that demand for information is exploding. The Internet has made it incredibly easy to get information on just about anything. Now that you know you can get your hands on that information, you want access to it, *now*. In fact, the more information you can get, the more you want. You also realize that most people are like you; the more information they can get, the more they want. This tells you that there is a huge demand for bandwidth. Companies like Cisco Systems and Broadcom have been beneficiaries of this demand. So have semiconductor chip makers such as PMC-Sierra and Texas Instruments. As demand for information explodes and customer needs become more sophisticated, companies have emerged that supply tools to help people manage, measure, and understand this information, such as Doubleclick and MediaMetrix.

In the health care arena, the single biggest demographic phenomenon is that of the aging populations of industrialized nations. When people get older, they become susceptible to all kinds of health problems. In the United States, the aging generation known as the baby boomers is a bulging market of 70 million people that cannot be ignored. To the boomer generation, quality

of life is hugely important. When you consider an aging generation for which quality of life is very important and juxtapose
against it the increasing incidence of age-related diseases like diabetes, you realize that there may be an opportunity for companies
that are targeting these needs. MiniMed, a San Francisco-based
company that has received FDA approval for an implantable insulin pump for diabetes, is one such company. Because its pump is
implantable, it enables people to go about their normal routine
without being slowed down by less "friendly" insulin injection solutions. Another company that has benefited from the aging demographic is VISX, the manufacturer of optical laser surgery
systems.

Although you certainly don't have to work at a tech start-up to
be able to identify and understand these market trends and opportunities, working in a tech start-up puts you closer than most to
the solutions that these markets will demand. You can learn about
the specific competing solutions that companies are developing to
address market needs. You have a superb vantage point from
which to predict winners and losers. This enables you to identify
companies that represent attractive employment and investment
opportunities.

Furthermore, having a bird's-eye view of new marketplace developments makes you increasingly valuable, not just to a tech
start-up but also to an array of other companies, large and small.
These companies will also be evaluating new opportunities and
will need expertise to help them make decisions about whether to
enter specific businesses. Your knowledge about what will work,
what won't work, and why will be tremendously valuable to
them.

Learning You Can Trade On

There are virtually infinite directions in which you can expand
your knowledge and experience base within a tech start-up. There
are three key areas in which you will learn at a tech start-up, no
matter what you do in the future. Although you will learn more
about these three areas in just about any job you might take, you
will not learn as fast as you will in a tech start-up.

Learn the Lingo—and Actually Understand It. Within a tech start-up, you may find yourself learning an entirely new vocabulary. Every industry seems to have its own alphabet soup. If it's an e-commerce company, maybe you're learning about TCP/IP, ANSI, OLAP, MOLAP, or ROLAP. If it's a semiconductor chip company, you might be learning about SONET, WDM, DWDM, ATM, and ATE. If the company is in health-care services, maybe the language consists of HMOs, PPOs, MCOs, TPAs, or IHDNs. The vocabulary for drugs will consist of totally different terms.

In a tech start-up, not only will you learn the lingo faster, you will actually know what it means. Your ability to succeed will depend at least in part on your knowledge of the lingo, what the terms mean, and how they relate to one another. Because industry lingo is always changing, you should not expect to know all the terminology before stepping into a tech start-up. What matters is your ability to pick it up fast.

Learn Competition at the Trench Level. For feeling the heat of the competitive fire, you can't beat a tech start-up. You know from other arenas of life, such as sports, other jobs, and games, what competition is like. But there is nothing like being in the trenches of a tech start-up. Crises happen all the time. Because nothing in a tech start-up will ever be perfect, situations will test you almost entirely in the way you respond. How do you respond when you are giving a software demonstration to a really important prospective customer and your system crashes? How do you navigate your way through a demonstration when you know that there's a killer bug somewhere in that software that your engineers worked all night trying to fix but couldn't? What do you do when your start-up has just launched its new, novel medical device, and you find out that some huge company has just launched its own version? Many successful tech start-up companies have faced these exact situations, often repeatedly.

Learning in the heat of battle within a tech start-up teaches you lessons that you will internalize deeper and faster than those you will learn elsewhere. The lessons you will extract from dealing with the competition at the trench level are a big part of the accelerated learning curve you will experience within a tech start-up.

Learn How to Do Deals.   A major portion of any role within a tech start-up will involve negotiation or dealmaking of some type. You stand to learn more about human interaction within a tech start-up than in most other situations. The reason for it is simple. You will be doing more, and therefore interacting with more people on more projects, and doing so more often than you would elsewhere. Interpersonal influence and negotiation will make up a big part of your accelerated learning curve within a tech start-up.

Your interactions with people in a tech start-up will encompass many widely varying situations: interviewing and hiring, interacting with and selling to customers, dealing with colleagues on teams, interacting with management and the board, dealing with potential partners, negotiating potential deals, and so forth. Judy Schneider points out that there's really no room for egos in a tech start-up and that the atmosphere is quite egalitarian. Part of the challenge is learning how to get the job done with other people who may have widely different backgrounds, interpersonal styles, and motives.

Much of this interaction can be uncomfortable. You will probably be trying to get things from people who do not report to you, don't need to care about you, and may know more about the topic in question than you do. You will find yourself continually trying to convince people of your point of view. In such situations, where the potential for conflict is high, it is always helpful to remember that you're both playing for the same team and that the team stands to benefit from a resolution. The same holds true for external discussions as well as internal ones, if the subject at hand is a potential partnership. In any event, practice makes perfect, and there is no better illustration of that than in negotiation and influence within a tech start-up setting.

WRAP-UP

You want to maximize the experience at any start-up you choose to pursue. However, doing so does not mean that you stop paying attention to the broader career and business marketplace around you. Indeed, you should pay closer attention in a tech start-up situation because you will be closer to the trends than most people. You can trade on that expertise and experience in future career opportunities, investments, and expanding your network.

14

THE LONG AND
WINDING ROAD AHEAD

"Instead of thinking about a specific kind of career, unless you've just got a passion that you need to follow, think in terms of skills and things that you like to do. Don't think about going to work for . . . a company as a career. But think . . . 'I'd like to work with people. I'd like to write code. I'd like to do creative things. I'd like to see results quickly for what I do. I'd like to conceptualize, and I don't care if I see results quickly'. . . . {Think about} skill sets . . . that fit your personality."

—JUDY SCHNEIDER, FORMERLY VICE PRESIDENT OF
CONTENT, COMMUNITY, AND PERSONALIZATION, ONHEALTH,
NOW CONSULTANT

You will spend many years performing many different jobs over the course of your working life. You may work in different industries. You almost certainly will work for different companies. Although no one likes to be forced to look for a new job, moving around among jobs and companies has become far more commonplace today. Corporate layoffs have taught people that there is there no job security anywhere. Moreover, people have learned that they can get ahead by switching companies. They have a greater ability to get the promotion and higher salary they seek if they look outside their current company. Ironically, it seems that many large companies doubt the abilities of their own people. With increasing frequency, they seem to prefer to look for senior-level talent outside the company than to hire it from within. The message to internal employees is clear: "Senior management doesn't think you're qualified for the job."

No wonder, then, that tech start-ups hold so much allure for people who are familiar with this corporate mindset. For people who have already succeeded on some level within their careers, the notion of joining a start-up, with a potentially higher degree of responsibility than they had previously, combined with significant potential upside from stock options, is extremely attractive. People who are confident in their abilities have no fear of looking for another job if the start-up fails. In today's economy, competition for talent is fierce. And although a tech start-up won't provide a complete escape from politics altogether, there is certainly less time for it.

MULTIPLE JOBS, MULTIPLE CAREERS

"A career is what you have just before the doctor pronounces you dead, and you look back at what you had. In any of the fast-paced centers, a career is history. You never know what is going to be reality next year."

—Alan Kitty, President and CEO, LinkTank, L.L.C.

Many career experts today tell you that you can expect to have anywhere from five to seven careers—*careers*—not just jobs, over the course of your working life. As people live longer, this is becoming even more true. Today's career climate is changing significantly. In many ways, it is changing for the better.

Although the notion of a career certainly holds meaning for specific professional fields of study such as law, accounting, or medicine, the term itself holds less meaning for those in the start-up universe or elsewhere, who may switch functions or employers frequently. That is because increasingly, people do not expect to spend their entire working lives doing just one thing, which is what the word "career" implies.

Even those who are trained as professionals in a specific field are increasingly pursuing careers in others. Doctors and researchers are usually the entrepreneurial brains behind biotechnology start-ups.

Accountants are highly sought after as CFOs for tech start-up companies. Lawyers are increasingly attracted to entrepreneurial and business opportunities, and have an ideal background for roles such as business development within tech start-up companies. University professors are increasingly trying their hand at entrepreneurial efforts as the founders of tech start-up companies.

As recently as the 1980s, there was much less crossover in terms of what people did with their training than there is today. Historically, if you trained in a particular field, you practiced it in a fairly narrow manner for the duration of your career. Today, there is much greater receptivity to people doing different things. Just because you trained in one field does not prohibit you from trying something else. Many different disciplines have applicability to business situations today.

That people are doing jobs in areas different from those in which they trained is a reality that is probably here to stay. Because knowledge in numerous fields is exploding, there is simply no way any one person will have the required training to keep up with the technology, be able to package that technology into a company, and get it off the ground. That is why tech start-ups need people with different backgrounds and education. Although these people may lack formal training in a specific area, they are able to learn rapidly. Today's marketplace demands this ability. Whether or not you intend to pursue many different job functions or "careers" over the course of your working life, that option is open to you.

Is This a "Job" or a "Career?"

As you may have gathered from the interviewees in this book, your tech start-up experience can be either a job or a career. How you use the tech start-up experience is up to you. It's what you make of it. You've seen different examples of how people treat the start-up experience in the context of their careers. There is no right or wrong career model; there is only the one that is right for you.

The Job Scenario. You can make a career of doing one thing for different companies. The role of CFO is a good example. Let's say that you obtained your CPA in college, and you have a few years of accounting and financial experience, maybe working for one of the major accounting firms. You could easily spend your entire career just playing the role of CFO at tech start-up companies, moving from one tech start-up to the next. Not a bad gig.

The Career Scenario.   You also might have training in a particular field and have different "careers" over the course of your working life. Let's say you're a doctor, trained in medical school. Perhaps, after several years of practicing medicine in a clinic, you become bored and decide to do medical research for a start-up biotech company. Maybe over the course of working at that company you find that you are needed to help negotiate licensing agreements with larger pharmaceutical companies for compounds your biotech company is developing. You have moved from the research lab into business development, an area that requires a significant amount of business and legal knowledge. Within the space of two different work situations, you have now had three different jobs and three different "careers."

These examples demonstrate that having different careers implies doing different jobs. Conversely, you can do one job for many companies. Both career strategies are viable in the tech start-up universe, and they apply to people with training and backgrounds in all kinds of fields. The beauty of tech start-ups is that you probably have more opportunity than you do elsewhere to try different jobs.

If It Doesn't Fit, Should You Call It Quits?

Definitely. Although it can be difficult to know exactly the right time to leave, if you are totally miserable at a tech start-up, you probably have lost your motivation to show up to work. This can happen for many reasons. Life is too short to endure such a situation for very long. Judy Schneider notes that although the tech start-up involves enormous hard work, "it should be fun, and you should be able to laugh at stuff." She says that it's important to stay in touch with how you're feeling, something that can actually be quite difficult when you're working so hard.

Adrianna Paradiso observes that it can be difficult to know right time to leave, but you have to be able to make that judgment. If you have planned your exit strategy, you have some fairly specific ideas about when to make that decision. John Lindsay observes that if you're still learning on the job, even if other conditions within the start-up aren't great, you may want to stick around to gain more experience. That can work, provided the company doesn't tank.

Prabha Fernandes notes that it's best not to burn any bridges. If you must leave, do so on the best possible terms, as you would attempt to do with any job. Emotions can run a little hotter at tech start-ups, so manage the situation to the best of your abilities. Who knows? Maybe some of your colleagues there will wind up with you in your next situation.

Bruce Pomfret was looking for a job after less than a year in a tech start-up that tanked, having to explain what happened. I myself was in a fairly similar situation. Although this can be daunting, the issue of timing should not be a factor. You should deflect any concerns about the short duration of your start-up stay by noting that in today's hyper-speed marketplace, winners and losers are determined faster than ever before. In addition, a year in a tech start-up is probably worth at least a few years' experience in other types of job situations.

The corporate layoffs that happen every so often have indeed taught us that competition is king. If a firm is victimized by competition, its employees must find jobs elsewhere. However, competition is also king for the career searcher in today's marketplace. So, while employers have always asked you the question: "Why should we hire you?" now more than ever is the time for talented people to ask the inverse of that question of potential employers: "Why should I work for you?" Today's job market is so competitive that it is only appropriate for you to explore your options selectively.

Three Key Things You Can Take Away from the Experience

You will take away much from a tech start-up experience. Everyone's experience will be different, but there are at least three things you should keep in mind as you go through it:

- having fun
- expanding your network
- leveraged learning experience

These three are definitely interrelated. They will help you understand the benefits you stand to gain from the experience but will also serve as checkpoints along the way in your tech start-up adventure.

Having Fun.   Given the diverse personalities and interests of people working in a tech start-up, chances are good you'll have a lot of fun along the way. Whether it's in the form of company picnics, sports events, beer bashes, or while you're actually doing *work*, the likelihood of having fun is high. It should be, because if you're not having some modicum of fun, it may well be time to go.

Expanding Your Network.   The tech start-up's people—as well as its contacts—will undoubtedly become part of that ever-increasing network that you hope to build. Rather than building a large network of people within just one organization, you will build a web that expands outward from your firm.

Hopefully many of these people will be exceptionally accomplished. Because of their fast pace, tech start-ups attract a wide array of personalities. Many such people will be very bright, creative thinkers who have an incredible range of backgrounds and experiences. They may be highly accomplished in their professional pursuits and personal interests. They can be intense. Hitting the jackpot in an IPO won't typically be the first reason they give you for why they joined the firm because they're much more realistic than that, but they will wholeheartedly assert, "Hey, if I make a few million bucks along the way, that'd be great, too." You want your network to include a lot of exceptionally accomplished people.

Leveraged Learning Experience.   Not only will you learn at an extremely fast pace based on your own experience within the tech start-up, but you will learn from your colleagues as well, who are also on an incredibly steep learning curve. You will reap the rich insights from the experiences of your colleagues. Therefore, you will tend to learn at exponential speed.

In addition to developing an appreciation for high-energy and exceptionally accomplished people, you will also learn your own organizational preferences—types of culture, management styles, and job roles—that appeal to you. You may have the opportunity to work with a mentor, someone whom you identify as an advisor, who volunteers to help you shape your career vision and guide your direction. You will be able to draw from the broad experiences of such people.

Thinking About a Career Game Plan

Your career plan should, of course, be a major consideration in your decision to join a tech start-up. It isn't so important that you know *what* you'll be doing twenty years from now as it is to know the *kinds of things* you'd like to be doing, the role you'd like to have, and the markets that appeal to you. Once you have established those reference points, think about the roles and experiences you'd like to have along the way. Think about both the short term and the long term.

Short Term. Imagine yourself in a tech start-up company three to five years from now and consider the scenarios. First, there's you on the beach, a fairly unlikely scenario. Next, there's you working as hard as or harder than you did on day one; in fact, not much has changed, a more likely scenario. Finally, there's you looking for a job somewhere else because your company tanked, also a more likely scenario.

You've heard about the mere kids who are worth millions because their company had an IPO and they became instant millionaires. You've also read about start-ups that get gobbled up by giants like Microsoft, IBM, and Oracle, and their entrepreneurs become the latest residents on Easy Street. You've also read about them in the biotech, telecommunications, and hardware worlds. There is an incredible amount of luck to each of these scenarios, a lot of risk, and an awesome load of hard work. John Lindsay's only comment regarding his windfall from the USData IPO is that he was incredibly lucky. It can happen. Hopefully, it will happen to you. But don't fixate on whether your options will ever become worth more than the paper they're printed on. That can drive you nuts. Focus instead on amassing all that great cutting-edge experience. That will help you be prepared for working as hard as or harder than you did on day one.

Although the firm's business plan had rosy projections for the three-to-five-year time horizon, in reality things haven't quite lived up to the forecast. The great thing about that three-to-five-year time frame is that for most firms, that's about how long it takes to figure out if it will sink or swim. That's not always the case, but if you think it will take longer than that, you had better really love what you're going to be doing. If you're still in business three to five years from now, be thankful you're still in business! Your company has obviously done a few things right along the way. But, at the end of that time frame, you still may be looking for a job somewhere else.

Your having to look for a new job may result from the firm's going out of business or your deciding that the firm isn't going to hit the big time and leaving while the getting is good. In either case, you need to think about how to prepare yourself for this very real possibility. Because you've already planned an exit strategy, you already have a good idea about how to prepare yourself for this possibility. There are several positive points for you to highlight about your experience in positioning yourself for your next job:

- *You're a risk taker:* You take calculated risks, and this is to your advantage no matter what. Great countries and companies were built on people taking risks, and you shouldn't be interviewing with firms that don't value the ability and chutzpah to take risks.
- *You're strategic:* You can help companies plan, execute, and grow. Recruiters will value your ability to think strategically.
- *You want an expanded role:* With your insight about what didn't work at your last firm, you can position yourself as seeking more responsibility to influence a firm's situation more broadly than you could in your last experience.

Long Term. Think about being ninety-five years old and looking back on your life. What would you like to have accomplished? Write it down. You are going to live a long time, and you will work in many different situations. Every new position you take should help you build greater knowledge, experiences, and skill sets. You definitely don't have to do just one thing over the course of your work life, unless one thing is all you really want to do. You will have choices, so it is important to choose wisely. Of course, most mistakes are fixable, so don't be afraid to take risks. As long as you are learning, any situation should bolster your career.

Advancement and Expectations

With each new position you take, you should seek to advance in whatever ways are most important to you at the time. Salary, job title, number of reports, experiences, and new skill sets are but a few parameters. The tech start-up experience may not necessarily be able to help you advance along all of your key parameters at any given time, but it will probably help you advance along at least a few of them very fast. Moreover, if the company succeeds and you have made valuable contributions, the company's growth will provide you with great opportunities to advance yourself in a multitude of ways.

As you consider joining a start-up, it is especially important for you to manage your expectations about advancement in the form of promotions. You need to be content with your situation going in, because it may be a few years before any opportunities for such advancement arise. If you have an expectation that you will be promoted in some way based on performance milestones, get it in writing in your offer letter.

Assign Yourself a Higher Value Based on Your Tech Start-Up Experience

You should absolutely assign yourself a higher value based on your tech start-up experience. Your wisdom and insight from such an experience will pay dividends for you over the course of your entire career, no matter what type of organizations you work in. You will be setting sail in uncharted territory in a start-up setting. Not only will you be acting on imperfect information virtually all the time, you will also frequently have little idea as to what your final destination looks like. In solving problems, you will likely try a variety of approaches before settling on a preferred course. You will make refinements along the way, gaining input from various resources. By the time you make a decision that is set in stone, or at least something close to it, you will have built a solid supporting base.

Start-up companies desperately need objective, "outside-the-box" thinking to solve problems because resources are so constrained that new approaches are required. It is no wonder that tech start-ups today are creating revolutions in their marketplaces. They simply *have* to create such upheaval to survive. For the resource-constrained start-up, the costs of doing business in the traditional manner are simply too great.

WILL THERE BE A MARKET "SHAKEOUT" OF INTERNET COMPANIES?

People observe with awe the fortunes that have been created, seemingly overnight, at Internet start-up companies that have gone public over the past few years. However, given the lofty-looking stock market valuations of such companies these days, people start to think about a market "shakeout," almost in the same breath. Many say to themselves, "Gee, I'd sure like to make it big at a company like that, but isn't the bubble going to burst for many of these publicly traded Internet companies?" Indeed, as of this writing, all major stock indices have plummeted from their recent highs.

It's difficult to gaze into the crystal ball to see exactly what will happen in the stock market over the next few years. Many Internet-oriented start-ups have gone public but do not have any profits, and many of them lack significant revenues. Does a shakeout seem possible? Sure; in fact, a shakeout of tech start-ups is happening all the time. But that's exactly why you shouldn't be concerned about a "market" shakeout. Just as they are dying every day, new tech start-ups are being born every day. For every start-up that dies, there's another to take its place. Unprecedented levels of wealth have brought about the new economy, and that wealth is in relentless search of growth opportunities. That means more start-ups. If and when successful start-ups categorically stop delivering the superior IPO returns that they have been generating, then we will have reason to worry. But at present, all indications are that investor demand for new, *proven* IPO stock issues is solid. One cautionary note is in order. The recent stock market gyrations probably imply that there will be a higher level of investor selectivity around technology companies in the future. In other words, greater investor emphasis will be placed on a company's "proprietary" or "unfair" advantages. In my opinion, that's as it should be.

Business to Consumer E-Commerce Markets

Although it's dangerous to make sweeping predictions, some sectors of the Internet definitely will produce a few winners and many more losers. Most Wall Street analysts believe that the "business to consumer," or B2C e-commerce market, where companies like Amazon.com, eToys, and eBay compete, will shake out. There *will* be a few winners in major B2C categories. The economics of these businesses depend on high-volume purchases offered at deeply discounted prices. As a result, the market can support only a few of these companies *at most* in any one category. Indeed, eventually there may be only one competitor in some B2C categories. In trying to forecast the future in B2C, analysts point to industries like the automotive industry in the early twentieth century. Although there were hundreds of auto manufacturers in the United States after the birth of the auto industry, there are only three major ones today. There are similarly few manufacturers of automobiles in Europe and Asia.

Business-to-Business E-Commerce Markets

In contrast to B2C, the "business to business," or B2B e-commerce marketplace, is far larger in dollar volume and is less crowded in terms of competitors. Given the size of the B2B market, there appears to be room for more competitors. However, Internet-focused start-ups that offer online markets for businesses will find themselves competing increasingly with established suppliers who are banding together to protect their interests. Because "old economy" companies are now using the Internet to integrate their suppliers more closely with their business processes, start-ups that serve B2B markets in some way will need to add value beyond simply facilitating online purchasing.

Companies that sell infrastructure software to businesses are well positioned. Such software systems, although often deployed over the Internet, are more proprietary in nature than online e-commerce offerings, and the barriers to entry are much higher. Although the products of these companies are typically very expensive, a company that serves customers successfully becomes entrenched. A couple of examples of such companies are Siebel Systems in the customer relationship management (CRM) software market and i2 in the supply-chain software market. There are many, many companies serving enterprise markets, and a lot of them are, or used to be, start-ups.

Hardware Arms Suppliers

Companies such as semiconductor manufacturers and producers of computer, network, and device hardware are basically the "arms dealers" to the companies that compete online. They also supply major consumer markets with devices to access the Internet. I like the analogy that these companies function like Levi Strauss did in the mid-1800s, supplying blue jeans to today's gold rush prospectors. Many of these companies will win no matter what happens. In the online universe of companies with no profits, well-known Levi Strauss companies such as Cisco Systems, Intel, and Dell are generating real revenues and real earnings. What's that, you say? None of those companies is a start-up? Not today they aren't! They're all adult companies, making big bucks. But they were all start-ups at one time.

Biotechs

How do the biotechs fit into all of this Internet stuff? There are at least a couple of similarities between biotech and the Internet.

First, biotechnology is a knowledge industry. The key assets of biotech are people and their intellectual horsepower. In addition, just as many Internet start-ups are trying to discover the right business model for success, biotechnology is a discovery business. Biotechnology can also teach us something about stock market shakeouts, because it had its own shakeout in the early 1990s. At that time, a great number of biotechnology companies went public, many of which lacked both revenues and earnings. They used the money raised from their IPOs to hire the teams they needed to develop their products. Many biotech companies went public at valuations that were huge given that they had no revenues or earnings. These stocks all fell back to earth when it became apparent that there were tremendous risks associated with their drug-development programs. Even today, only a handful of biotech companies are actually profitable. Many biotech stocks have never attained the same heights that they realized in their IPO. Many biotech companies merged or went out of business.

However, there are still many biotech companies around. Generally, those that remain are much more efficient and are more poised to capitalize on their technology and achieve profitability. Moreover, computer technology has made drug discovery far more efficient than it has ever been before. Therefore, much of the promise of biotech is still to be realized. Many believe we will realize unprecedented economic benefits from biotech over the coming decades.

What shakeouts tell us is that it is important to calibrate expectations of a technology, company, or industry. If the biotech industry serves as any example, clearly it shows that expectations can get too far out of line. The biotech industry has been anything but a failure. However, the expectations for it were enormous. Although many people lost a lot of money on biotech stocks, there is still a great deal of money to be made in biotech. However, investor expectations in terms of opportunity, risks, and timing must be managed carefully.

Why You Do Not Need to Fear a Shakeout

You don't need to fear a market shakeout for several reasons. If you apply rigor and diligence to your decisionmaking process, you will only join a start-up that you believe has excellent prospects for success. A company with inherently excellent prospects for success should not get shaken out. Moreover, you should be joining a tech start-up first and foremost for the experience it will give you.

WRAP-UP

Hopefully, this book has given you much to think about. The idea of joining a tech start-up is pretty scary in some ways but incredibly exciting in others. The most important assurance you need to give yourself when you consider joining a tech start-up is that irrespective of the firm's outcome, you will land on your feet. If you are secure in that, then you are mentally prepared to join a tech start-up.

You cannot afford to take your career lightly. However, your career need not be mundane, boring, or routine. In fact, it should be fun before anything else. If you know that a certain start-up will afford you tons of fun in addition to great experience, chances are good that other pieces are in place as well. Sound strategic direction, management team, and company culture are all key to making a start-up experience fun.

To be sure, you will also work very hard at a tech start-up. But if you're excited about the firm's vision, it won't feel like work all the time. What you are doing will feel bigger than work; it will feel like you are changing the world. Best of luck to you as you consider joining a tech start-up. The fact that you are reading this book tells me you are on the verge of doing some very exciting things, whether it's with a tech start-up or not. Let me know how it works out!

RESOURCES

Following are resources that I think are well worth checking out. While undoubtedly they constitute a small fraction of what is available, I consider them to be better than most that I've seen. They offer you assistance in both finding and assessing career opportunities in the tech start-up universe. They also contain a gold mine of information about industries, economic outlook, and hiring trends. I have tried to group them into discrete categories based on their focus, but as with most things from the World Wide Web, they do not lend themselves easily to classification and often have more than one focus. For those that offer help in more than one category, such as career listings and career guidance, I've noted it. For all resources, I've added my commentary about each so you know what to expect if you decide to use them. Most of the career search or guidance sites below enable you to post your résumé online or submit it to an employer or resume database.

CAREER GUIDANCE: RESOURCES FOR TECH START-UP AND NEW ECONOMY CAREERS

Careerbuilder (www.careerbuilder.com) is a career guidance and search site that has partnerships with Microsoft, CareerEngine, MediaCentral, ComputerJobs.com, and Bloomberg.com. This site is intuitive and easy to use and has won numerous awards. The site offers its own Web guide for finding useful resources organized by topic, as well as articles on numerous career-related topics. It claims to provide access to over 2 million jobs, virtually every job on the Internet, by searching not only all of its own databases but also those of every major search site on the Web. The site also enables users to register for a personalized search agent that alerts them when jobs match their criteria.

Career Magazine (www.careermagazine.com) is operated by National Career Search. It is positioned as a full-service, one-stop shop for the career needs of both working professionals and college and M.B.A. career searchers. The site is formatted like a magazine, featuring columns and advice, but also facilitates the career search process with its own employment database, links to recruiters, and on-campus recruiting events and schedules. It also enables candidates to post their résumés and features a recruiter directory. Additionally, it has its own online bookstore.

Career Resource Center (www.careers.org) is oriented towards career searchers interested in employment with technology companies. The site offers links to career guide Web sites, learning directories, employer directories, small/home office resources, career services, and various others. It also offers career guidance on search strategies, interview strategies, the career life cycle, and career challenges. The director of the Career Resource Center is Marc D. Snyder, co-author of *How to Get a Job in Seattle and Western Washington* (4th ed., 1998), published by Surrey Books in Chicago.

Career Resource Homepage (www.rpi.edu/dept/cdc/homepage.html) is a Web site developed in conjunction with Rensselaer Polytechnic Institute. It serves as a portal to other career-related resources, including job search sites, professional societies and other organizations, career services at various universities, and Internet news groups. It also contains links to other resources. It is an intuitive and easy to use site.

High Technology Careers/Incpad (www.hightechcareers.com) features career, employment, and job search articles from *High Technology Careers Magazine*. It includes articles on a broad spectrum of career topics and career trends. It also offers a virtual job fair.

Job Choices Online (www.jobweb.org/jconline) is published by the National Association of Colleges and Employers (NACE). It offers career advice on interviewing, writing letters and résumés, and "real life" perspectives from the working world. Its target audience is both college students and graduates in the working world.

JobWeb (www.jobweb.org) is sponsored by the National Association of Colleges and Employers (NACE). For college graduates, it offers employment outlook information in terms of jobs and salaries. It also offers information for career services and human resources professionals.

The National Association of Colleges and Employers (NACE) (www.jobweb.org/nace), formerly known as the College Placement Council, Inc., promotes itself as a "bridge between higher education and the world of work." In this role, it describes itself as having three constituencies: over 1,600 member universities and colleges from across the United States (and their career services professionals); over 1,600 employer organizations (Fortune 500 service and manufacturing companies, fast growth, medium size, and start-up companies; and federal, state, and local government agencies, and their human resources and employment professionals); and over 1 million students and alumni, who use and rely upon NACE publications and services yearly. NACE publishes *Job Choices*, a career search and guide magazine both in hard copy and online.

WetFeet.com (www.wetfeet.com) bills itself as the leading site on the Web for researching your job and managing your career. The site offers its own research on various industries and sells its own more detailed industry profiles though its online store. It provides free condensed industry overviews that are accurate and informative. It also features articles on a range of career topics, including résumés, interviews, search strategies, jobs, and professional fields. It provides an expert advice feature in which you can e-mail career questions and "the Expert" will respond to you. The site also provides links to other career Web sites.

CAREER SEARCH: RESOURCES FOR TECH START-UP AND NEW ECONOMY CAREERS

CareerCentral® (www.careercentral.com) is dedicated to matching people with career opportunities. The site offers free, confidential membership that includes information about job opportunities that fit members' backgrounds and skill sets even while they may be happily employed. On the flip side, the site offers client company recruiters a way to identify qualified candidates. The company has expanded on its original focus on M.B.A. graduates and now offers similar services for general business and marketing jobs.

CareerMosaic (www.careermosaic.com) is a leading career search Web site, featuring over 100,000 jobs at a time. The site categorizes jobs by function and offers content for selected "communities": Accounting & Finance, Health Care, Human Resources, Insurance, Public Sector, Sales & Marketing, and Technology. The site also offers company profiles, features online job fairs, and contains an international gateway. The site is quite popular, as evidenced by its 4 million plus site visitors per month.

CareerPath.com (www.careerpath.com) is a career search Web site that contains job advertisements from leading newspapers in the United States. The company itself is backed by six major newspapers—*The Boston Globe, The Chicago Tribune, The Los Angeles Times, The New York Times, The San Jose Mercury News,* and *The Washington Post*—as well as other media companies. The site also pulls job listings from the Web sites of leading employers. It offers company profiles, a job fair finder, career counseling, industry information, a salary search feature, and other services. Career seekers can search it by geography, newspaper, job type, and keyword.

Headhunter.net (www.headhunter.net) contains job postings from corporate recruiters. It also allows recruiters to search its database of résumés, offers links to companies, and features news items. Its database contains roughly a quarter of a million jobs at any given time. Although the search capabilities of many sites enable you to customize your search based on type of industry and geography, Headhunter.net enables you to customize by salary range and education. The site receives roughly 3.6 million visitors per month.

HotJobs.com (www.hotjobs.com) is a career search site that is particularly strong in the high-technology fields of computer hardware, software, e-commerce, and communications. The site features a new companies section, information about career fairs, and an online jobs magazine. The site is highly intuitive, easy to use, and provides good content.

JobBankUSA.com (www.jobbankusa.com) offers databases of employment opportunities and recruiters, career advice, and a host of resources. These include newsgroups, career fairs, assessment tools, and relocation tools.

Monster.com (www.monster.com) is a popular career search site that offers a searchable jobs database and personalized tools such as a search agent, expert career search and management advice, and free newsletters. The site's job database contains over 200,000 jobs worldwide at any given time. Monster.com has sites in the United States, Canada, United Kingdom, Netherlands, Belgium, Australia, and France, with sites to launch soon in Germany and Singapore. The site's jobs are categorized by industry.

ValleyJobs.com (www.valleyjobs.com) is a career search and guide site for Silicon Valley and the San Francisco Bay area. It offers the ability to search by geography, job category, and keywords. It features brief profiles on hot and pre-IPO companies, as well as articles on various relevant topics from sources such as *Newsweek*, *The San Francisco Chronicle*, *The San Jose Mercury News*, *Interactive Week*, and *Computerworld*. Many of these articles offer career guidance. Valleyjobs.com provides links to government jobs, newspapers, and online news sources. The site also has a sister site, SVDaily.com, which offers daily news about Silicon Valley.

Yahoo (www.Yahoo.com/Business—and-Economy/Companies/ Computers/Employment) offers links to dozens of information technology recruiters, as well as for virtually every other industry. Although it lacks any particular career search emphasis, its industry-specific career search and recruitment sites have definitely improved over time, offering increasingly comprehensive, albeit general, information.

INDUSTRY-SPECIFIC CAREER SEARCH AND INFORMATION RESOURCES

Biotechnology

Australian Biotechnology Association (www.aba.asn.au)is the leading trade association for biotechnology in Australia. Its Web site contains news, a calendar of events, a directory of organizations, links to other resources, and a recruitment service.

BioIndustry Association (www.bioindustry.org) is a leading association for the biotechnology sector in the United Kingdom. It is a superb site for obtaining industry news and offers a calendar of events, membership information, and various publications for sale. Some services are available to members only, such as an opportunities exchange.

BioPharMed (www.biopharmed.com) is a recruiting site that specializes in biotechnology, pharmaceutical, and medical device industries on a global scale. The site offers an employment database and career guidance services for candidates. It serves both start-up ventures and larger, established corporations.

BioSpace (www.biospace.com) serves the biotech community, offering a career center and an employment database. It also offers highly comprehensive news for investors and industry participants.

BioTactics (www.biotactics.com/career/html) offers a comprehensive set of resources for career seekers in the fields of biotechnology and medical devices. It includes a database of positions; an online newsletter; links to other employment sites; and advice on salaries, employment outlook, relocation, negotiating, networking, and personal development.

Biotechnology Industry Organization (BIO) (www.bio.org) is the largest trade organization serving the biotechnology community in the United States and around the world. The organization represents companies of all sizes. The BIO site is arguably one of the first places for career searchers to go to obtain information on virtually all issues important to biotechnology. It offers a superb overview of the biotech industry in general and provides key industry statistics and information on biotech company financing. It also provides overviews of ethics in biotechnology, legislative issues, and the biotech drug development process, and links to a variety of Web resources.

E-Commerce, Information Technology, and the Internet

Association for Interactive Media (AIM) (www.interactive.org) is the nonprofit trade association for Internet business users. Its membership comprises companies whose goal is to maximize the value of the Internet in business and consumer communities. AIM has a threefold mission: to support interactive media interests at the federal level, to promote consumer confidence, and to provide business to business networking opportunities. AIM's Web site offers free electronic newsletters, a job search service for senior-level positions in media, links to Internet market research organizations, a calendar of events, and links to a variety of sources: industry news, various AIM programs, Internet political resources, consumer resources, and more.

Association for Women in Computing (www.awc-hq.org) is a nonprofit professional organization serving women with an interest in information technology. It focuses on advancing the interests of women in the fields of computing, business, science, education, government, and the military. The association provides opportunities for professional growth through networking and programs on technical and career topics. The site offers news, chapter information, and links to other Web sites of interest.

Association of Internet Professionals (www.association.org) is a leading professional association of the Internet industry. Its mission is to represent the global community of Internet professionals and serve as a forum for ideas, people, and issues shaping the future of the Internet industry. Its corporate membership spans both large and small (pre-IPO) companies. The association has chapters in France, the United Kingdom, and the United States. Within the United States, there are chapters in many major urban areas. The association's Web site offers industry news, a member list, a calendar of events, chapter activity and contacts, a list of its programs, and an online store.

British Computer Society (www.bcs.org.uk) is dedicated to providing service and support to both individuals and employers in the IS community. It seeks to promote the study and practice of computing. The society's Web site provides industry news and offers resources for education and professional development. It also offers a career search service in partnership with PlanetRecruit.

CompInfo-Center.com (www.compinfocenter.com/home/htm) is a fantastic starting point for finding important information about the computer and communication industries. Although the Web site serves primarily buyers and sellers in the IT/IS community, it is an enormously useful resource from a career search standpoint because of its rich content and links to hundreds of industry resources and trade organizations. The site also offers an employment service.

CompTIA: The Computing Industry Association (www. comptia.org) is an established association representing 7,500 computer hardware and software manufacturers, distributors, retailers, training, service, telecommunications, and Internet companies. CompTIA's public policy office mission is to advance and protect the interests of the computing industry at federal and state levels. One of CompTIA's recent public policy successes was enactment of legislation that placed a moratorium on Internet taxation activity at the state level. CompTIA has task forces on Public Policy, E-Commerce, and Information Technology Services. Its Web site offers news, an online store, and a calendar of events.

Information Technology Association of America (www. itaa.org) is a trade association that represents interests in computers, software, telecommunications products and services, Internet and online services, systems integration, and professional services companies. It serves all companies in its industries, from the largest behemoths to the smallest start-ups. The association Web site provides news and information about the IT industry and its issues, ITAA programs, resources, divisions, and affiliates. The ITAA has four major divisions: software, IT Services, Information Services and E-Commerce, and Enterprise Solutions. The Web site provides links to a rich variety of global Web sites focusing on government, industry, trends, markets, and statistics, which are of tremendous value to career searchers and industry newcomers.

Mobile Computing and Communications (www.mobilecomputing.com) bills itself as "the single most influential publication providing information critical for volume buyers of mobile technology to make sound purchase decisions." This industry resource chronicles trends in the mobile computing field and provides performance overviews of new products, as well as news about upcoming product launches. The magazine features industry veterans who write on a variety of topics: new mobile technology, alternative workplace, mobile technology and travel, and Internet connectivity. It also provides comparison reports and a buyer's guide for selected product categories. The Web site provides industry news and a calendar of events.

U.S. Internet Industry Association (www.usiia.org) is a nonprofit trade association dedicated to promoting the growth and development of Internet commerce, content, and connectivity. It serves the corporate community by providing information and advocating on behalf of its members in areas of open access, privacy, copyright, taxation, self-regulation, and electronic commerce. The Web site offers industry news, a careers section, publications, and links to other resources.

Semiconductors

Fabless Semiconductor Association (FSA) (www.fsa.org) is the leading semiconductor association, serving over 200 companies. The FSA's vision is to establish the fabless business model as the dominant semiconductor business model (outsourcing of wafer fabrication/manufacturing due to high costs of building that capability internally). Easy to navigate, the FSA site offers a section on employment opportunities with member companies, a calendar of events, committee information, and industry news. The site also offers links to numerous semiconductor trade associations.

Semiconductor Equipment and Materials International (SEMI) (www.smi.org) is a global trade association representing the semiconductor and flat panel display equipment and materials industries. Its membership comprises more than 2,000 companies that generate more than $65 billion in sales. SEMI has numerous offices in Asia, Europe, and the United States, and helps member companies expand global marketing opportunities and improve access to customers, industry, and governments. SEMI's Web site provides industry news, industry and market statistics, information on public policy, and a calendar of events. It also provides links to a variety of resources, including conferences, expositions, business education/technical programs, and employment resources.

Semiconductor Industry Association (SIA) (www.semi-chips.org/main/html) is a leading trade association for the computer chip industry. Its mission is to provide leadership for U.S.

chip manufacturers in areas of trade, technology, environmental protection, and worker safety and health. The SIA seeks to achieve free and open markets worldwide, maintain U.S. leadership in technology, drive state-of-the-art programs for safe working conditions, and maintain top ranking in worldwide market share. With its counterpart organizations in Europe and Japan, the SIA Statistics Committee plans and implements policies established by the World Semiconductor Trade Statistics Program. The SIA Web site offers rich information on the semiconductor industry, including product definitions, world market sales and shares, and sales forecasts.

Semiconductor Online (www.semiconductoronline.com) is an online community sponsored by VerticalNet. Semiconductor Online seeks to be a leading source for technology, operations, product management, and regulatory information for the semiconductor industry. The site is highly user friendly and easy to navigate. It provides rich industry news and analysis, product information, an online marketplace, and a professional center. The professional center offers career search and recruitment resources, training resources, and other forums and event information.

Telecommunications and Multimedia

Internet and Telecoms Convergence Consortium (formerly known as Internet Telephony Consortium, ITC) (www.itel. mit.edu/itel/newind.html) is a collaboration sponsored by various companies and selected academics, largely from the Massachusetts Institute of Technology (M.I.T.), who jointly pursue research on technical, economic, strategic, and policy issues brought about by the convergence of telecommunications and the Internet. ITC is a policy-neutral forum that integrates a wide range of companies and academic disciplines. Member companies are all sizes of firms in software, computing and communications, and telephone and Internet services industries. Participants in the consortium work collaboratively to understand and define future technologies, industry and market structures, and prices. The goal of the collaboration is to grow new forms of multimedia communication that bridge the Internet and telecommunications. The ITC Web site provides links to and resources on a variety of topics, including policy resources, software, news, equipment providers, IT standards, and news groups. The site also has posted dozens of ITC publications relevant to many topics in the telephony/Internet field. These studies, which are free of charge, are an awesome source of knowledge and information about the telephony/Internet space.

Multimedia Telecommunications Association (MMTA) (www.mmta.org) is a subsidiary of the Telecommunications Association (TIA—see below). MMTA seeks to support market growth and drive convergence of communications and computing. The site offers industry news, an events calendar, and information about research and education.

Telecom Information Resources on the Internet (www.china.si.umich.edu/telecom) maintained by Professor Jeffrey MacKie-Mason and Juan Riveros at the University of Michigan. Largely designed as a reference resource, the site contains links to hundreds of sources relating to technical, economic, public policy, and social issues in telecommunications. Links are listed under general categories such as Associations, Bandwidth Markets and Providers, Broadcasters, Internet Economics, and Network Security and Cryptography. The site also offers a Career and Job Information resource that lists several general career Web sites as well as those specific to telecommunications. Moreover, it lists recruitment firms that specialize in telecommunications. Without a doubt, this is one of the top reference sites for telecommunications resources on the Internet.

Telecommunications Industry Association (TIA) (www.tiaonline.org) is a trade association serving 1,000 companies that provide communications and information technology products, materials, systems, distribution, and professional services in the United States and globally. Through its subsidiary, the MultiMedia Telecommunications Association (MMTA), and in conjunction with the Electronic Industries Alliance (EIA), TIA represents the telecommunications industry. The TIA Web site provides superb information in a variety of areas: industry news, public policy, shows and events, standards and technology, international affairs, and resources.

OTHER GENERAL RESOURCES

Computer and Communication (www.cmpcmm.com/cc/orgs/ html) is sponsored by Webstart Communications. Webstart has three key focus areas: content, advertising, and confederations. Its organizations page lists several hundred links to organizations all over the globe in the fields of broadcasting, communications, computing, fiber optics, multimedia, radio communications, software, and telephony.

VerticalNet (www.verticalnet.com) is a superb site for Internet communities covering a number of different industries, such as advanced technologies, communications, environmental, healthcare/science, and manufacturing and metals. VerticalNet offers industry news, white papers written by industry leaders, directories, and job listings. Its community focus enables professionals to exchange ideas, search for career opportunities, and stay current on industry events. Each business community site provides links to other industry-specific Web sites of interest.

RESOURCES FOR STOCK OPTIONS AND COMPENSATION

IPOfn Online™ (www.ipofinancial.com) is oriented around pre-IPO companies and financing. As the site notes: "Initial Public Offerings (IPOs) have created more millionaires than any other segment of the stock market." The site provides research and news on companies that are about to go public. Of particular value to the career searcher is its glossary of terms, which contains a wealth of information relating to company stock, ownership, and going public. Scroll about two-thirds of the way down the home page to find the link to the glossary.

The National Center for Employee Ownership (NCEO) (www.nceo.org) is a nonprofit membership and research organization that aims to be the leader in providing accurate and unbiased information on employee stock ownership plans (ESOPs), employee stock options, and employee participation programs. The center's Web site does a fair job of explaining different types of stock options, how they work, and the pros and cons of each. Although the detail can get fairly technical, the site may help if you have basic questions relating to some aspect of stock options. Perhaps more important, the site also sells online publications produced by the NCEO. These publications presumably provide answers to questions that remain unanswered after perusing the NCEO site.

INDEX